IMAGES
of America

MIDCOAST MAINE

THE CUNNINGHAM COLLECTION

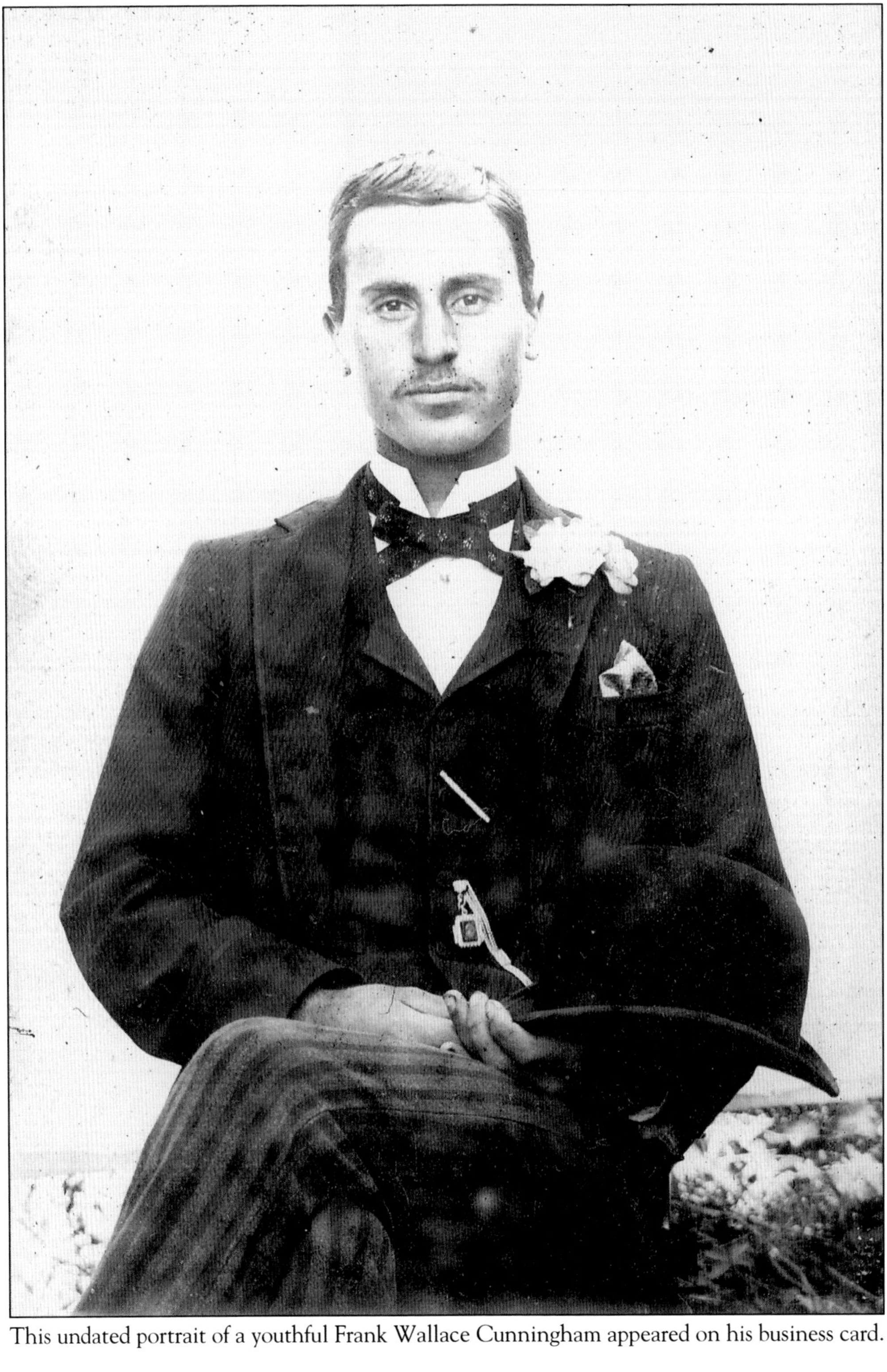

This undated portrait of a youthful Frank Wallace Cunningham appeared on his business card.

IMAGES
of America

MIDCOAST MAINE
THE CUNNINGHAM COLLECTION

Joseph W. and Jeremy T. Dieffenbacher

ARCADIA

ISBN 0-7385-3641-5

First published 2004

Published by Arcadia Publishing,
Charleston SC, Chicago IL, Portsmouth NH, San Francisco CA

Printed in Great Britain

Library of Congress Catalog Card Number: 2004106611

For all general information, contact Arcadia Publishing:
Telephone 843-853-2070
Fax 843-853-0044
E-mail sales@arcadiapublishing.com
For customer service and orders:
Toll-free 1-888-313-2665

Visit us on the Internet at www.arcadiapublishing.com

On the cover: Taken in 1913 by Bert E. Cunningham, this photograph shows a backwoods long-lumber sawmill, its nine-man crew, and their two horse teams.

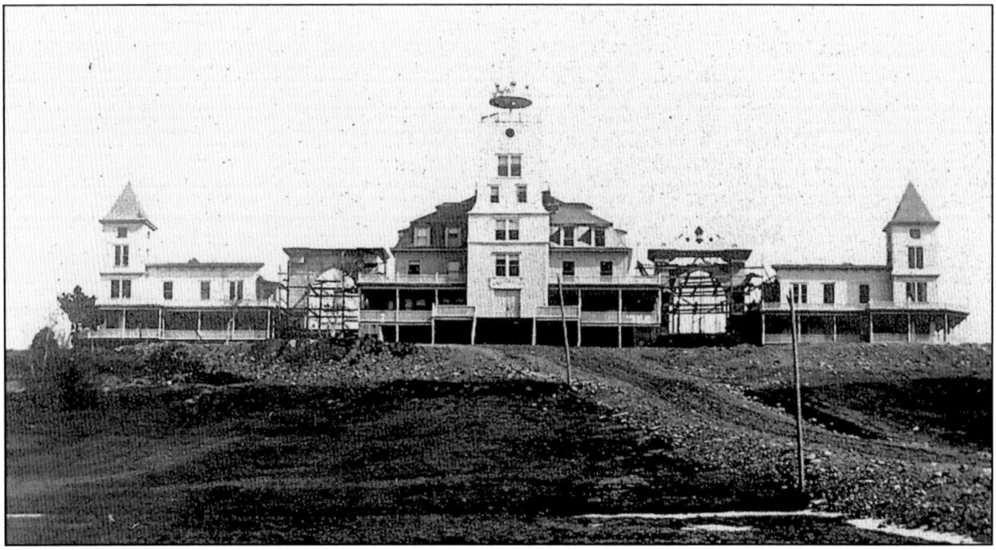

Taken in 1905 by F. W. Cunningham, this photograph shows the Reverend F. Sanford's impressive Holy Ghost and Us Temple, located in Durham.

Contents

ACKNOWLEDGMENTS

An endeavor such as this is never the effort of one or even two people and could not be accomplished without the assistance of a great many others. While it is impossible to name everyone who has contributed time, knowledge, or expertise to this work, there are some who deserve special recognition.

First of all, we would like to thank Susan Dieffenbacher, wife and mother, for her invaluable support and assistance in researching and assembling this work. Her countless hours of diligent work have undoubtedly contributed to the accuracy and readability of the final product.

We give a special acknowledgement to Ralph and Priscilla Bond of Jefferson. Without their incredible knowledge of the history and geography of Jefferson and Damariscotta Lake, our work would undoubtedly have been immeasurably more difficult and time consuming.

Special thanks are also given to Francis Cross of North Waldoboro, whose insight and humor contributed greatly to our understanding and appreciation of his "neck of the woods."

We were also aided greatly by the memory and knowledge of George Worthing. The recollections of his lifelong residency of Liberty, combined with his keen insight, contributed immensely to our work.

We were aided in our research by the staff and resources of numerous libraries and historical societies throughout the midcoast area and beyond. Some knew of our quest, while others did not. Regardless of their insight into our ultimate goals, all preformed their duties and jobs to the best of their abilities and collectively were a wonderful resource. Our thanks to all those unrecognized by name.

We have made every effort to research carefully the information and claims made within, but undoubtedly, mistakes can and will be made. Memories become hazy, photographic images can be misinterpreted, and sometimes the research done by others in years past, but relied upon today, may be faulty. Whatever the cause, if any errors exist, we politely beg the indulgence and forgiveness of our readers.

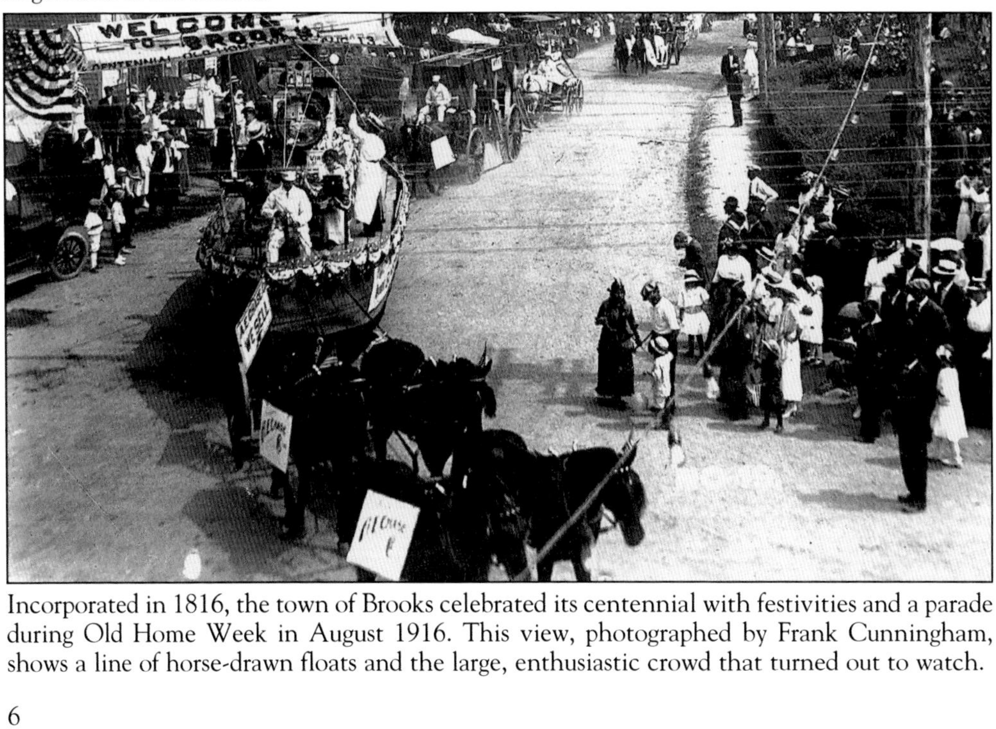

Incorporated in 1816, the town of Brooks celebrated its centennial with festivities and a parade during Old Home Week in August 1916. This view, photographed by Frank Cunningham, shows a line of horse-drawn floats and the large, enthusiastic crowd that turned out to watch.

INTRODUCTION

Frank W. Cunningham was born in Washington, Maine, in 1866, one year after the Civil War ended. His younger brother, Bert, followed in 1873. The life that they knew in rural midcoast Maine during the late 19th century was much different than the life experienced by those living here today. The predominantly agrarian economy was heavily dependent upon manual labor, as evidenced by the population figures of 100 years ago. Nearly every township in the area experienced a population spike in 1850, followed by a slow but steady decline thereafter as farms disappeared and mechanization began playing a more prominent role. Today's census figures, while showing some growth, have remained fairly steady for nearly two generations.

The midcoast communities that Frank and Bert Cunningham knew were, by necessity, self-reliant. Each town or village had, either within it or nearby, all of the industries or resources needed to maintain itself. As with any early American settlement, the most important resource was running water, which was needed for power. Rivers that could be dammed sprouted mills of every description—sawmills, gristmills, and mills designed for the manufacture of everyday implements such as ax handles and barrels. Around these mills grew the small communities that fed them and were in turn fed by them. Those communities most often became known by the name of the original builder of the mill and carry those monikers today, long after the last remnants and memories of the structures have faded.

The infrastructure of the small inland towns, villages, and settlements was nothing like what is found today. Dirt roads, more like paths in many cases, were the norm. Horse-drawn wagons and buggies were the standard mode of transportation for both people and material. Railroads existed in the midcoast area, but the services were far apart and not convenient for most daily trips. Travel that takes hours today took days a century ago. Add to that the effects of winter and wet weather on both the roads and the travelers, and one can see how extended isolation was a way of life in years past.

Popular and pervasive social events and organizations temporarily dispelled the isolation of the farming communities of a century ago, however. The Grange, formerly called the Patrons of Husbandry, was organized in Maine in 1873. It was started as an organization to spread information and ideas about modern farming methods and evolved into a social group of the highest order. Monthly meetings, dances, and excursions all brought people together. Local "bees" were a popular and necessary element of community life when large tasks needed to be completed. Similar to an Amish barn raising in character, these communal events were considered not only a charitable deed but a duty as well. Included among the popular events that occurred during the years that Frank and Bert lived and worked were the centennial celebrations taking place all over the area. These were large and extravagant events that generally engaged nearly everyone in the community and the surrounding areas. People traveled great distances to participate in and observe these festivities.

As insular as the settlements of the midcoast were a century ago, they were also the destination of choice for some people. Those living in the larger cities of Maine and beyond would regularly summer in rural areas, boarding in private homes or small rooming houses. The areas around Lake St. George in Liberty and Damariscotta Lake in Jefferson were particularly popular destinations for those seeking to escape the summertime heat of the city. As is the case today, these tourists provided much needed income for the people and revenues for the areas they visited.

This was the world that Frank and Bert Cunningham lived in—an isolated rural area, attractive to outsiders, proud in its self-sufficiency, and eager to partake in all that life had to offer. It is unknown how these two brothers first became interested in photography or where they learned the art, but what is known from their incredible legacy is that they were good at it. The images that they have left behind show moments of a life that no longer exists, frozen in time for us to examine today. Many of the structures and panoramas that they photographed no longer exist or have been irrevocably altered. The people we meet in portraits have been gone many years, but we can look into their eyes and we see them smile at us from beyond the grave. Many of the Cunningham images have unintentionally captured activities in the background, taking place beyond the subject matter. These "gifts" provide us with another glimpse into a past rich with what was then considered mundane but has, with time, become special.

Frank Cunningham maintained a gallery in the town of Washington for many years but began his career on the "circuit," a nearly 300-square-mile slice of rural Maine. He would travel the dirt roads of the midcoast by horse-drawn buggy, stopping at farms and villages and taking photographs of whatever or whomever his customers desired. He maintained the glass negatives for all of his images and would sell subsequent duplicates in postcard or cabinet photograph form to anyone who wanted one, regardless of subject matter. It was because of this business practice that we are blessed with a relative abundance of his images today.

Frank's brother Bert was not as active a photographer and seemingly pursued other vocations during his lifetime. We do know that for a period during the opening years of the 20th century, brothers Frank and Bert worked together, even marrying sisters, Mabel and Ellen Morang of Washington. After the death of Bert's wife, Mabel, their formal working relationship ended, although Bert did continue taking a limited number photographs on his own for several years thereafter.

Whatever the exact nature of the relationship between Frank and Bert, what they accomplished together and on their own surely exceeded their own expectations. They have left behind, in their skillfully executed images, a legacy that transcends the original subject matter. They took the ordinary and created the extraordinary, made all the more poignant by the unforgiving passage of time and progress. We have much to thank Frank and Bert Cunningham for.

One

Liberty and Lake St. George

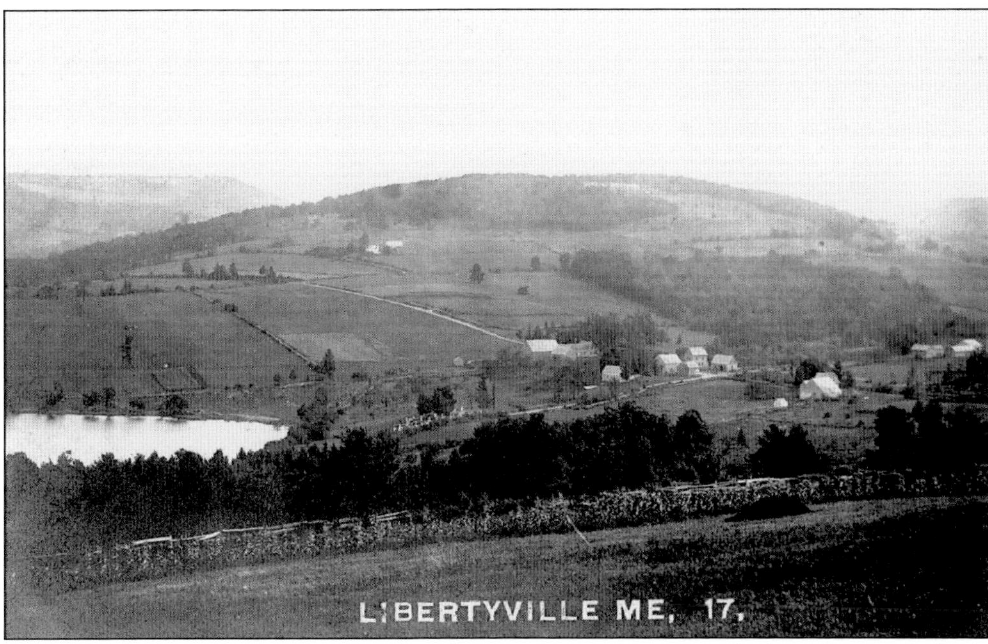

Known a century ago as Libertyville, the Sherman's Corner section of Liberty lies west of Lake St. George State Park. In this view looking southeast from the Stagecoach Road, Stickney Hill rises in the distance, a portion of Lake St. George is visible to the left, and the Belfast-Augusta Road passes through the center of the image. Visible to the right of the lake is Sherman's Cemetery, visible today alongside Route 3.

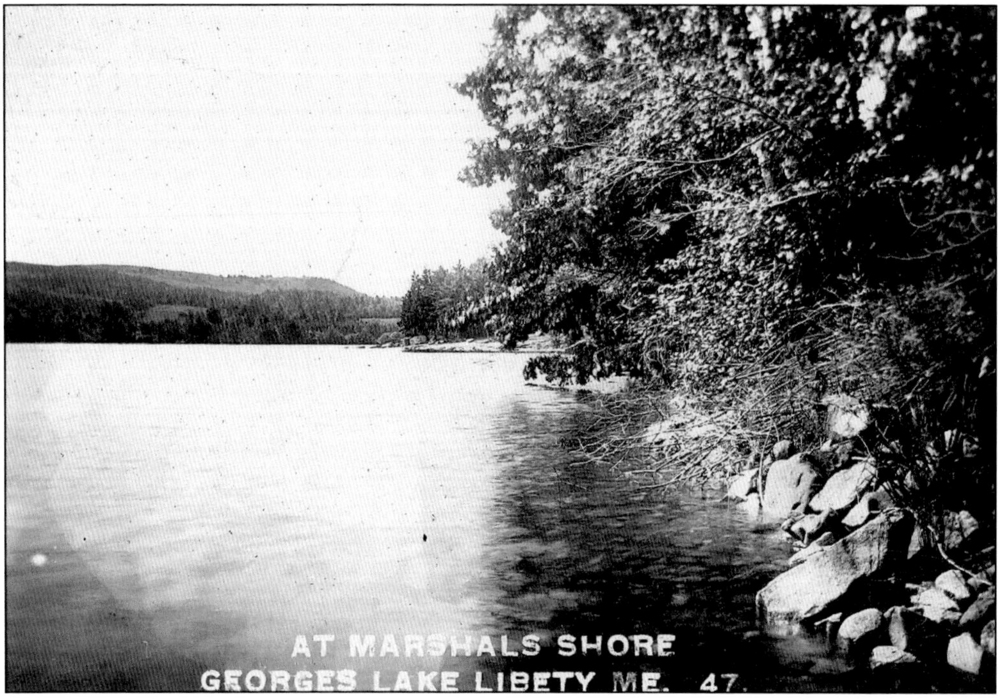

Marshall Shore was named for James Marshall, one of the early settlers of Liberty. Lying east of Sherman's Corner along the Marshall Shore Road, this area is the location of town-owned public lake access. This undated view, looking southeast, was taken on a small peninsula alongside the road, now privately owned. Visible at the center of the image is the rocky outcrop pictured in the next image.

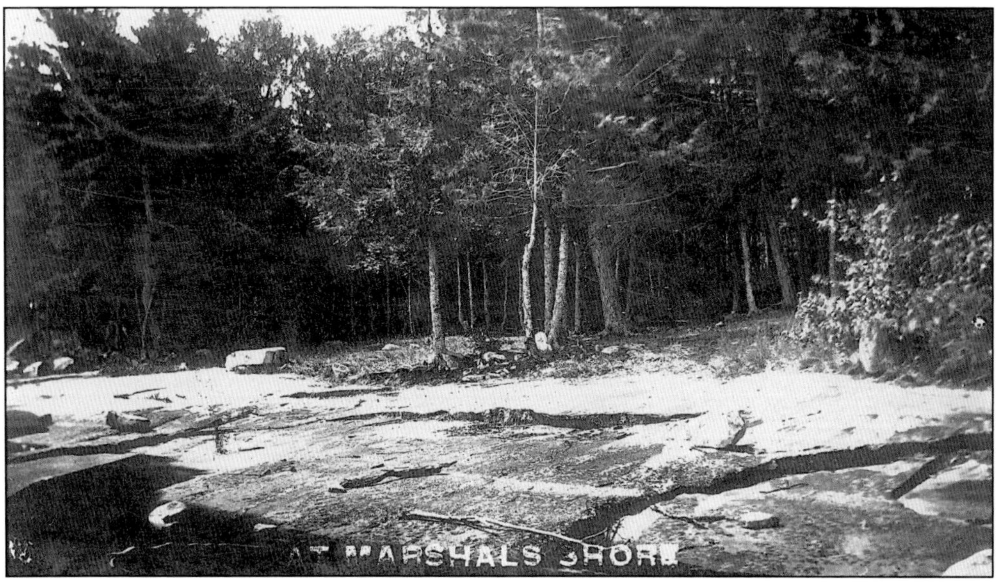

Surrounded by pine trees, this section of Marshall Shore is today a favorite summertime getaway location for locals. This rocky outcrop is its central feature and serves as the beach. Picnic tables, barbecue grills, and public restroom facilities are maintained by the town. The annual Liberty Volunteer Fire Department Fourth of July chicken barbecue is also held here.

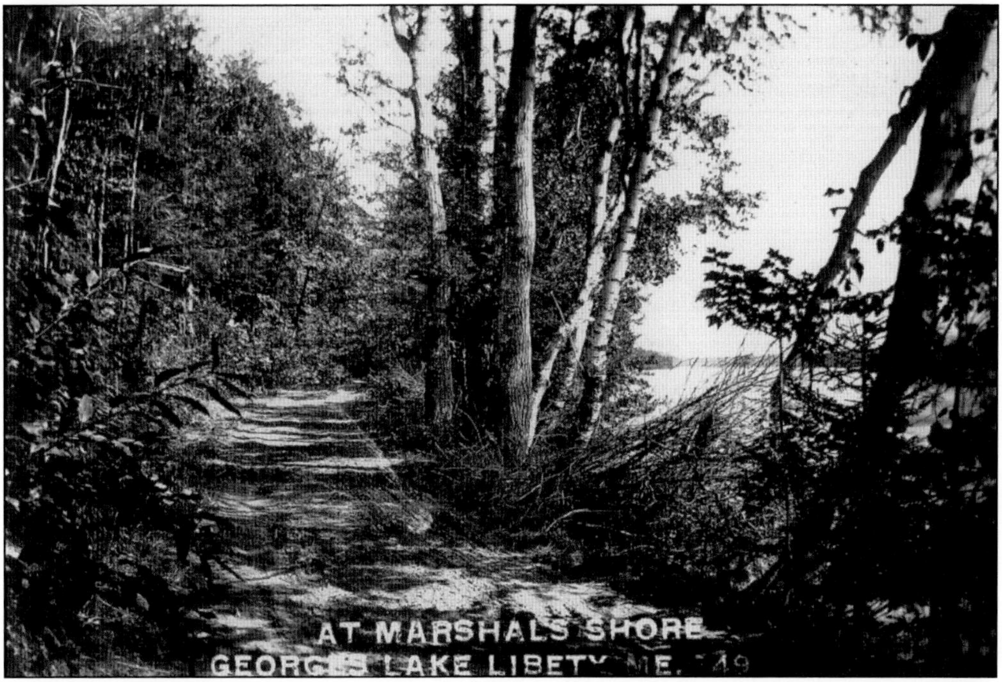

This is an undated photograph of the Marshall Shore Road, looking west, back toward modern Route 3. The beach area lies just out of view, to the right and slightly behind the camera position. While the road has been widened and paved since this image was taken, the overall scene has changed little. As in this view, the road passes within feet of the lake's edge, and trees still shade the road.

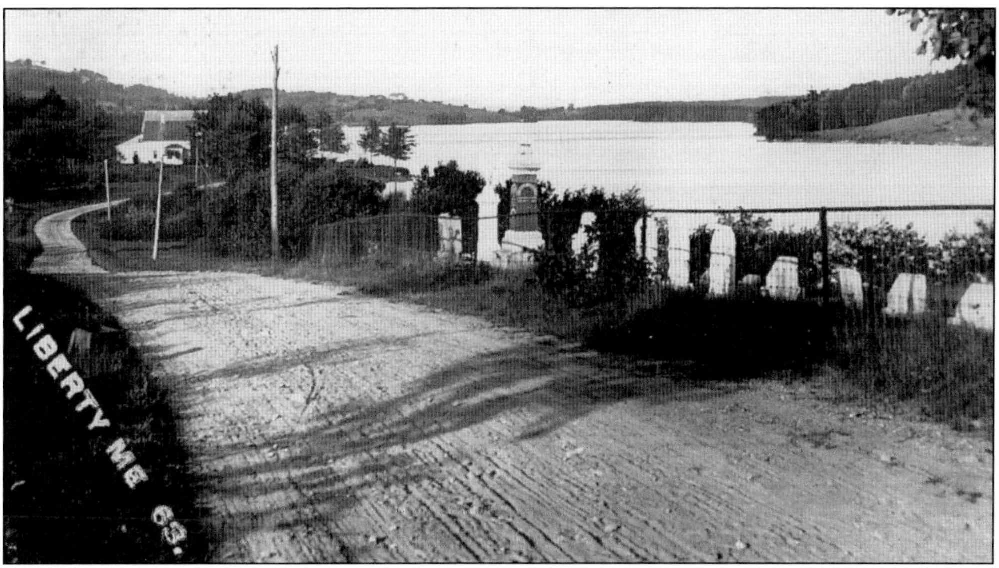

In this eastward-looking 1905 view along the Lake Road, Sherman's Cemetery stands on a small rise, with Lake St. George in the background. The original wire fence still surrounds the burial ground. The white house in the distance, less the lean-to addition at its rear, plus the barn visible just beyond, still exists. Modern Route 3, now paved and straightened, passes behind the house, rather than in front of it.

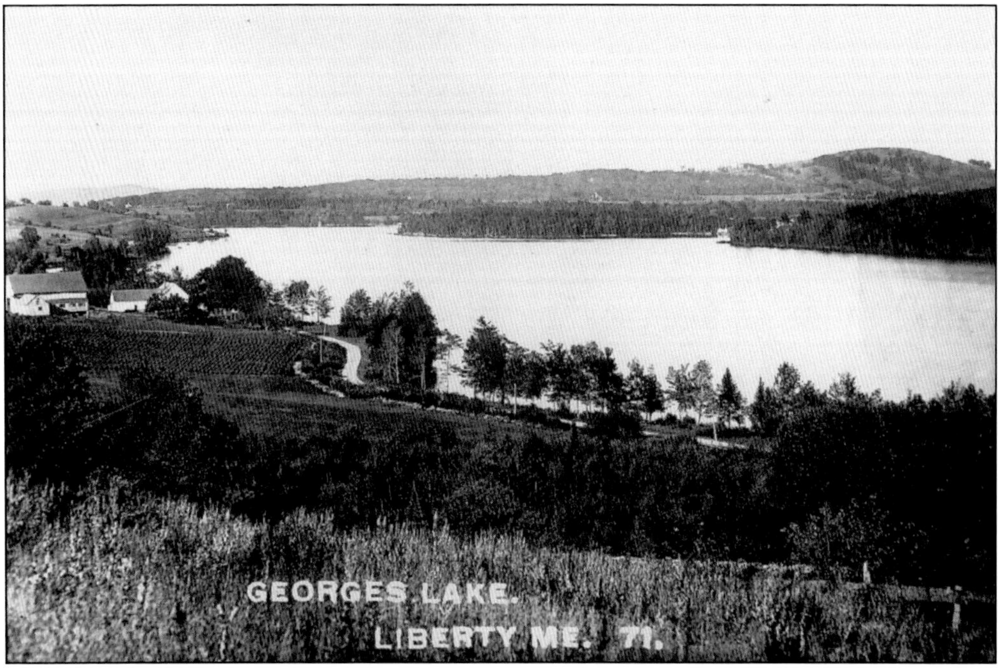

Taken from atop Bolin Ridge looking toward the northeast, this undated image shows the path that the Lake Road once followed, hugging the shoreline. The white farmhouse and barn to the left no longer exist. Seen in the center of the image is Hayes Island, with the tip of Sherman's Neck visible to the right. Haystack Mountain rises prominently in the distance on the extreme right.

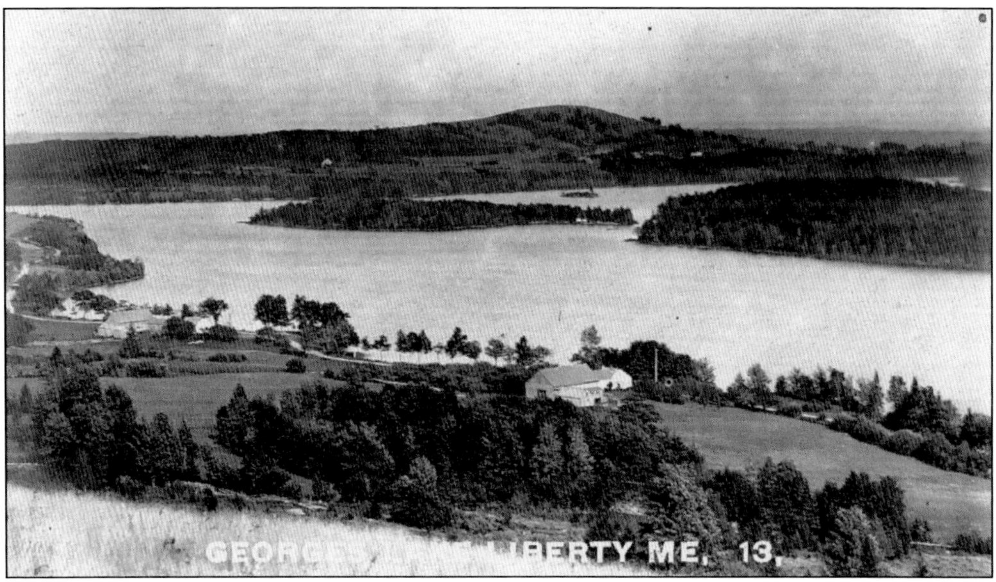

This is an earlier view of approximately the same scene, taken from farther up on Bolin Ridge. The farm in the center of the image is seen in the last photograph. The farm at the left exists today as part of Lake St. George State Park. Visible in the distance is Hayes Island, with Sherman's Neck to the right. Haystack Mountain rises in the distance, and Loon Island appears just below.

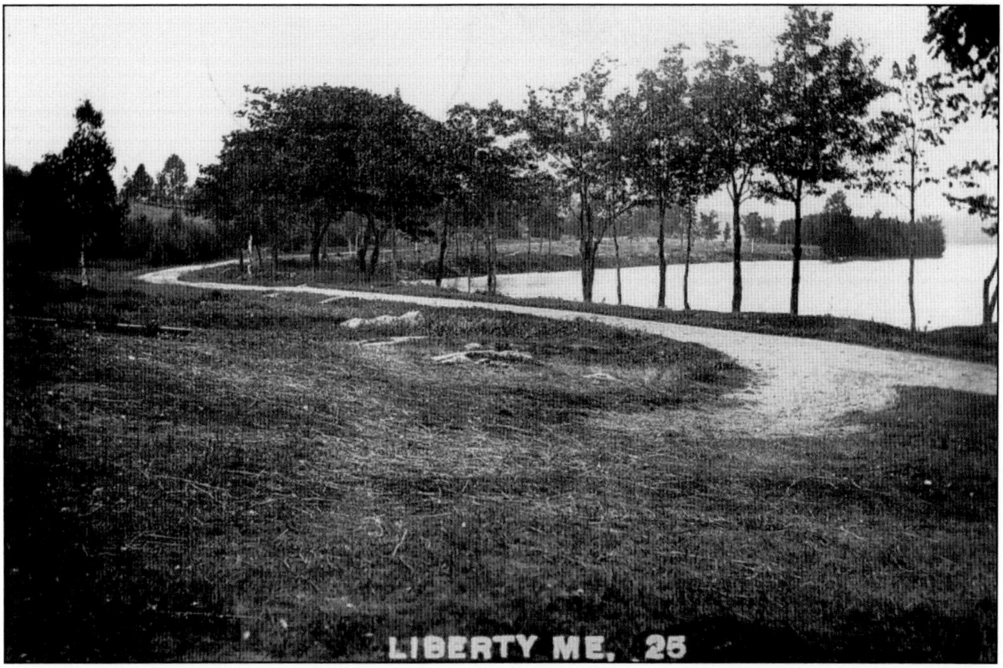

The former Lake Road once followed the eastern shoreline of Lake St. George from Marshall Shore to the Stagecoach Road. It has since been replaced by modern Route 3, but segments of the original road still exist. This photograph was taken from just beyond the farm that is now part of the state park, looking to the northeast. Now a trail leading to the swimming area, the road looks very much the same today.

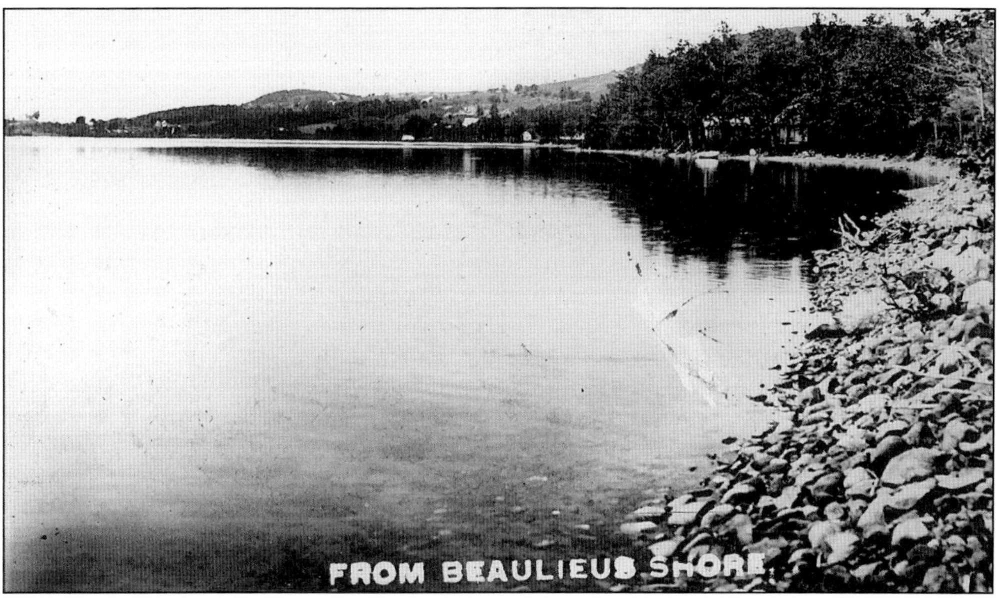

This location is now the swimming area of Lake St. George State Park. The view looks back toward the previous camera position. Bolin Ridge rises along the right in the distance, and Marshall Shore is just out of view to the left. The Lake Road, not visible in this image, is just to the right and follows the shoreline around the lake.

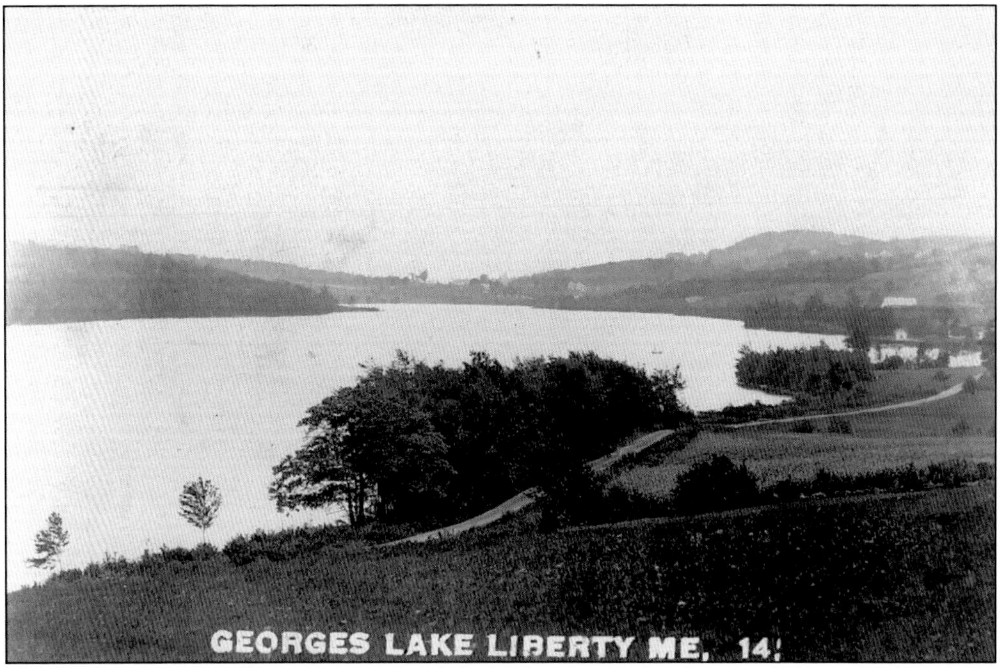

This is another early photograph of the Lake Road in the area of the state park. The present-day swimming area lies out of view, behind and to the left of the camera position. The peninsula visible to the far right of center is the one seen in a previous image. The farmhouse stands just beyond camera range on the right, and Bolin Ridge, cleared of trees, rises along the right-hand side.

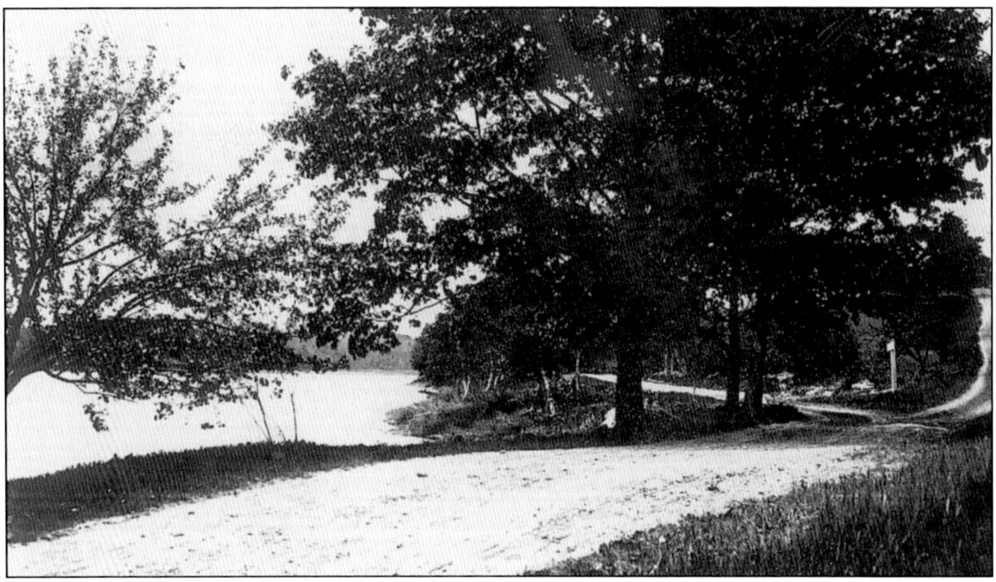

Formerly known as Kenniston's Shore, this area lies at the extreme northern edge of Lake St. George, near the intersection of modern Routes 3 and 220. In this view looking toward the southwest, the Lake Road sweeps off to the left and the Stagecoach Road climbs Bolin Ridge to the right. Across the lake, the tip of Sherman's Neck and Hayes Island is visible, partially obscured by trees.

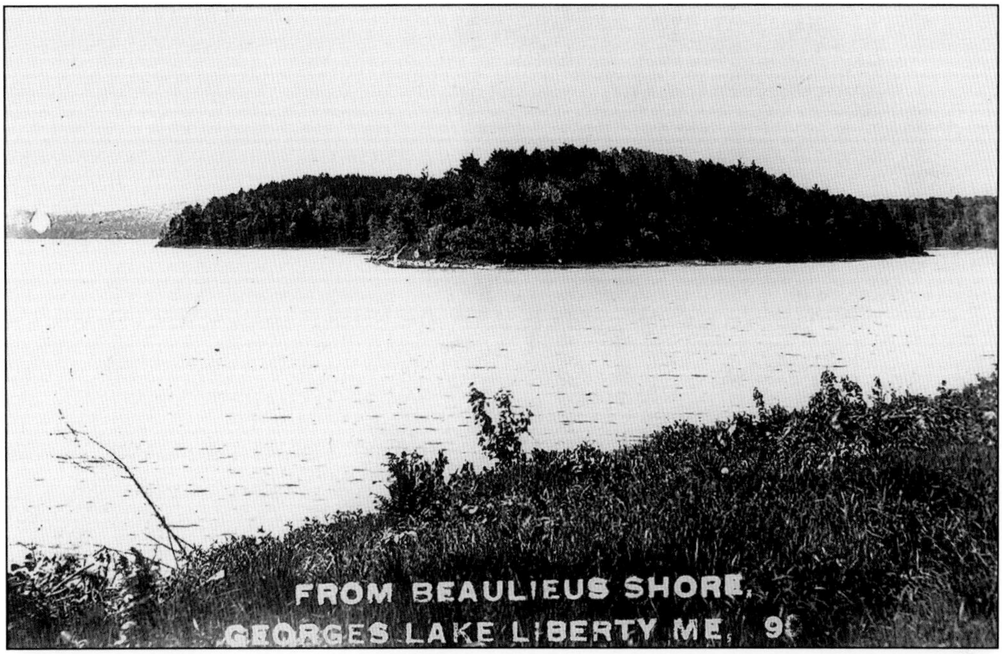

Adjacent to Kenniston's Shore lies what was once known as Beaulieu's Shore, paralleling modern Route 220 at lake's edge. Nearly inaccessible today because of tree growth, this view looks toward the southwest, with Hayes Island visible in the foreground. The tip of Sherman's Neck can be seen just beyond and to the left of the island.

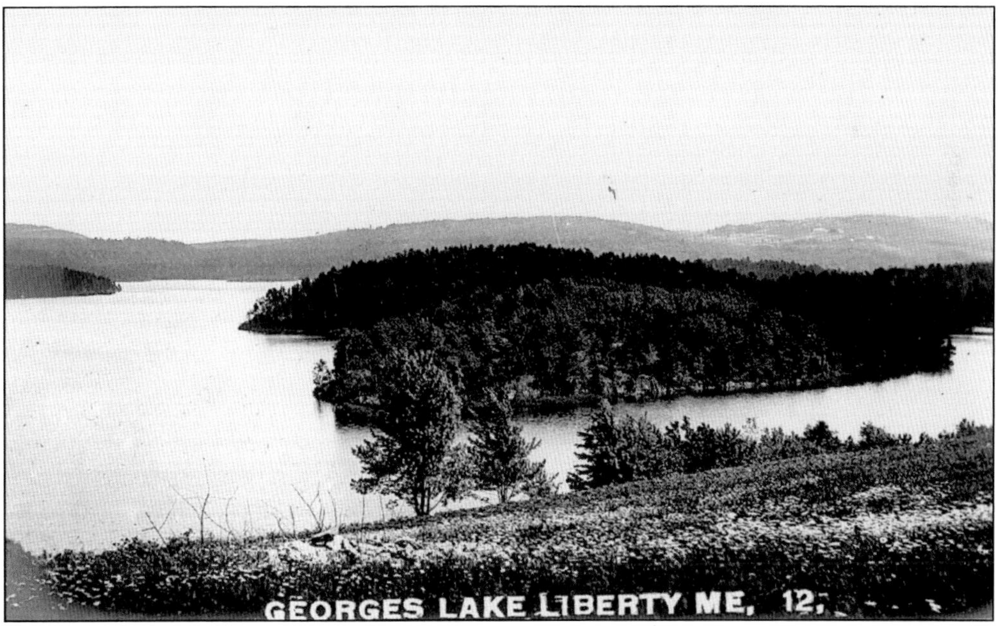

This view, looking in a more southerly direction, is similar to the last image but was taken from the elevation of the Stagecoach Road. Hayes Island is in the foreground here, Sherman's Neck is just behind, and barely visible beyond that can be seen the trees of Millstone Island. The eastern shore of Lake St. George is visible in the far distance.

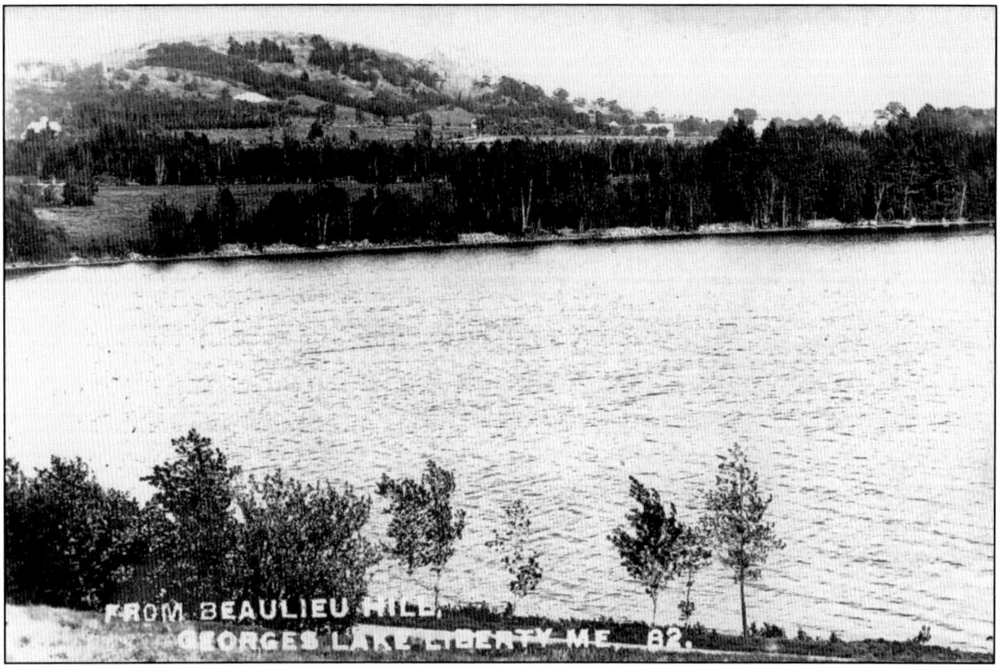

Taken from nearly the same camera position along the Stagecoach Road, this photograph looks east at the flanks of Haystack Mountain and at Beaulieu's Shore, in the foreground. A portion of the Lake Road can be seen along the extreme bottom edge of the photograph. Because of tree growth, this view is nearly impossible to duplicate today. The facing slope of Haystack, once nearly devoid of woods, is tree covered today.

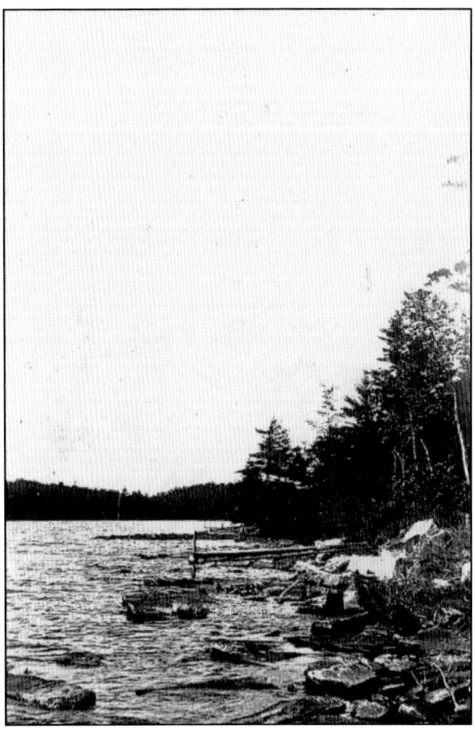

This 1914 photograph was taken from the western shore of Millstone Island, looking nearly due north. The eastern shore of Sherman's Neck stretches along the horizon, and two boat landings are visible at the center of the image. It is interesting to note, in this and several later images, that because of a drought, the level of the lake is down approximately two feet, exposing normally submerged rocks and altering the contour of the shoreline.

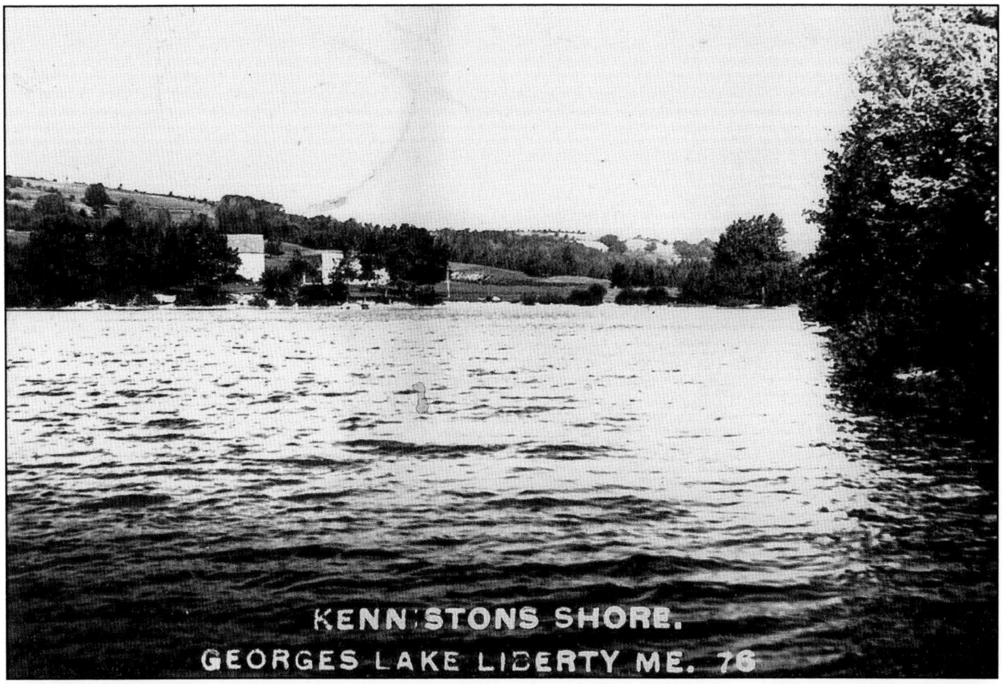

A view of Kenniston's Shore, this undated photograph was taken from Pinola Point, looking toward the northwest. Bolin Ridge and the location of the Stagecoach Road rise to the left in the distance, and Beaulieu's Shore lies straight along the right-hand edge of the image. The white farmhouse to the left of center, once owned by the Bagley family, still exists, although the large barn does not.

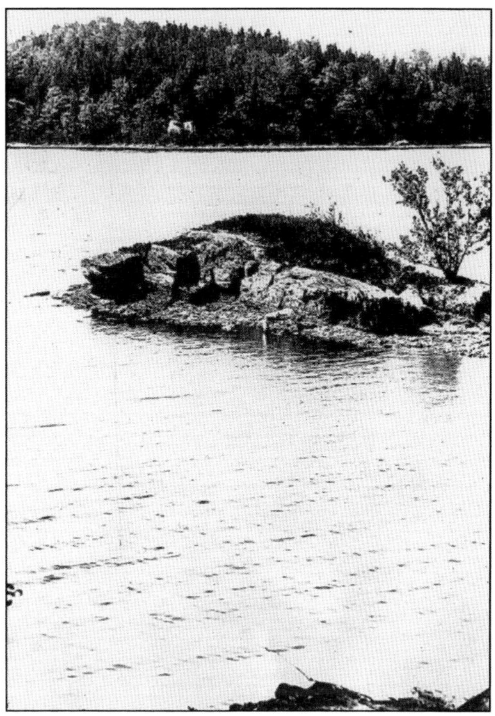

Located just off Pinola Point at the northern edge of Lake St. George, this small, unnamed island is visible today from modern Route 3. Taken from the point and looking southwest, this image shows Sherman's Neck in the background. In this view, most likely taken at the same time as the earlier Millstone Island photograph, the level of the lake is conspicuously down because of the 1914 drought.

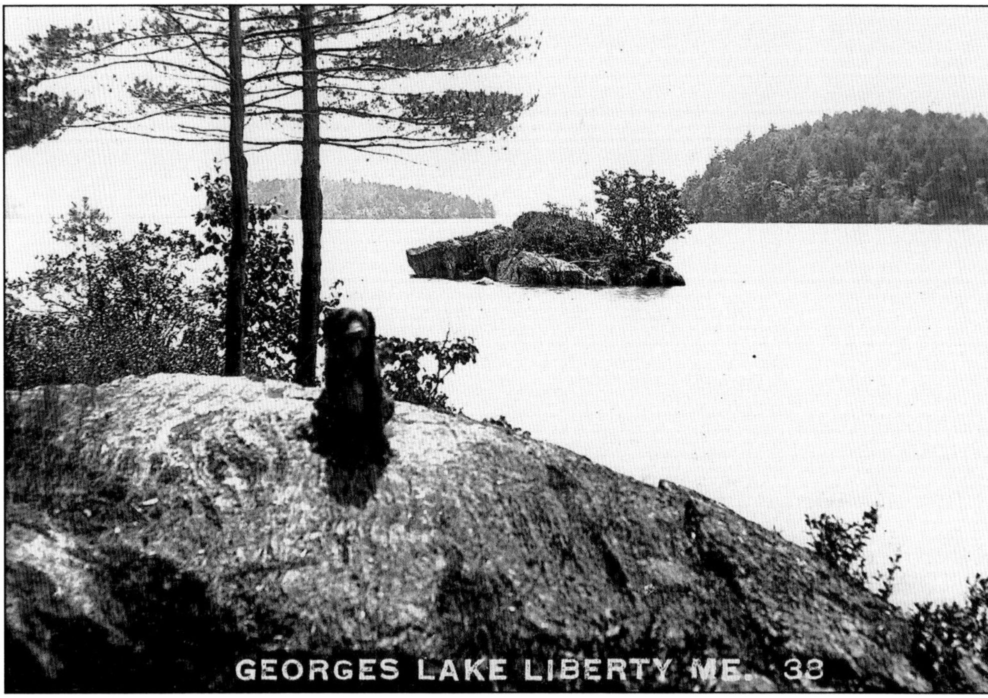

This is another view taken from Pinola Point looking toward the small island, this time in a more southerly direction. Visible in the distance are Sherman's Neck to the right, and Millstone Island to the left of center, directly beyond the dog. The water level of the lake in this earlier, undated photograph is at a normal height when compared to the 1914 image.

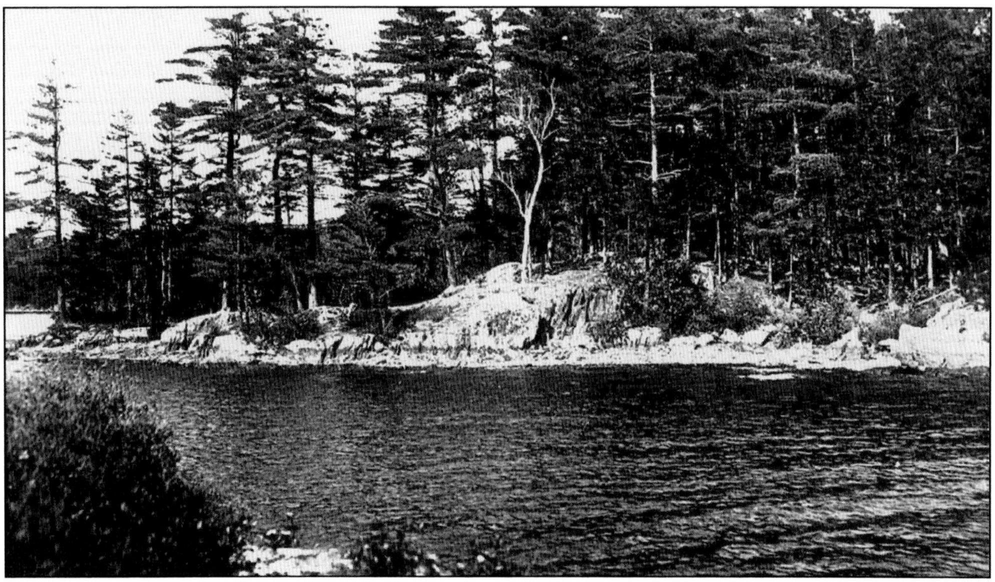
Another image taken during the drought of 1914, this view was recorded from the small island seen in the previous two photographs, looking northwest at Pinola Point. The water level drop is made obvious by the dark line along the shore, indicating the normal water level mark. As evidenced by its distinctive shape and prominent crack, the large rock to the left (near the tip of the point) is the same one the dog is sitting on in the previous photograph.

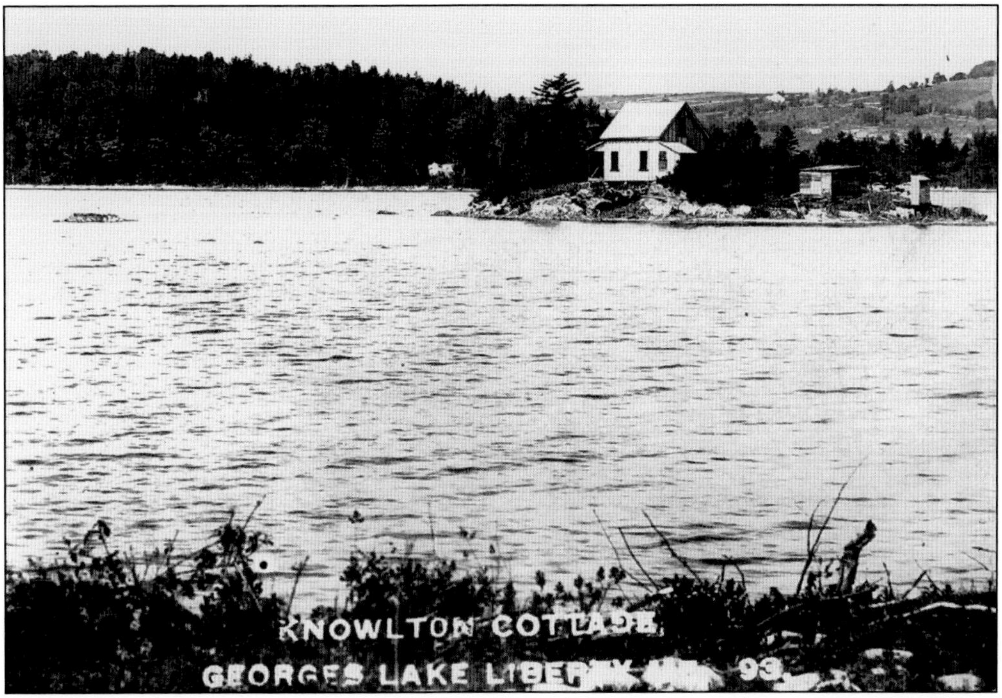

Taken from east of Pinola Point and looking toward the southeast, this 1914 image of Loon Island features the Knowlton cottage and its attendant outhouse. The tree line in the left background is the eastern peninsula of Little Pond, and the treeless ridge in the distance follows modern Route 220. The effects of the drought are apparent around Loon Island, and in the dark line appearing along the rocks on the far shore.

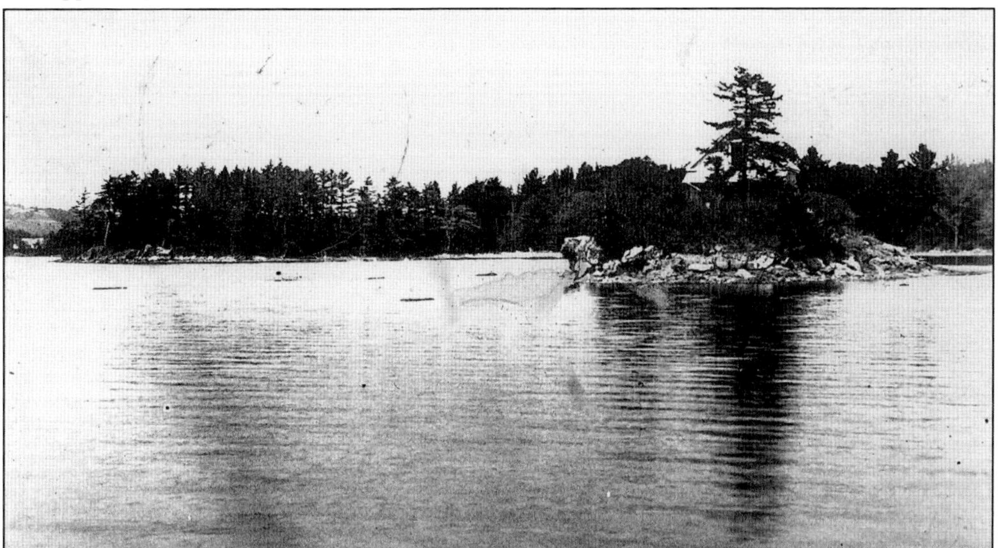

This photograph of Loon Island and the Knowlton cottage was taken from the shore, south of the entrance to Little Pond. Just out of sight to the left lies Green Island, with Pinola Point in the left background. Barely visible on the left and in the far distance are the buildings of the Bagley farm along Kenniston's Shore, and the rise of Bolin Ridge.

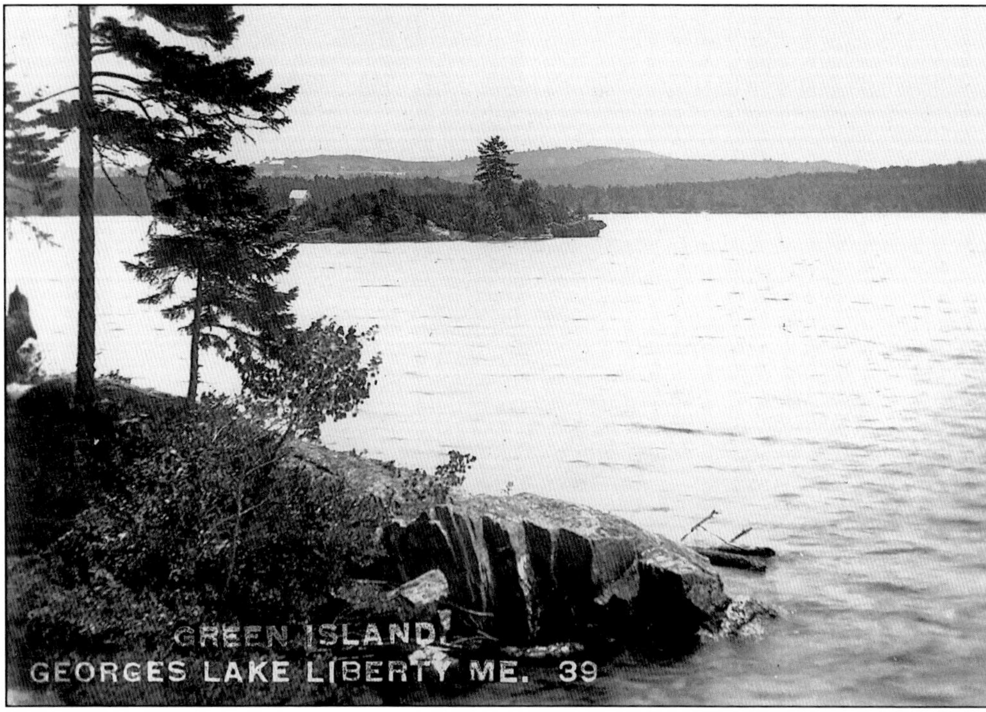

This undated view of Loon Island was taken from the tip of Green Island, looking toward the northeast. This image predates the construction of the Knowlton cottage. Hidden behind the island is the entrance to Little Pond. Haystack Mountain rises out of camera range to the right, and Pinola Point and Kenniston's Shore lie out of sight to the left.

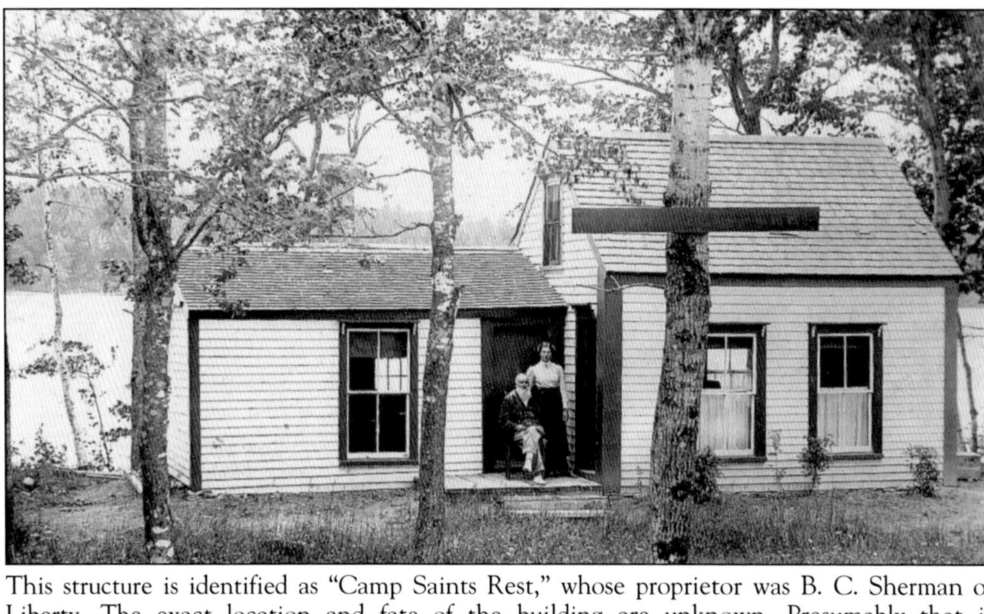

This structure is identified as "Camp Saints Rest," whose proprietor was B. C. Sherman of Liberty. The exact location and fate of the building are unknown. Presumably that is Mr. Sherman and his daughter pictured on the front porch. Judging by the proximity of the opposite shore in the background, this camp may have been located on Little Pond, along the present-day Roberts Shore Road.

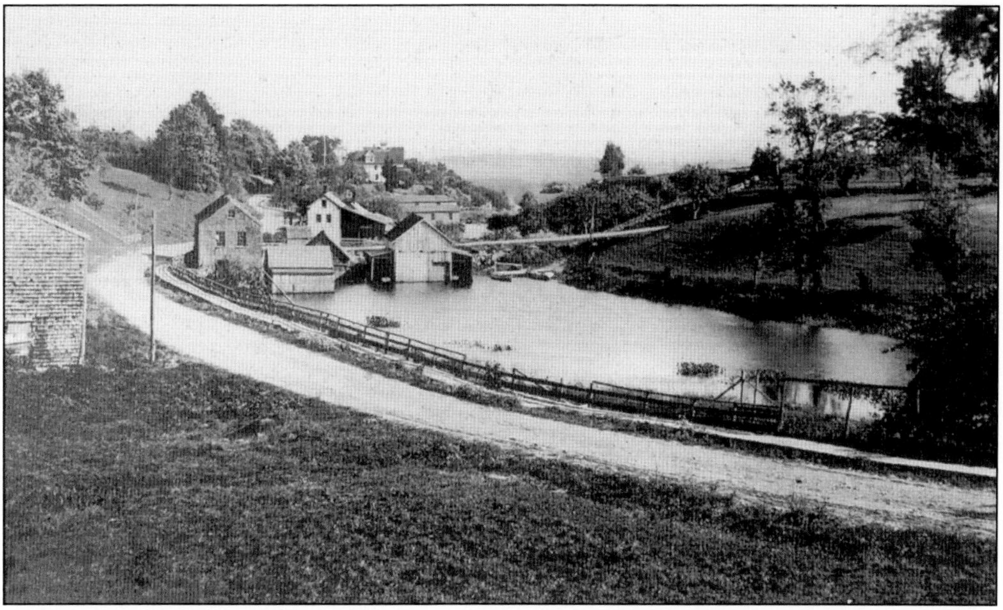

This 1906 view was taken looking south toward Liberty village, along modern Route 173/220. The water to the right is the channel leading into the St. George River. The buildings to the left of center are boathouses for the motorboats that provided ferry service around the lake. The wooden sidewalk visible on the right side of the street extended all the way through the village—about a mile distant.

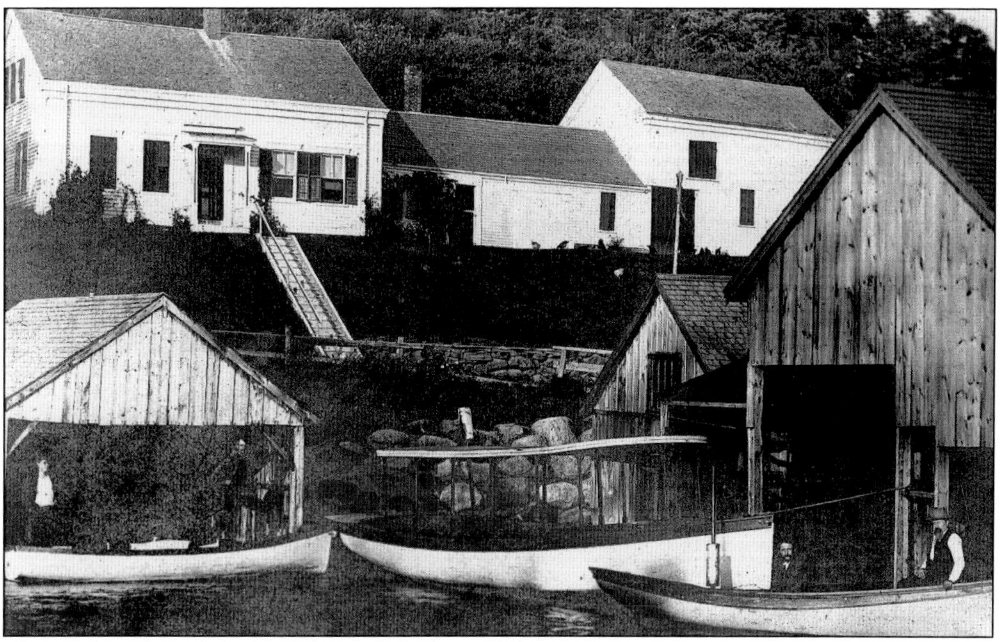

This early image of the boathouses and three of the steam-powered craft was taken from a boat in the channel. It was once a popular service to ferry tourists and picnickers to Marshall Shore, Sherman's Neck, and other locations along the lake from the landing just above the first dam on the St. George River. The house seen on the hillside still exists today at the intersection of Upper Main Street and the Pinnacle Road.

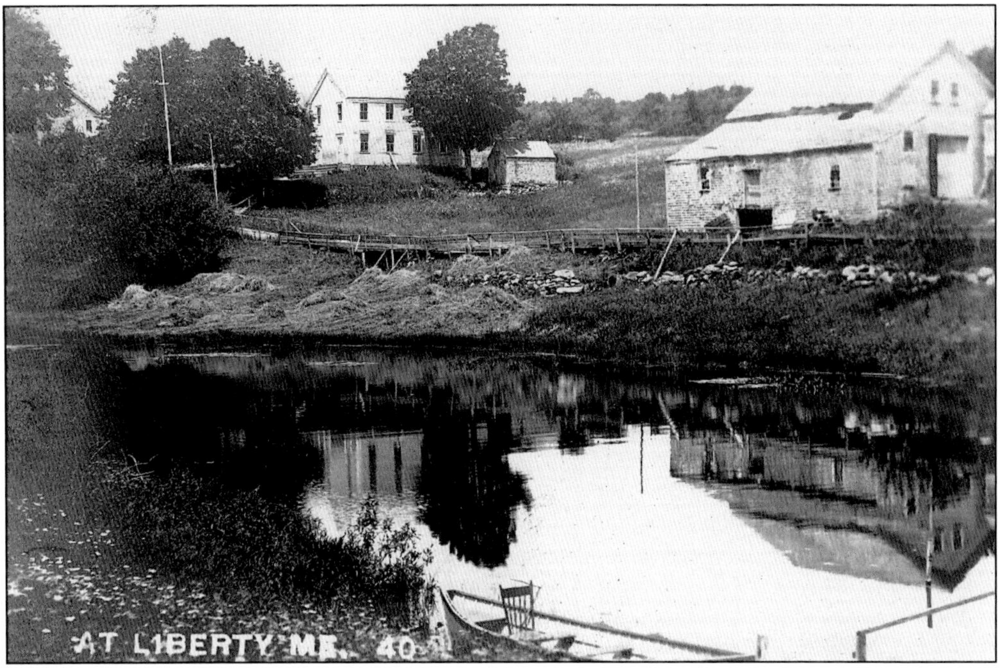

Taken from a small boat landing on the shore opposite the boathouses, this 1906 view looks uphill toward the northwest. The large building just to the left of center housed the village school. Directly across the street, mostly obscured by trees, stands the one-time dormitory building. Neither the school nor the large barn to the right exists today. Visible along the street is the wooden sidewalk seen in the last image.

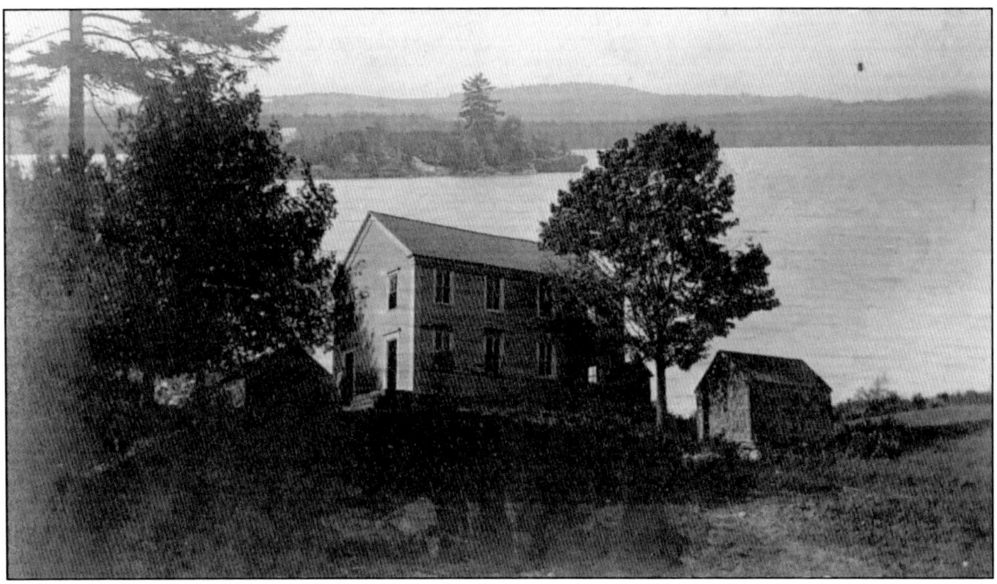

This photograph is an unusual double exposure of two different scenes—the first a view of Lake St. George, seen predominantly here as the background, and the second, a downhill image of the village schoolhouse, which makes up the foreground here. This image is interesting first in its very existence, and second, for the view it affords of the school structure itself and the associated outbuilding.

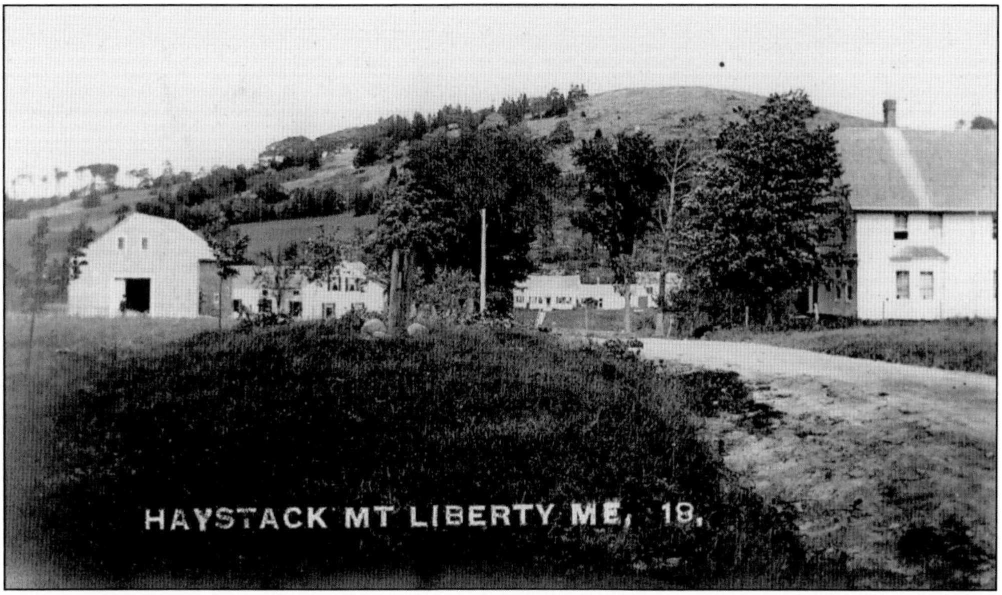

Haystack Mountain rises at the center of this 1905 image, taken looking northeast from modern Route 220. The long white house in the distance is the one seen in the earlier view of the motorboats. Neither the large farmhouse at the right nor the barn and house on the left has survived. This south-facing slope of the mountain is overgrown today and affords none of the following views.

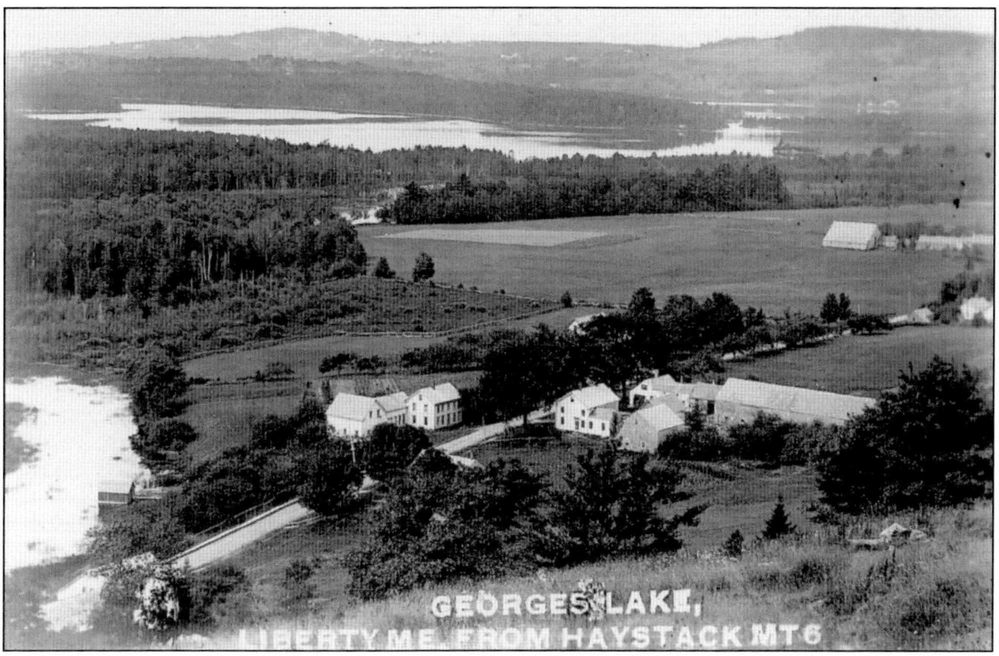

This early view from the summit of Haystack Mountain looks toward the southwest over Lake St. George, with Bolin Ridge in the distance. The extensive farm grouping to the right of center was the John Fuller farm, which burned in the 1920s. The dormitory building, now a private residence, is seen across the street. The schoolhouse, barely visible behind the trees, can be seen to the left of the Fuller farm.

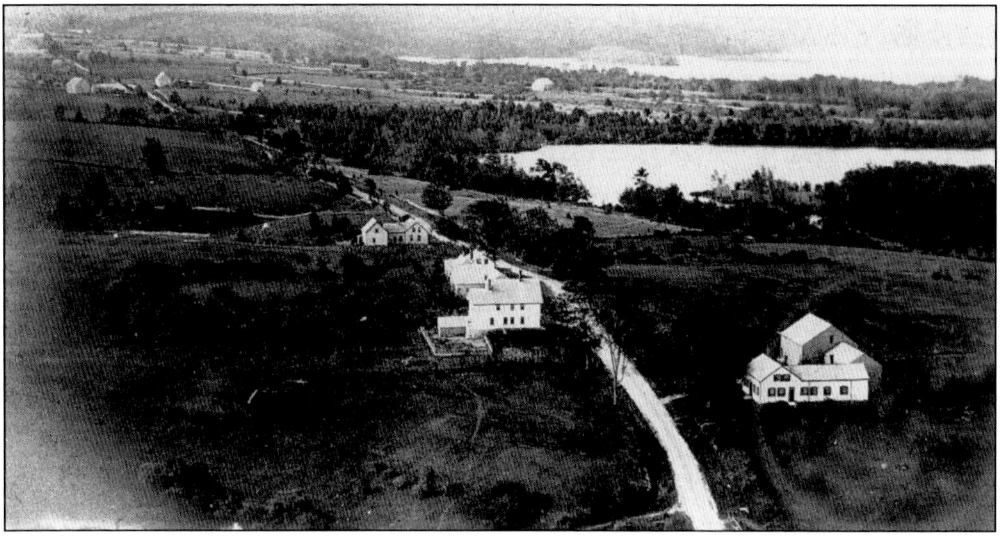

Another image recorded atop Haystack Mountain, this view looks almost directly south along the road to South Liberty, now modern Route 220. This 1904 view shows Little Pond to the right and the eastern shore of Lake St. George in the distance. The only structures surviving today are the small one to the left of center and one on the right side of the road, far off in the distance.

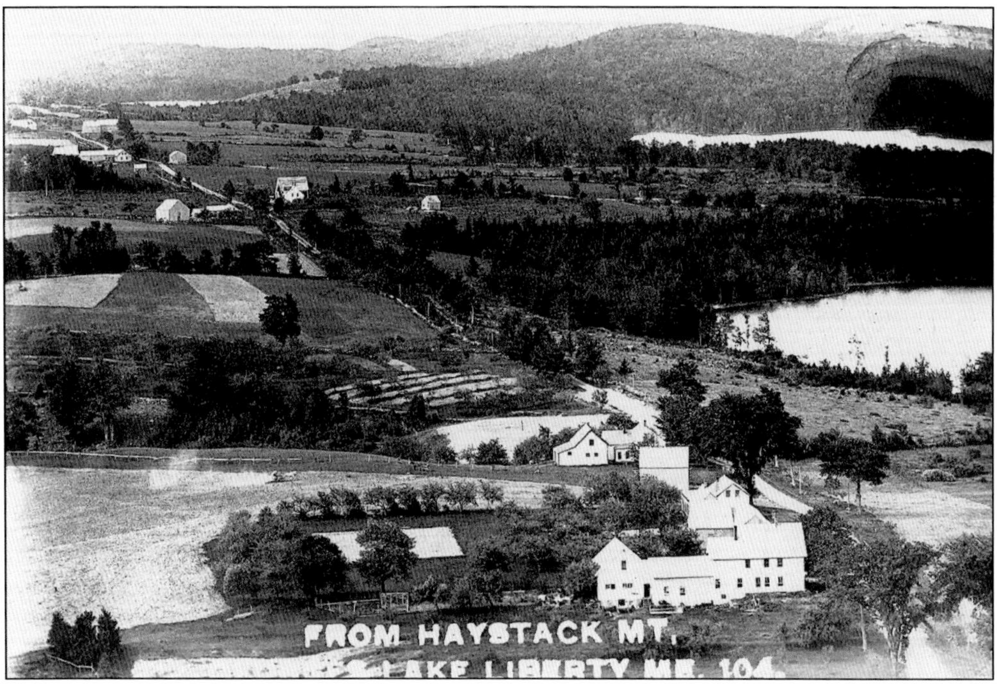

This 1914 image was recorded from a camera position a short distance east of and downhill from the previous view, looking toward the southwest. The most noticeable difference between the two photographs is the extensive additions to the white house in the foreground. The farmhouse just beyond it, which still exists today, has also received a new addition to its barn, and the one in the distance has a new, prominent dormer and barn.

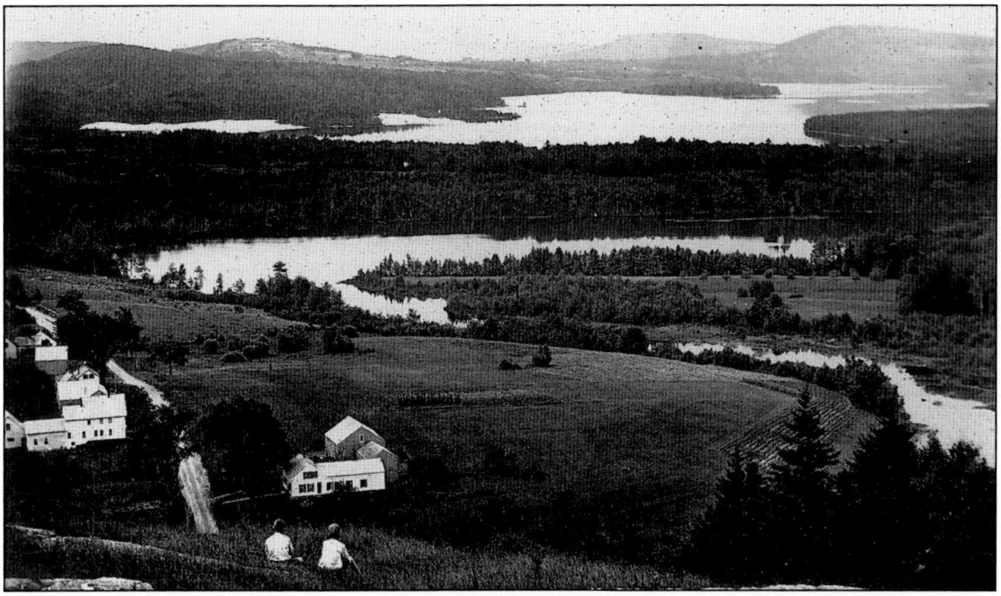

Taken from approximately the same camera position as the previous image, this view looks nearly due west. Bolin Ridge lies on the right horizon, with Lake St. George and Sherman's Neck visible just above center. Little Pond lies in the middle of the photograph, and the channel snakes its way from left to right. The structures and road in the left foreground are the same as those seen in the earlier views.

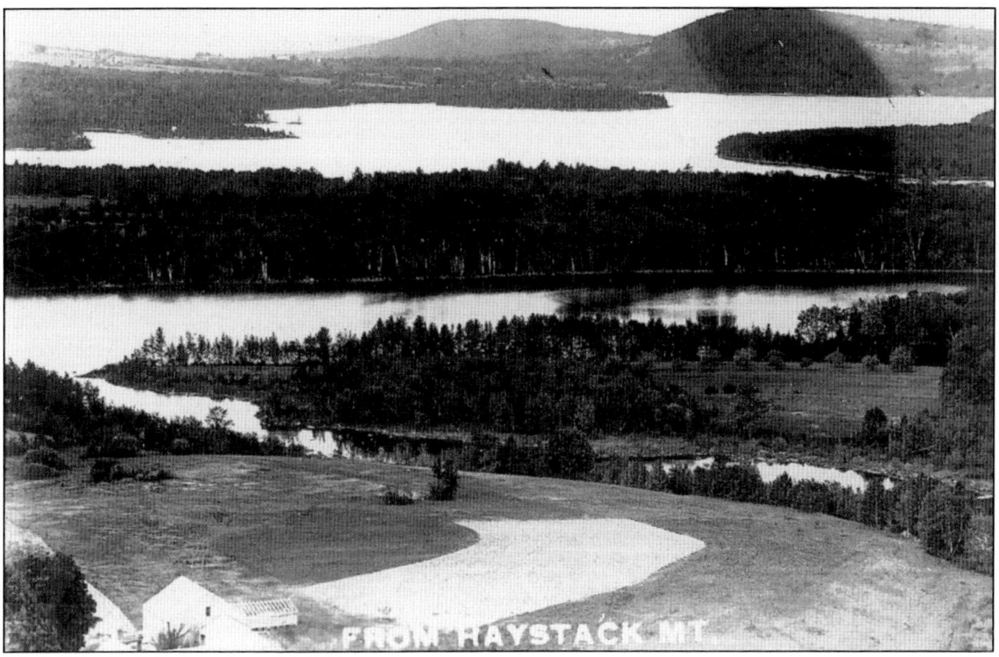

Another view looking westward, this image was taken later and from a lower elevation than the previous one. Once again, Bolin Ridge, Lake St. George, Sherman's Neck, and Little Pond are in the distance, with the channel stretching from left to right in the foreground. One notable exception from the previous photograph is that the barn visible at the lower left is receiving an addition, as yet unfinished when this photograph was exposed.

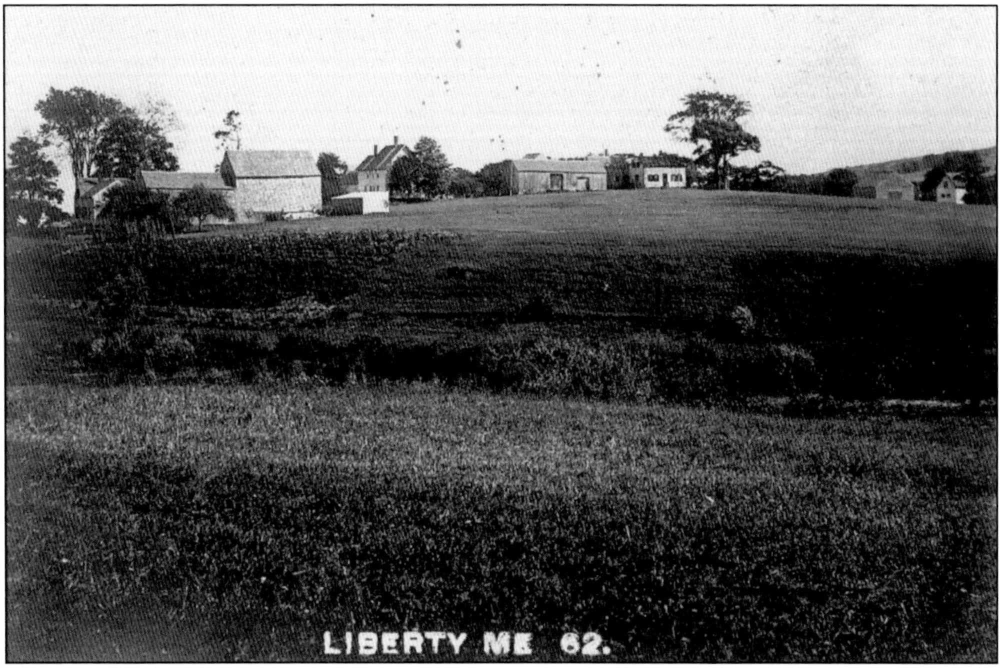

This undated image was taken alongside the road to South Liberty in the open field seen in previous photographs, looking east toward Liberty village. The only structure to survive to this day, although without its barn, is the small farmhouse at the extreme right. The balance of the houses and barns have long since disappeared.

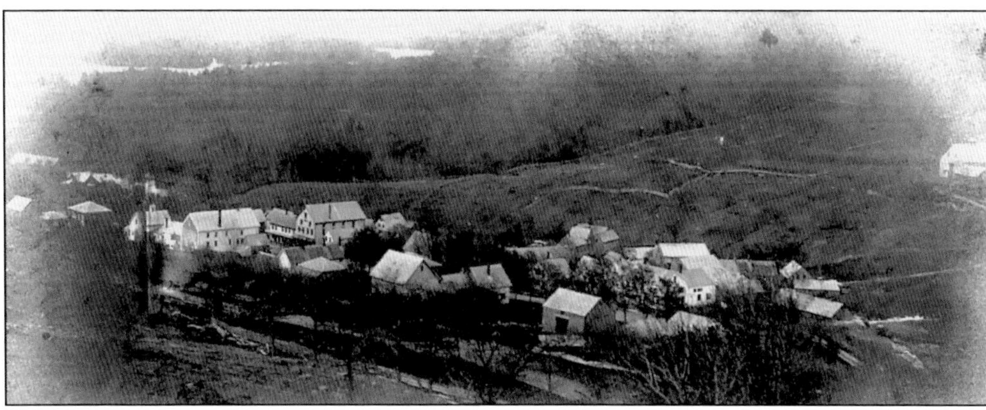

Taken from Haystack Mountain, this early view looks toward the southeast, over Liberty village. Many of the buildings have disappeared, but several notable exceptions still exist today. The farmhouse and attached barn at the center of the image are now the Liberty Graphics facility. The two large buildings facing each other to the left are the Liberty Tool and Davistown Museum buildings, while the foursquare building down the hill is now a private residence.

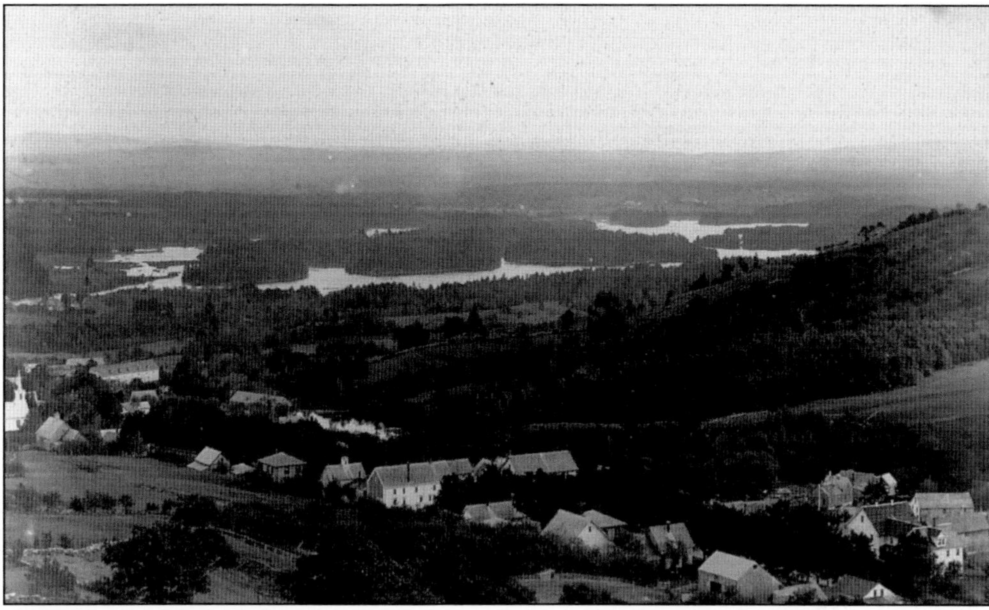

Taken from a slightly different angle and in summer, this later view captures essentially the same scene. Visible to the left is the Liberty Baptist Church, and Stevens Pond, with its many islands, lies in the distance. The long, multistoried white building with dormers to the right of the church is the tannery, later to become the novelty mill owned by the Vose brothers.

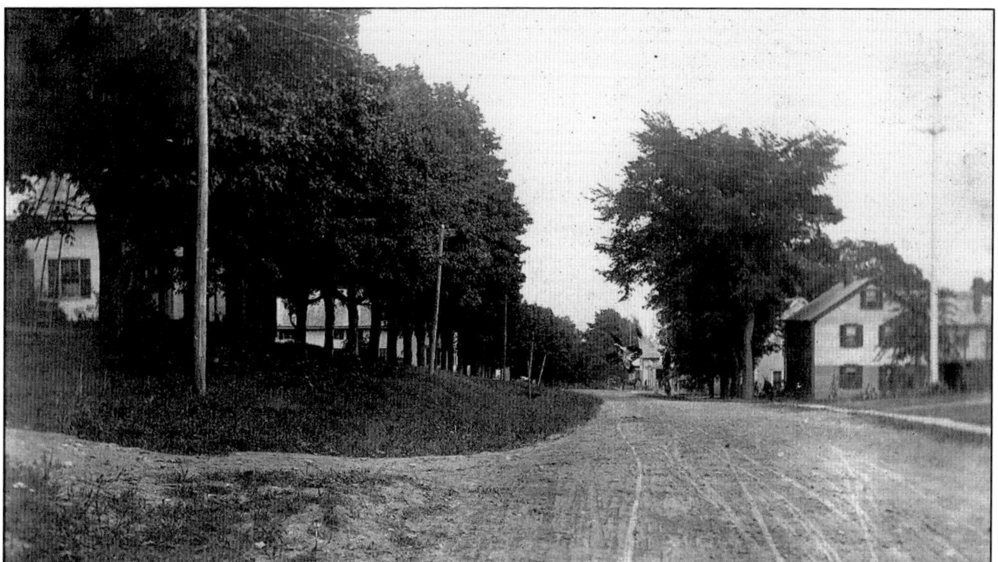

Looking down into the village along Main Street, this 1906 view was taken just above the current Liberty Graphics building (left), partially obscured by trees. The large house on the right burned in the 1920s. Farther down, the corner of the octagonal post office and the front façade of the Sanford House are visible in the distance. The wooden sidewalk continues into town on the right.

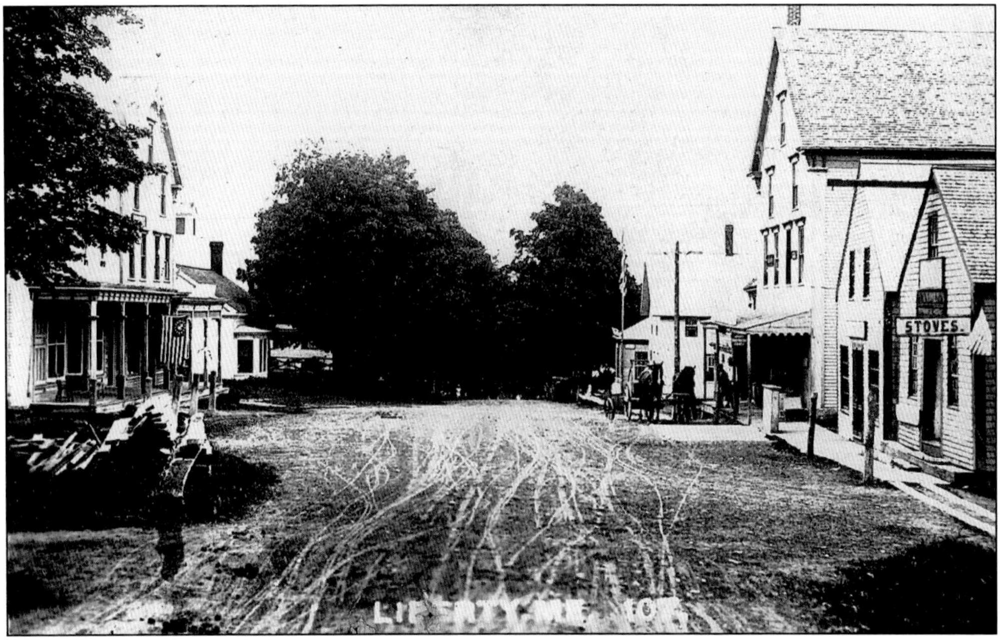

This undated view of Main Street was taken in front of the present-day Artisans Building, across from the new Community Hall. The Prescott Block (the first large building on the left) still exists, as does the small white house just beyond. On the right, the large general store exists today as Liberty Tool, and farther down, the white house and the old octagonal post office remain. None of the other structures have survived.

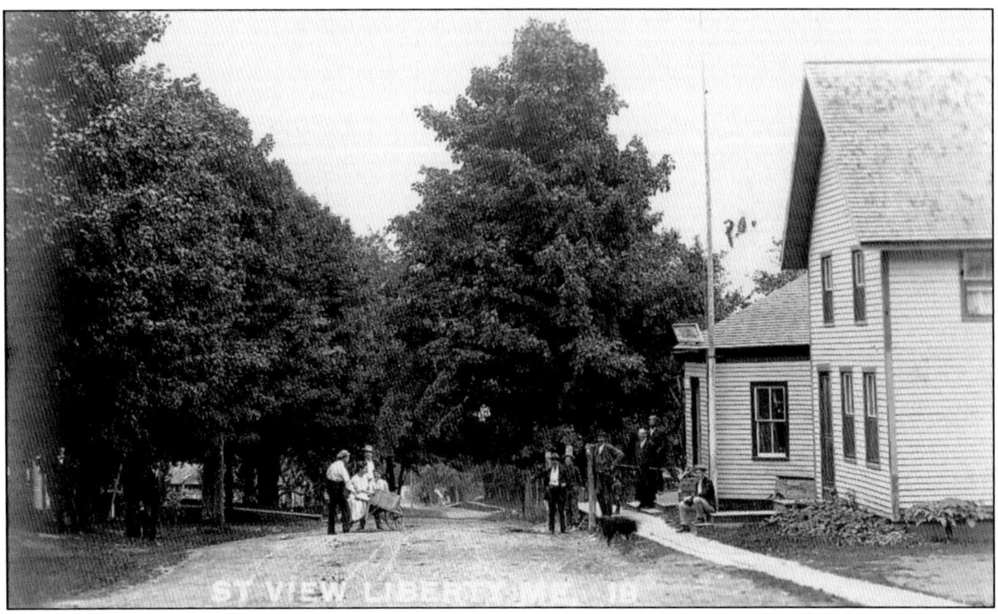

Taken from in front of the Sanford House, this undated image is of the old octagonal post office and the private residence just uphill, both of which still exist. There are thirteen people posing in this photograph, two men under the trees to the far left, two men and two women in the middle of the street with the wheelbarrow, and six men and a child on the steps of the octagonal building.

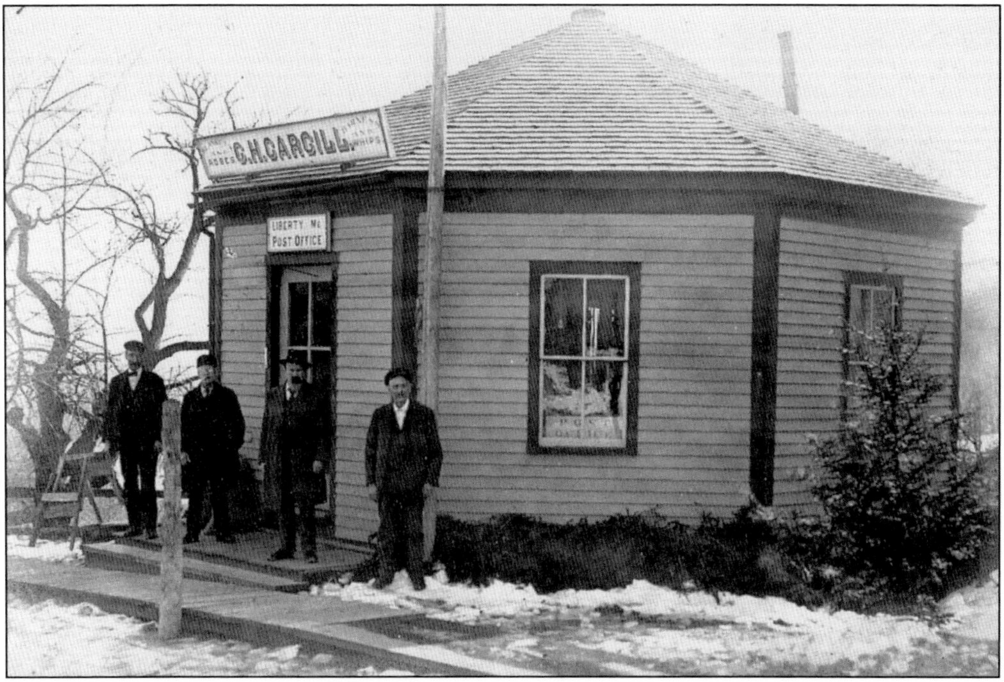

Rufus Carter built this octagonal building, now the home of the Liberty Historical Society, in 1867, for his harness-repair business. Purchased in 1878 by Gus Cargill for his own harness business, the building also served as the Liberty post office until 1960. During that time, it was touted as the only octagonal post office in the country. The identities of the four men posing for this winter view are unknown.

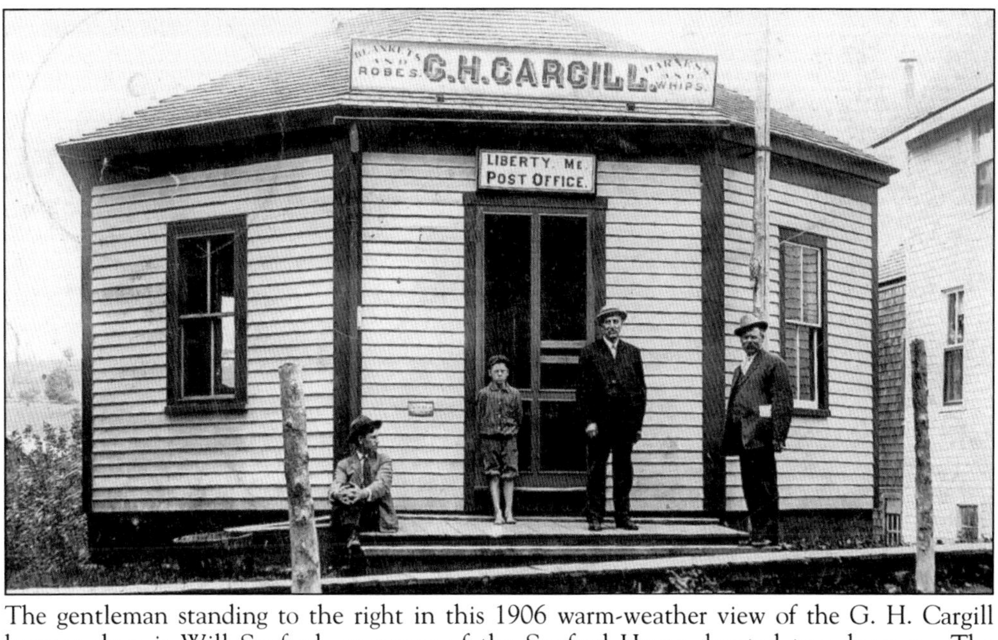

The gentleman standing to the right in this 1906 warm-weather view of the G. H. Cargill harness shop is Will Sanford, co-owner of the Sanford House, located two doors up. The identities of the other two men and the child are unknown. In 1973, the octagonal post office building was added to the National Register of Historic Places.

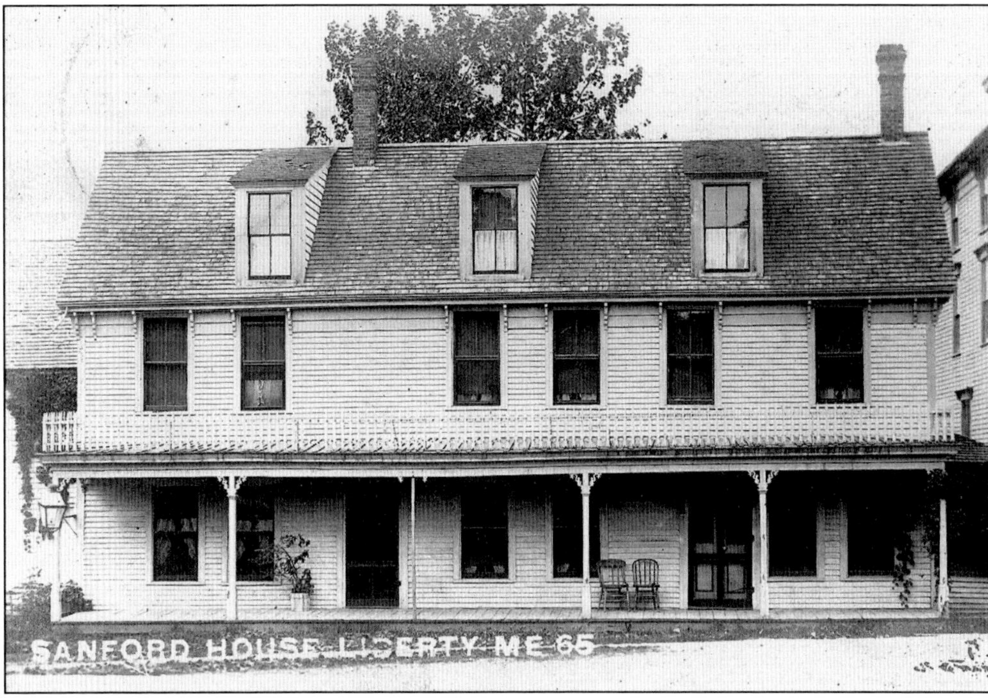

The Sanford House, originally run by Francis Chapman, was the first hotel in Liberty. Located on the site of the present-day Ivan O. Davis-Liberty Library, for years the hotel did a brisk business. A stagecoach layover stop on the Augusta-to-Belfast route and a favorite summer vacation area, Liberty at one time hosted many overnight and long-term guests.

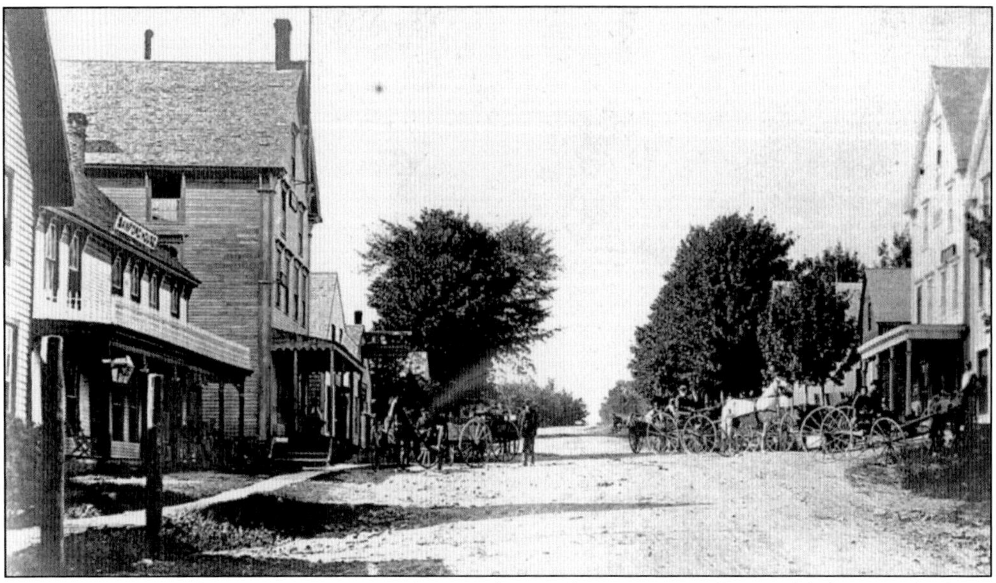

This 1906 view of Main Street was taken in front of G. H. Cargill's establishment, looking uphill. The Sanford House is visible on the left, next to the general store. Across the street are the Prescott Block and the current Artisan's Building. In this photograph, there are 10 buggies and buckboard wagons crowding this small section of town. The wooden sidewalk can be seen continuing through the village on the left.

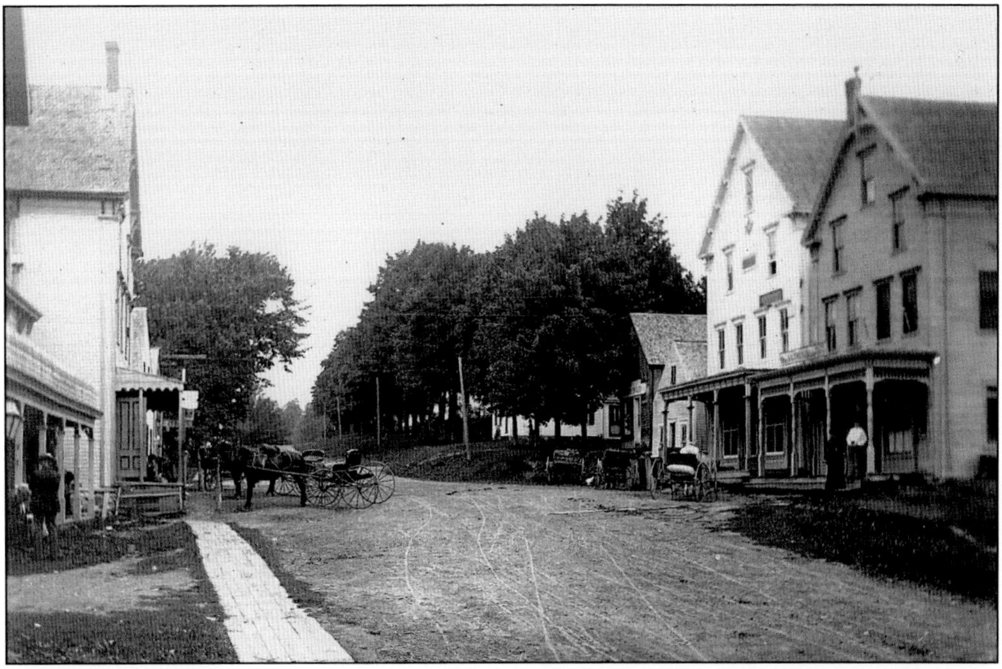

In this similar, undated view, there is much less traffic on the road—only six buggies. The large building to the right was, in later years, Merrill's Quality Store, a combination general store, gas station, and soda fountain. It was torn down in the 1940s in favor of a filling station. That structure still exists today but as an annex for Liberty Tool, now located where the general store (later an IGA) existed.

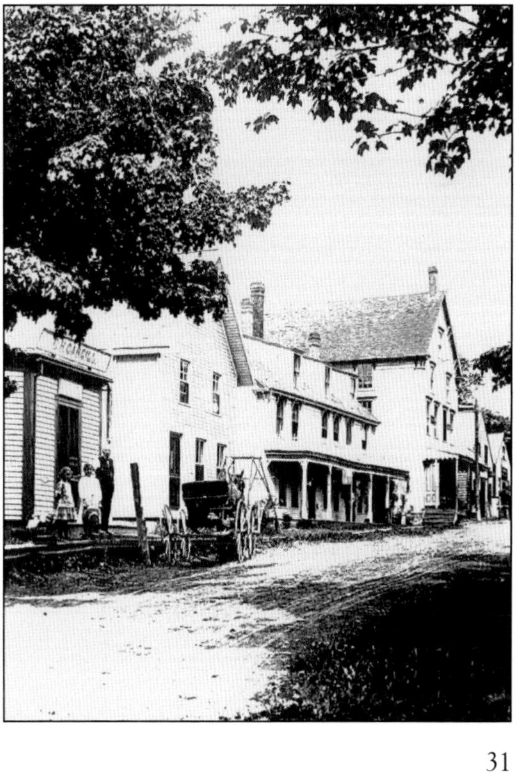

This final 1915 view of the lower section of Main Street captures Gus Cargill posing outside his shop with two unidentified young girls. The building at the far right just past the general store was Knowlton's "tin shop," where stove components, smoke jacks, and other metal implements were manufactured.

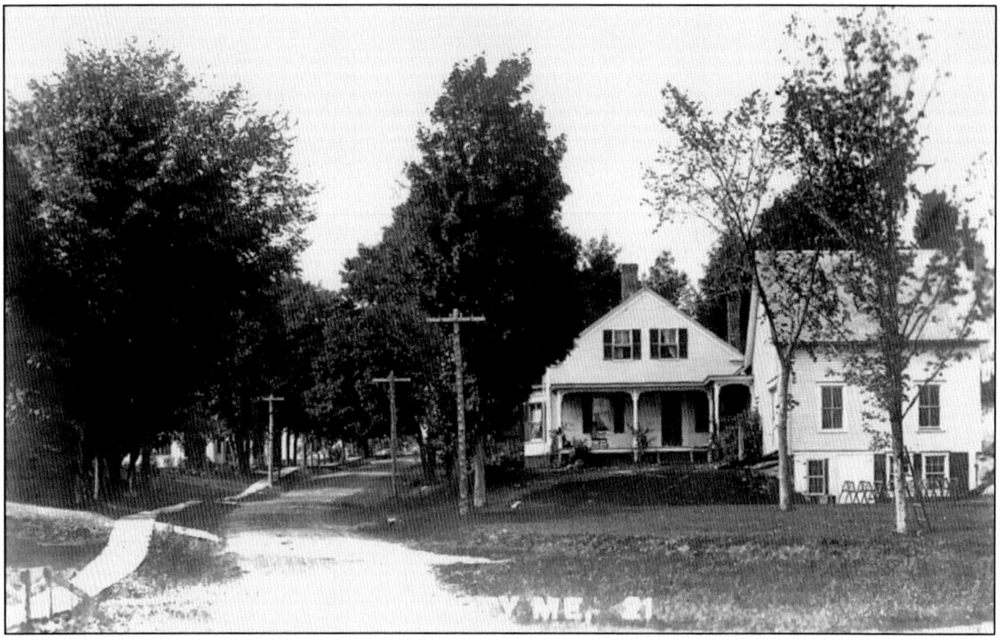

This 1906 view was taken near the Liberty Baptist Church, looking back uphill toward the village. The house and attached barn shown here still exist. The wooden sidewalk, having coursed its way through town from the school, is nearing its end at the bottom of the hill. Judging from the poles lining the street in this image, some households in the village had phone service but no electricity as of yet.

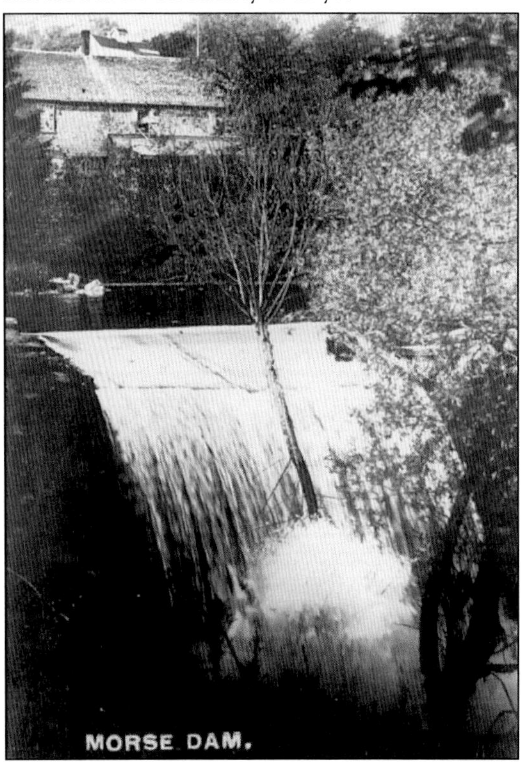

Morse Dam was one of several dams located along the St. George River as it coursed through town. As was generally the case in early America, water supplied the power for industry here. Along the river was an ax factory, a foundry, a machine shop, two tanneries, five sawmills, and a gristmill. According to the 1881 *State of Maine Gazetteer*, items manufactured here included cabinets, coffins, carriages, cultivators, horse rakes, saddles, harnesses, boots, and shoes.

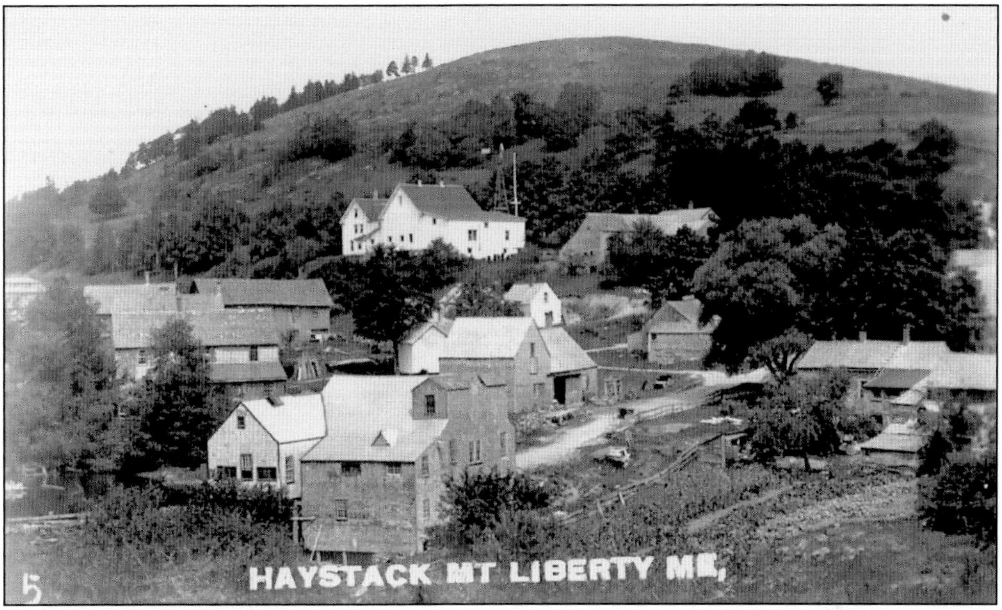

Taken in 1903 along the banks of the St. George River, this image looks due north toward Haystack Mountain. Main Street extends from left to right in front of the large white house in the distance. The buildings in the foreground lie in the area now occupied by the Community Hall, and almost all were involved in some sort of commercial enterprise. Visible in the foreground to the left is a millpond.

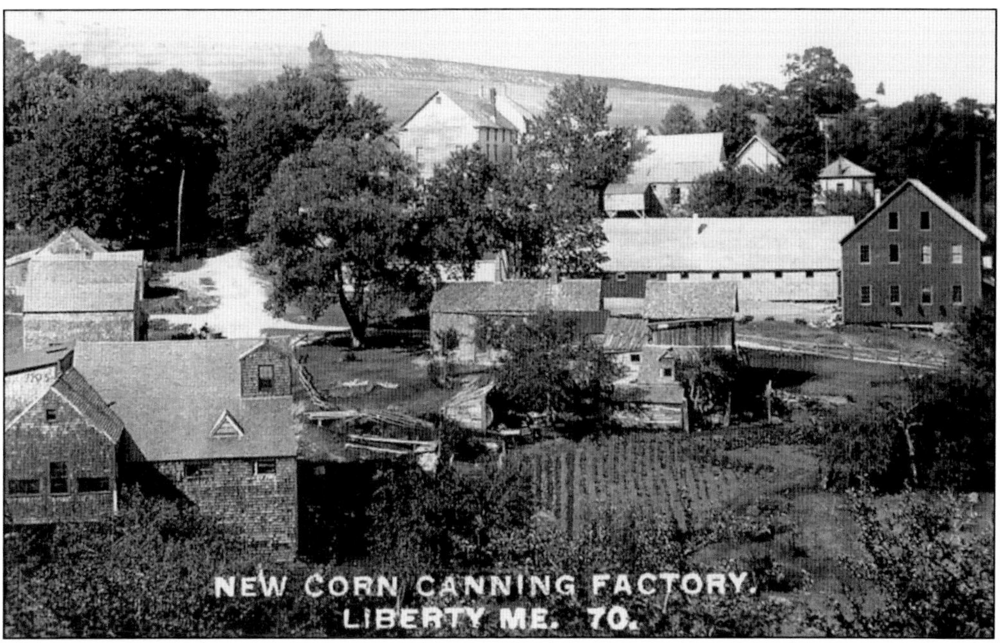

This is a 1905 image of the same area, taken from a short distance to the west. Prominent in this view are the two large business blocks on Main Street and the corn-canning factory to the right of center, all of which still exist today. Also visible just above the canning company is the octagonal shop belonging to Gus Cargill. The large mill to the left can be seen in the previous image.

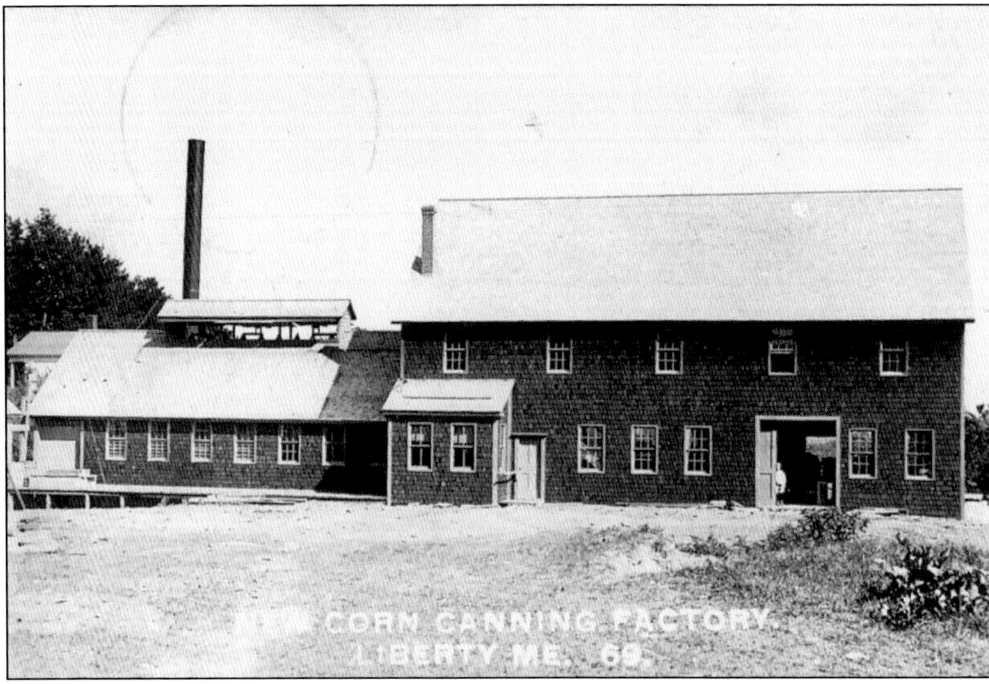

The Monmouth Canning Company factory building was constructed in 1905, the year this photograph was taken. Located along the Back Road on the banks of the St. George River, the factory was engaged in the seasonal business of canning corn, beans, and blueberries. During operation, the factory employed approximately 50 people at any given time. The local plant manager was John Sanford.

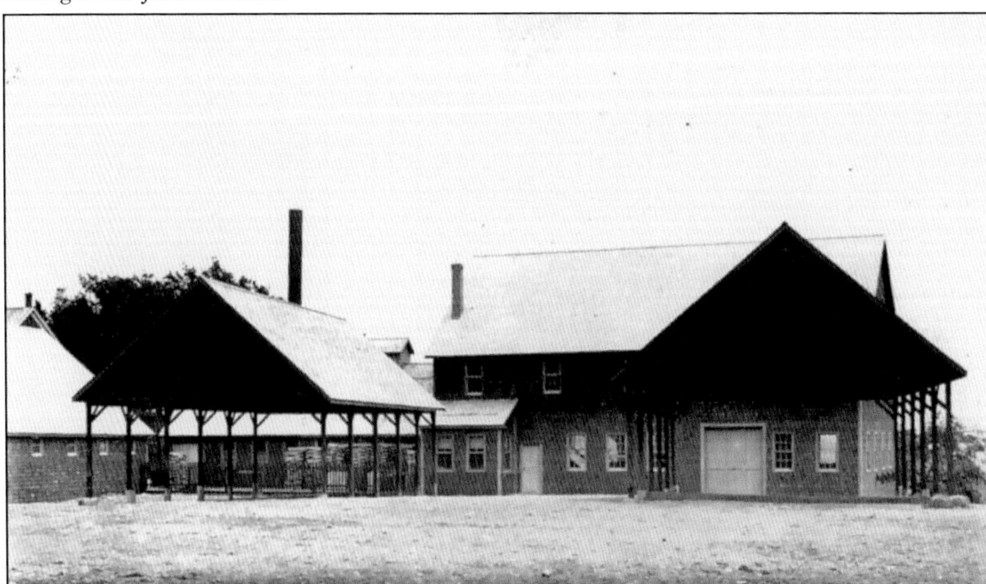
In 1906, a pair of corn sheds was erected beside the main packing building of the canning plant. Corn was unloaded from farm wagons here, where it was shoveled manually onto conveyors for the journey into the husking room. The factory building exists today as a private residence, and the owner operates a specialty construction business from the site.

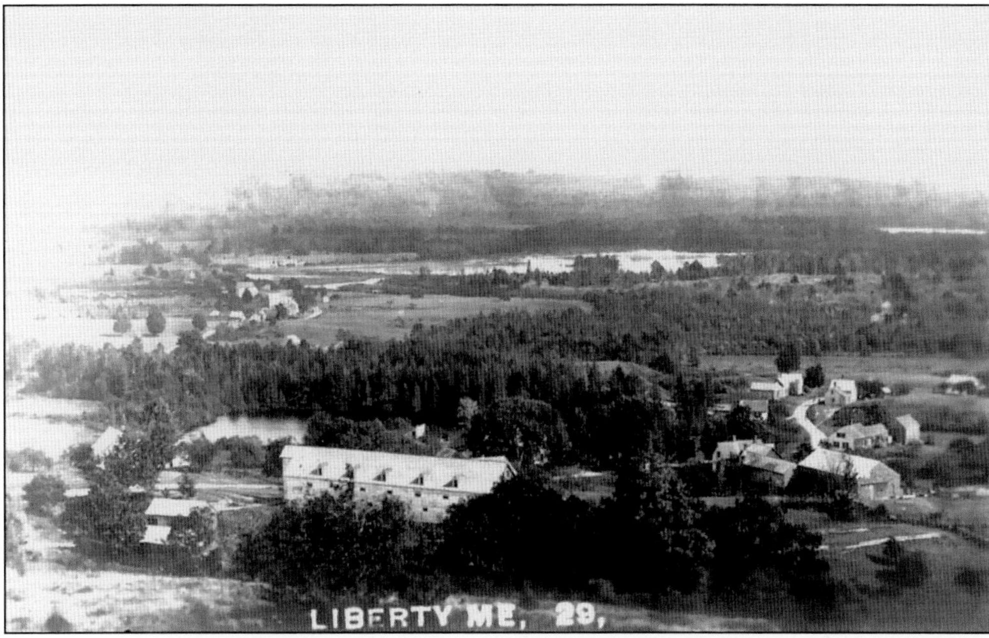

This is a 1905 view of the lower end of Liberty village, looking almost due east. The large building in the foreground is the tannery, later to be operated by the Vose brothers as a novelty mill. Main Street comes down the hill from the left of the tannery building, and the wooden sidewalk ends just out of camera range to the left. Trues Pond and Montville lie off in the distance.

This final image of Liberty is an early view of Stevens Pond. Located southeast of both Lake St. George and the village, Stevens Pond lies along modern Route 173, on the road to South Montville and Searsmont. There is a small parking area and boat ramp at the dam site, where the public has access to the pond today.

This is an undated wintertime image of the treeless, snow-covered slope of Haystack Mountain and the backside of the Main Street buildings. The St. George River lies in the foreground. Prominent in this view are the two large business blocks on Main Street, both of which still exist today. Also visible to the left of center is the octagonal harness shop belonging to Gus Cargill.

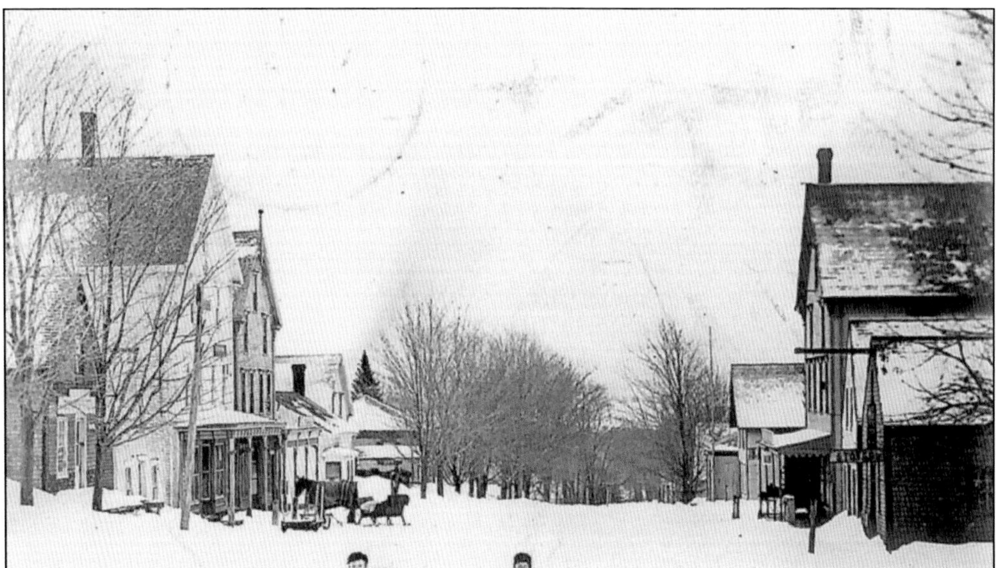

This snowy winter view of Main Street was taken in 1907 in front of the present-day Artisans Building, across from the new Community Hall. The large structure on the right is the current Liberty Tool building, while the white building on the left is the home of the Davistown Museum. Of particular interest are the children playing in the foreground and the horse-drawn sleigh to the left.

Two

South Montville, Searsmont, and Appleton

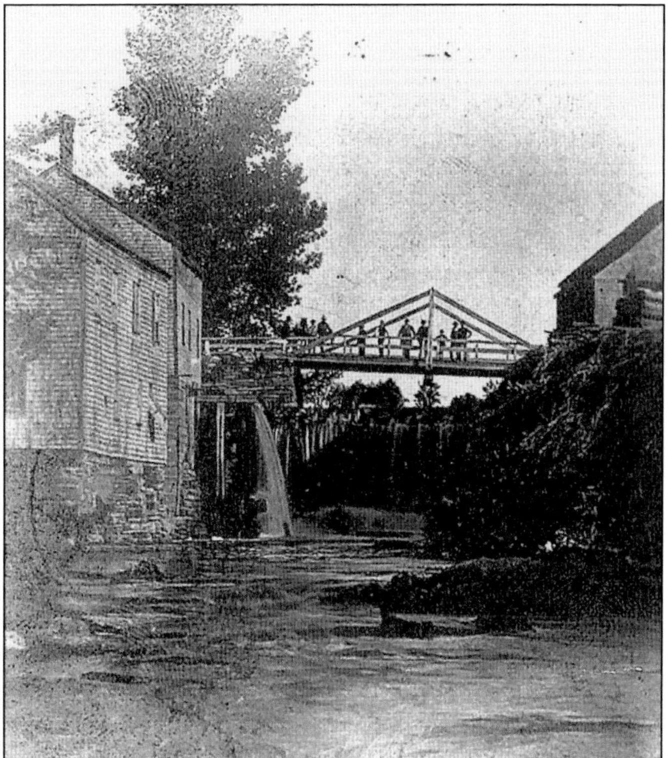

Located east of Liberty is the settlement of South Montville. Located just downstream from the modern Trues Dam, all that remains of this *c.* 1905 view are massive granite abutments rising on either side of the St. George River. Built in 1811 by Ezekiel True and washed away in a 1936 flood, this was the site of the first gristmill built in the town of Montville.

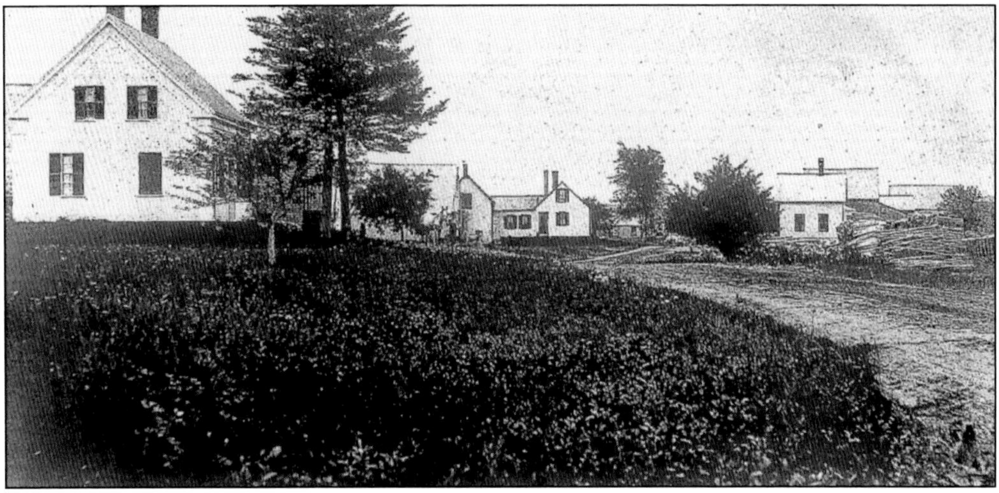

At the intersection of the West Appleton Road and Route 173 is the Woodsman's Mills section of Searsmont. In 1817, Smith Cram built a mill here astride the St. George River, which was later purchased by Edmond Woodsman. In this 1905 view, logs for the nearby sawmill are visible to the right. The large house to the left and the structure beyond the logs still exist, but the dwelling in the center has disappeared.

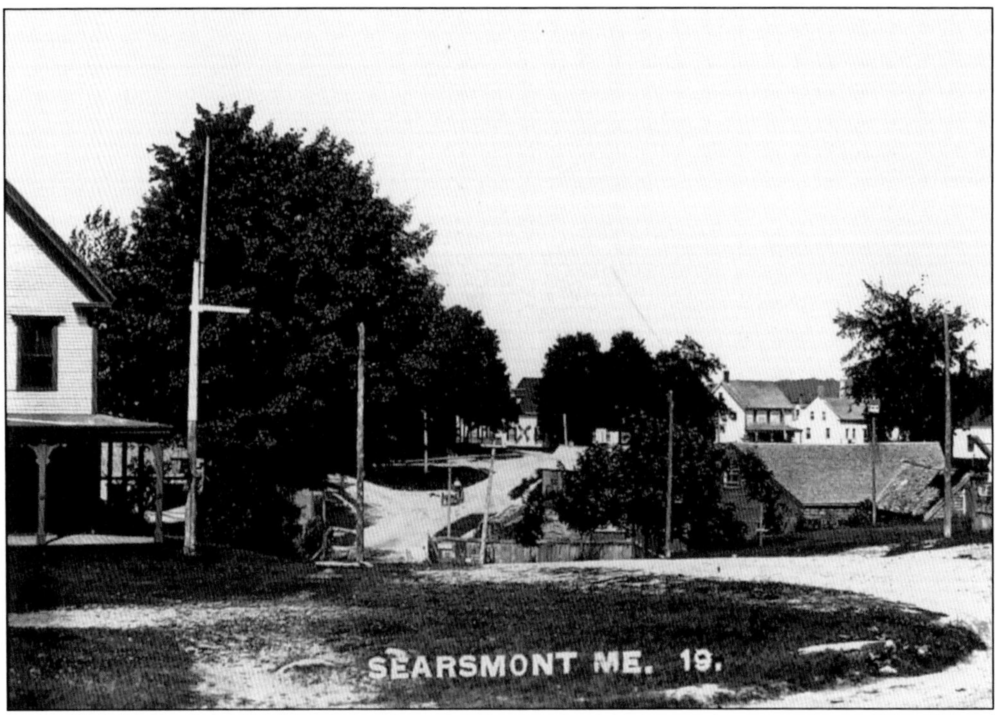

This image, taken at the junction of Routes 173 and 131, shows the view toward the Upper Bridge and the village of Searsmont. Nearly all the buildings visible in this 1904 photograph have disappeared, with the exception of the two-story building with the long covered porch in the distance—the site of the current Fraternity Village Store—and the private dwelling just to its left, barely visible behind the trees.

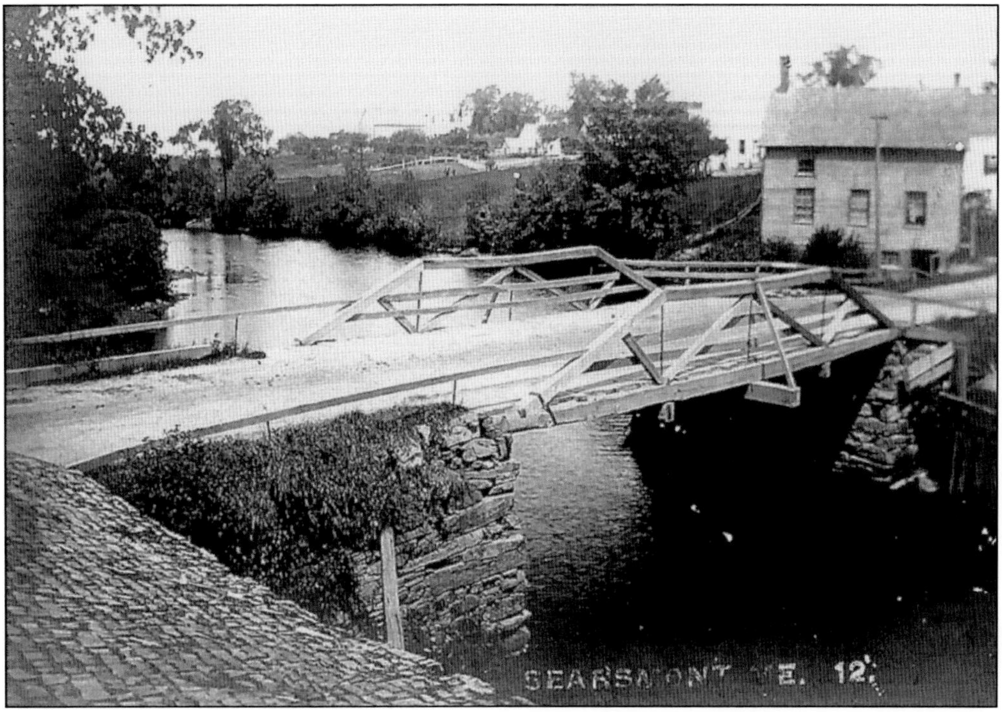

Taken looking upstream from atop the roof of the long, low building seen in the next photograph, this is an interesting view of the Upper Bridge as it crosses the St. George River. Included in the scene are the long-defunct casket factory, just beyond the bridge, and the backs of the structures located along the New England Road.

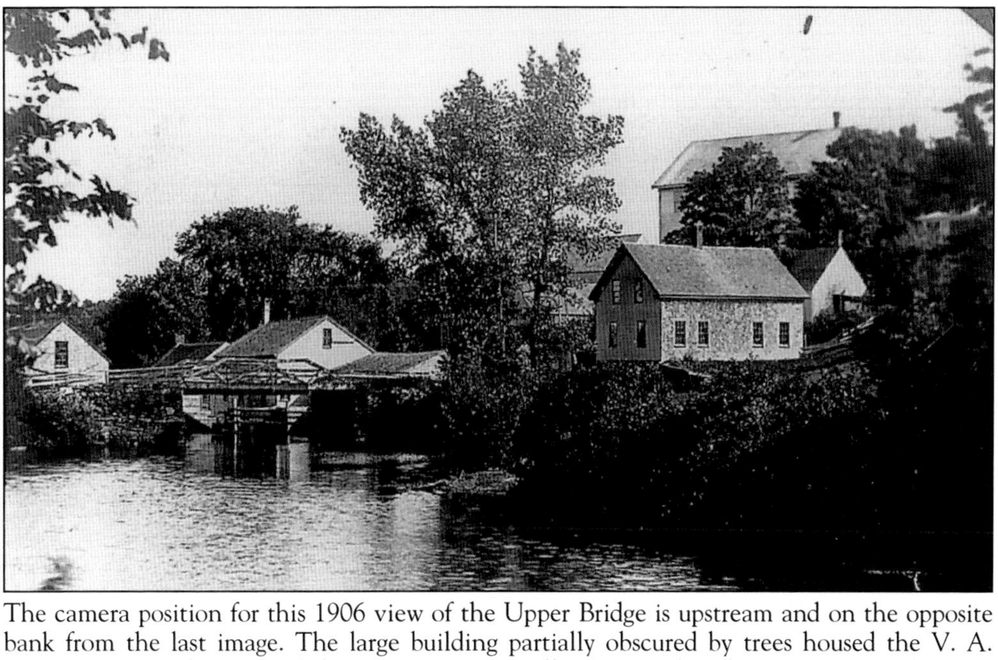

The camera position for this 1906 view of the Upper Bridge is upstream and on the opposite bank from the last image. The large building partially obscured by trees housed the V. A. Simmons General Store and the Searsmont post office. Located at the intersection of Routes 173 and 131, the building was demolished during the 1970s. Tablet Park now occupies the site.

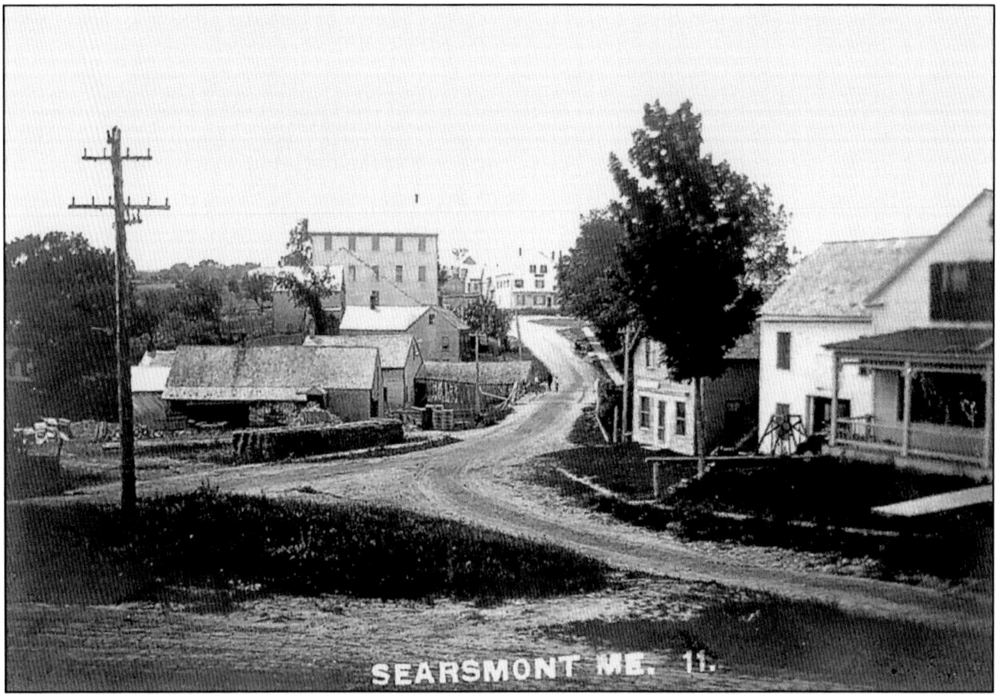

With the New England Road stretching off to the right and Route 131 to the left, this view looks back toward the Upper Bridge and the road to Appleton. The V. A. Simmons General Store is in the distance, the casket factory is to the right, and the stave mill, engaged in the manufacture of lime casks for the Appleton kilns, is to the left.

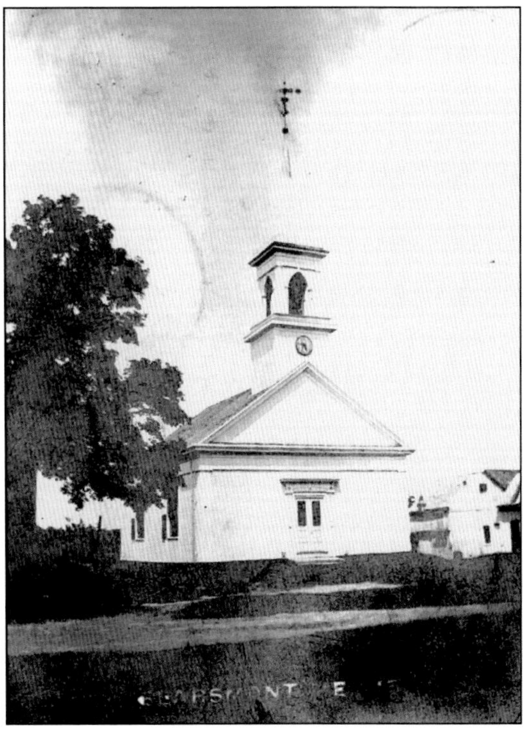

Built in 1845, the Searsmont United Methodist Church stands just east of the village. Visible in this 1904 view, but no longer operable today, the clock mechanism and face were donated by David Sears, a prominent citizen of Searsport and Boston, in memory of his father. The wooden face, now timeworn, is permanently on display at the Searsmont Historical Society.

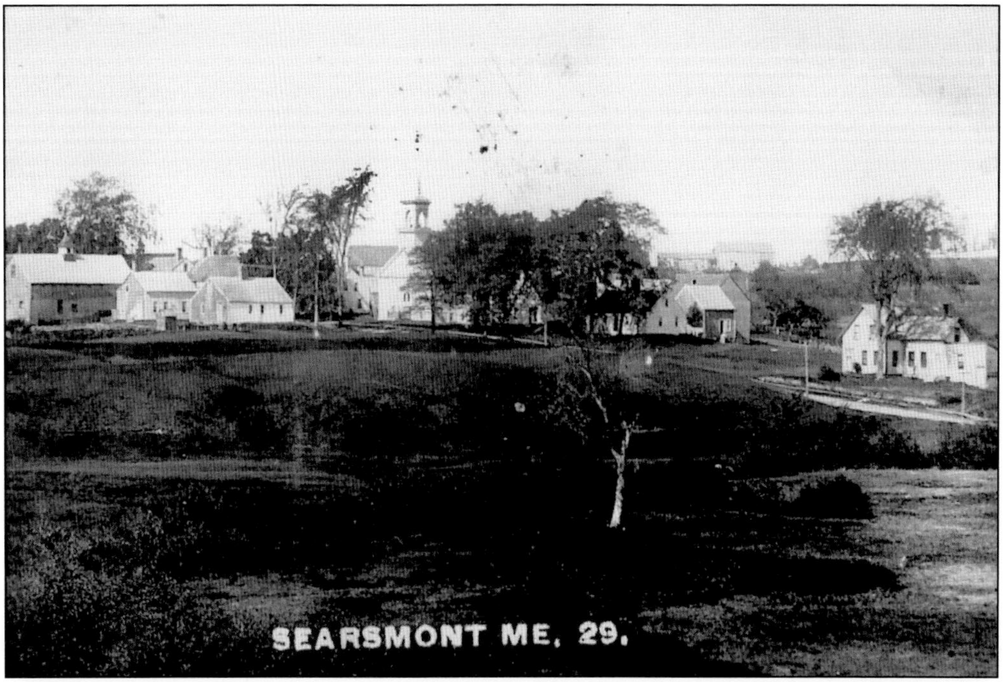

Taken in a field just behind the present-day post office, this view looks back toward the United Methodist Church. The barn with the cupola, the smaller structure just to its right, the house to the far right, and the house next to the church and partially hidden by trees all exist to this day. The original camera view is now obscured by tree growth.

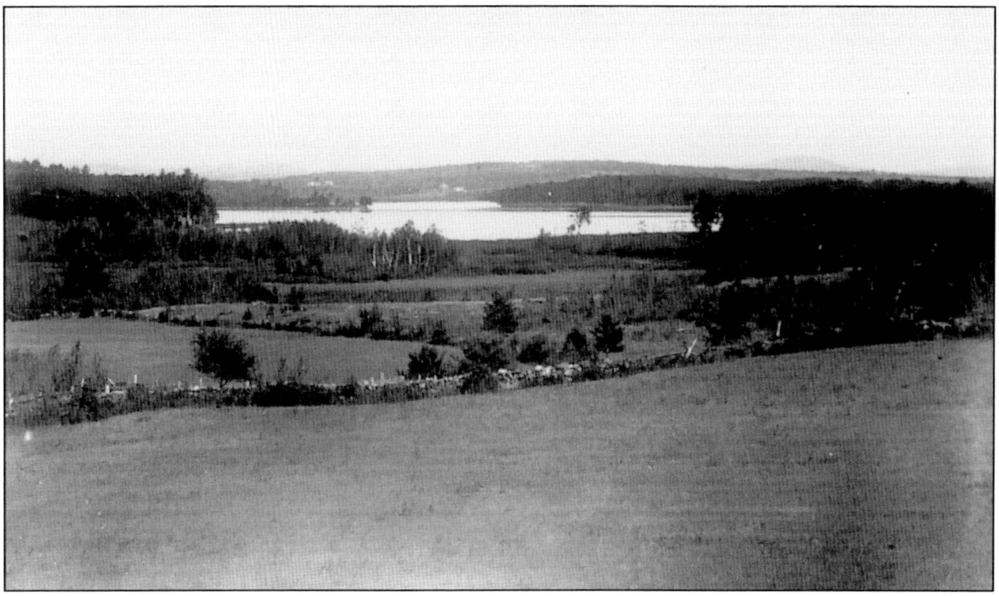

This 1905 view of Quantabacook Lake remains little changed today. While woodlands now obscure the original camera position, a closer location nearby reveals few additional houses visible. Located northeast of the village and sandwiched between Routes 3 and 131, the lake was and continues to be a popular vacation spot. Many area residents maintain summer camps on the lake, as do the Boy Scouts of America.

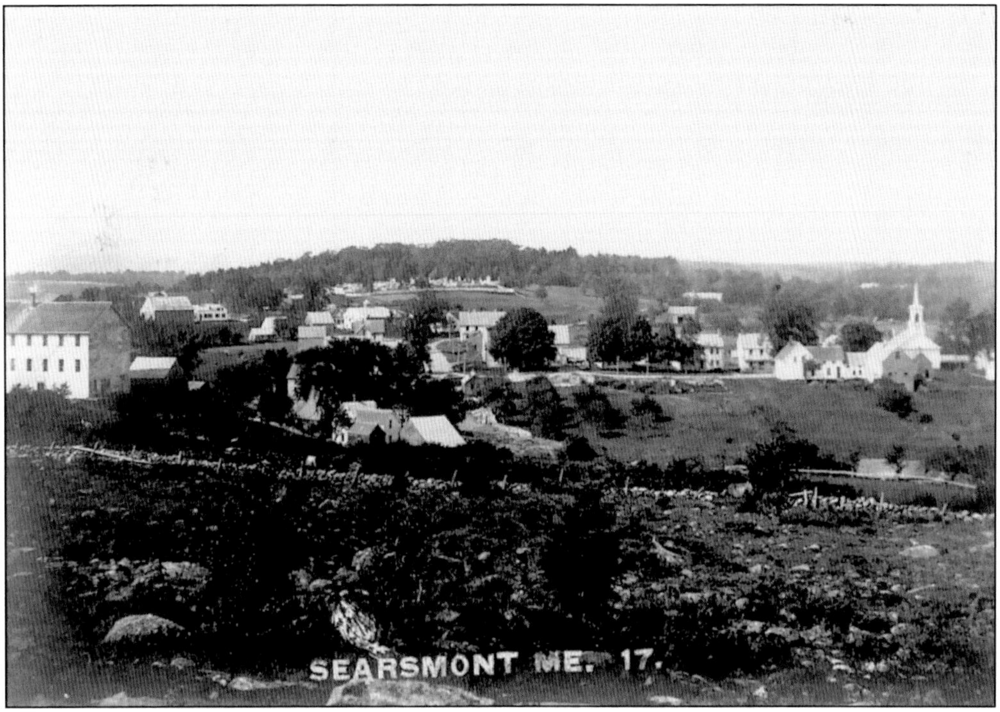

Taken in a rocky field just south of town along the Appleton Road, this 1906 view is blocked today by tree growth. Visible to the left is Simmons General Store, while the stave mill is just to the left of center, and the Methodist church rises on the right. Clearly visible on the hill in the distance are the monuments of the Oak Grove Cemetery.

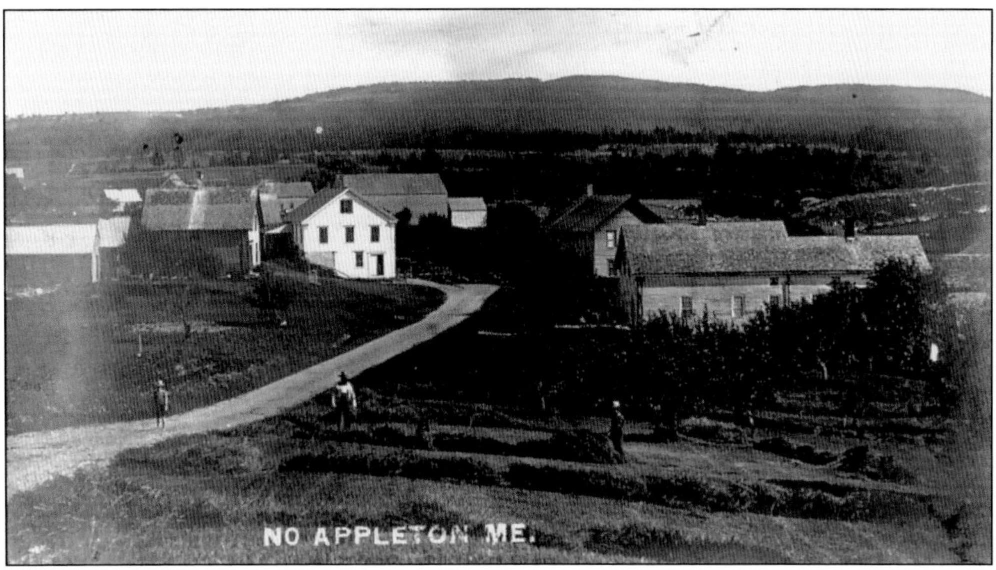

Located south of Searsmont along Route 105, the village of North Appleton was originally known as Packard's Mills. This view, looking south toward the St. George River, appears much changed today. The white house with the granite corner, located just to the left of center here, and the house to its left still exist, but nothing else remains. As with many other modern views, woodlands have reclaimed much of the landscape.

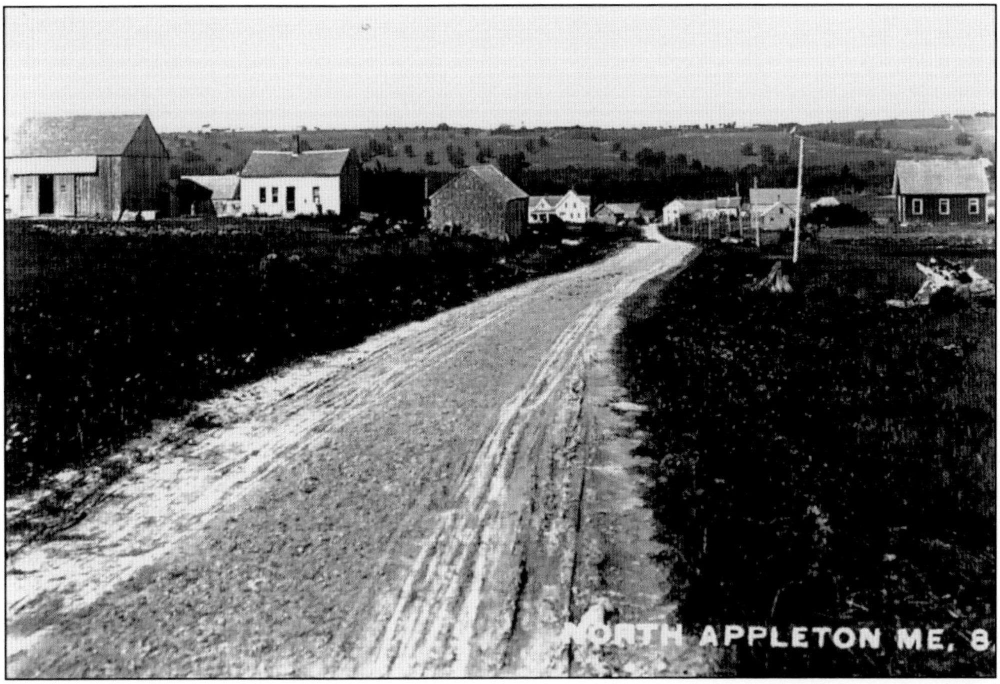

This view of North Appleton was taken from east of the settlement, looking west toward Appleton Ridge. The barn to the left still exists, although the farmhouse has since disappeared. The structure to the far right is currently a business establishment, and the farmhouse with the interesting double-peaked roof near the center of the photograph is still easily identified today. Tree growth along the entire ridge has obscured any remaining structures there.

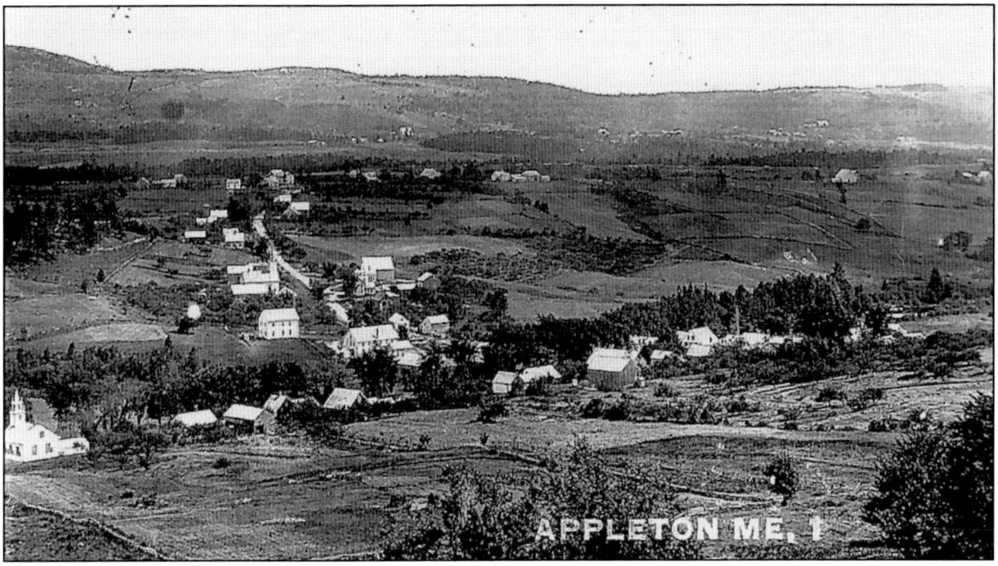

Appleton Ridge Road, constructed in 1812, was the original stagecoach route from Belfast to Wiscasset. This 1906 view was taken in a blueberry field atop the ridge, looking to the east. The village and McLain's Mills are at the center of the photograph, with the monuments of Pine Grove Cemetery visible just above the church. To the left, the 1816 Appleton Baptist Church, less its steeple, stands today.

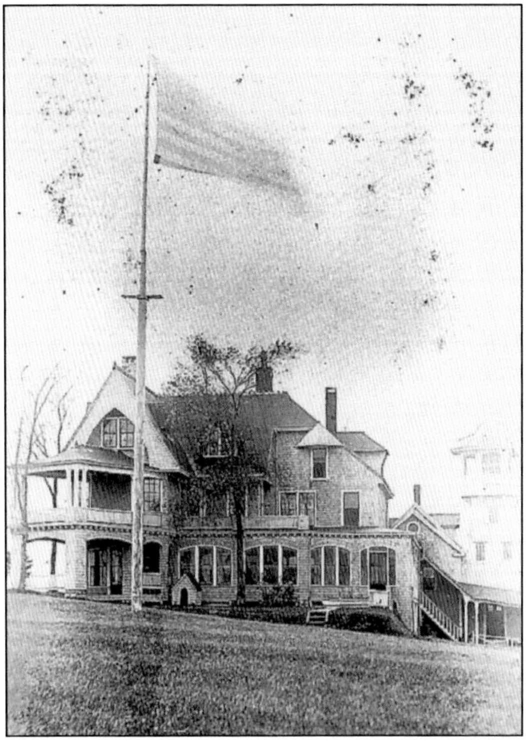

Prominently visible atop Appleton Ridge, overlooking Sennebec Pond to the south, Sullivan Heights is as imposing today as it was when completed in 1900. The 20-room home of Adalaine S. Oakes sported a 60-foot flagpole with a massive 15- by 30-foot American flag and was among the first homes in the area to have electricity installed. The house is still a private residence today and has been undergoing restoration.

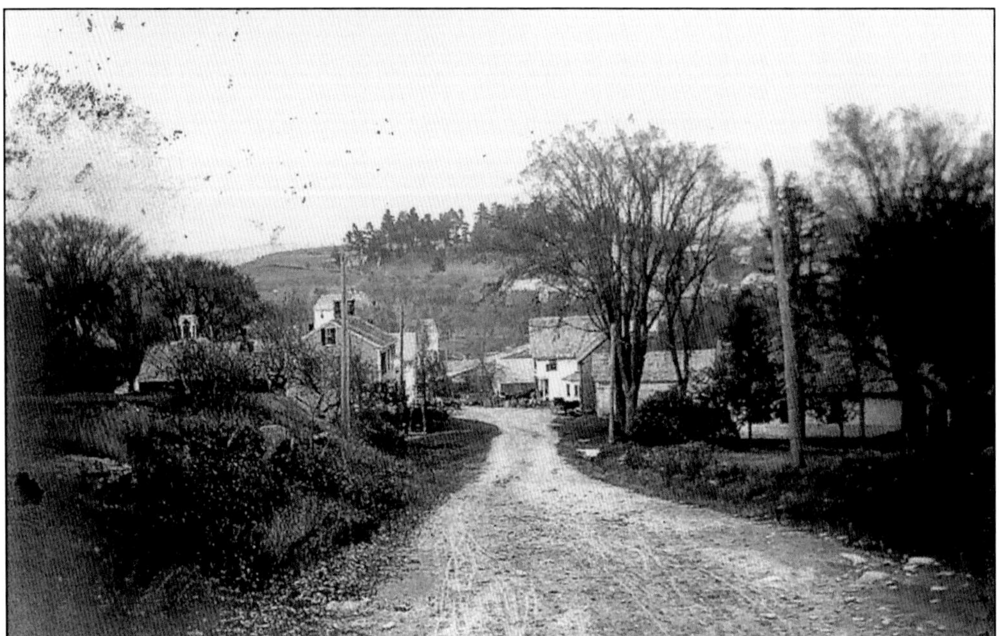

This 1904 view of Appleton village was taken from the Town Hill Road. The white corner building at the center of the photograph still exists and was a general store, as evidenced by the plethora of casks, boxes, and implements lining the street. The backside of Pine Grove Cemetery is visible in the distance, as is the steeple of the former Appleton Union Church, now the home of the historical society.

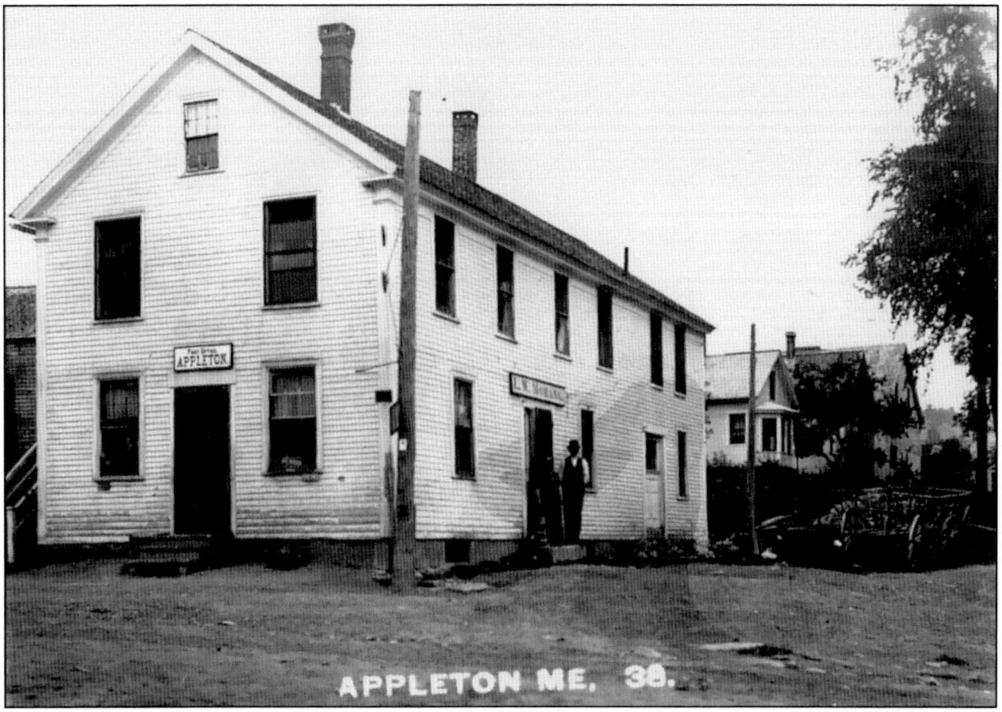

Located at the corner of the Town Hill Road and modern Route 105/131, this building once served as the Appleton post office, as well as the business and private residence of L. W. Morang and his family. The original building is easily recognizable today and remains little changed as a private home.

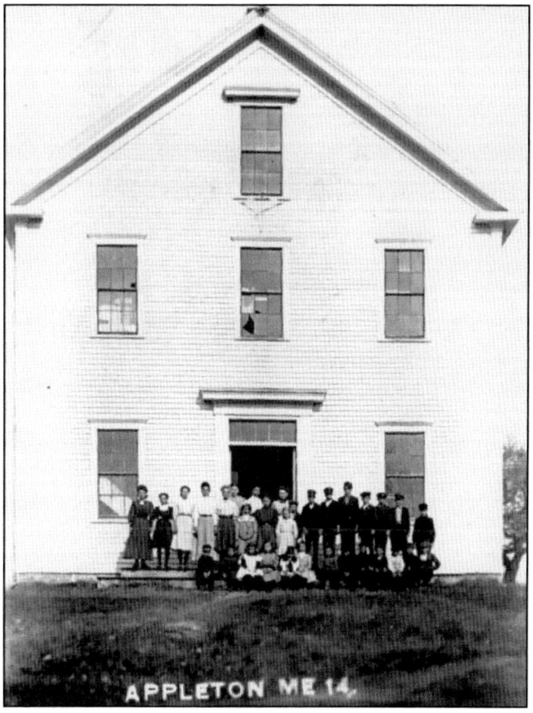

This undated image of the former Appleton school features 32 pupils and teachers gathered on the front steps. There is a wide range of ages present, all apparently dressed in their finest on the day of their portrait. A portion of the second floor of the schoolhouse was used for storage, and several broken windows are visible there. Burned in 1929, the school was located diagonally across from the post office.

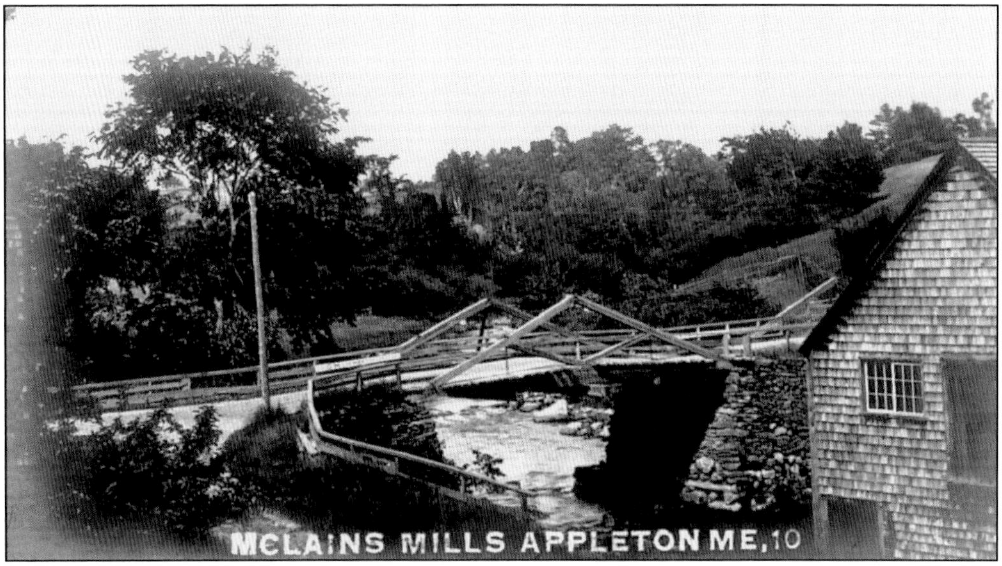

This 1909 view of McLain's Mills was taken from the village side of the St. George River, opposite what is now the library. A modern concrete bridge now spans the river at a slightly higher elevation, and the short road in the foreground was long ago abandoned. Stone retaining walls leading down to the river are clearly visible today and outline the road's former path. The building on the right no longer exists.

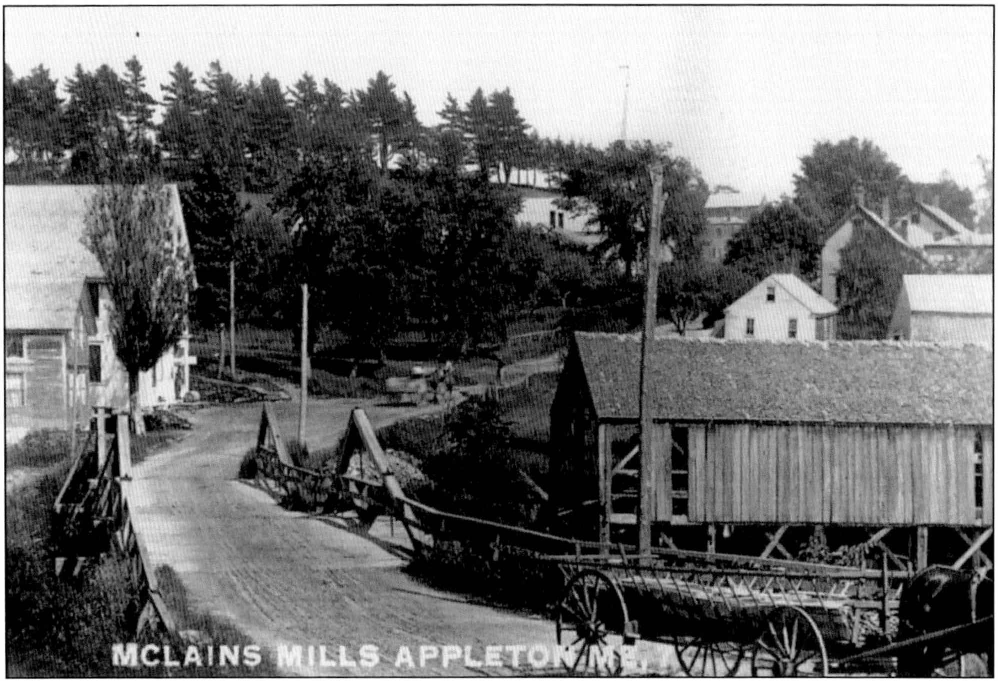

This photograph was taken in 1904 from a position just opposite the short road in the previous image, looking east. The long, low post-and-beam building to the right was a sawmill, located on the far bank of the river. The horse-drawn wagon in the foreground contains freshly milled lumber. Looking uphill, the monuments of Pine Grove Cemetery and the steeple of the Appleton Union Church are visible.

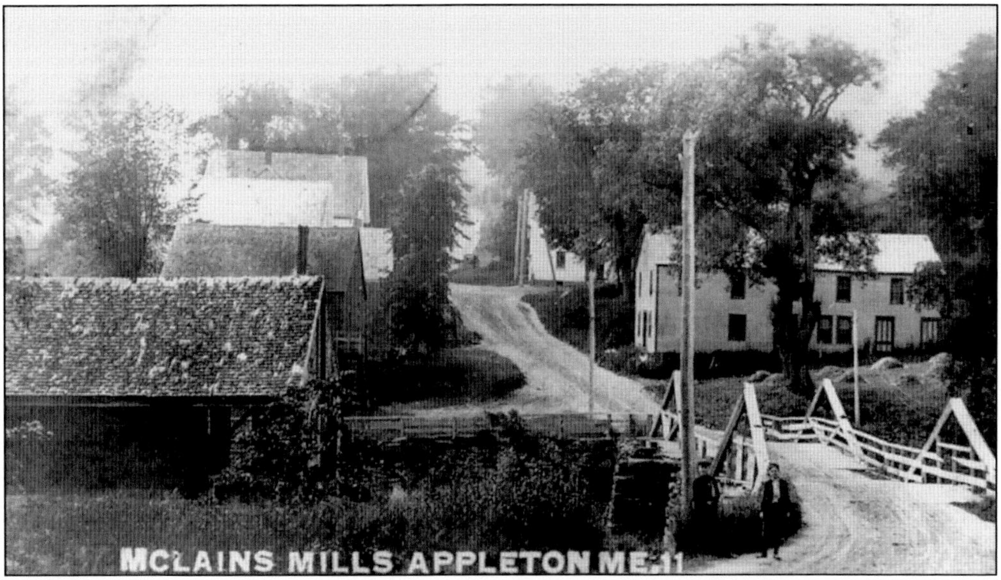

Looking west across the river toward town, this image captures both of the previous two camera positions. The sawmill in the left foreground and the next three structures no longer exist, but the long white building to the right of center survives as the library. Just beyond that, partially obscured by trees, is the former post office. Diagonally across from that, the roof of the general store can be seen.

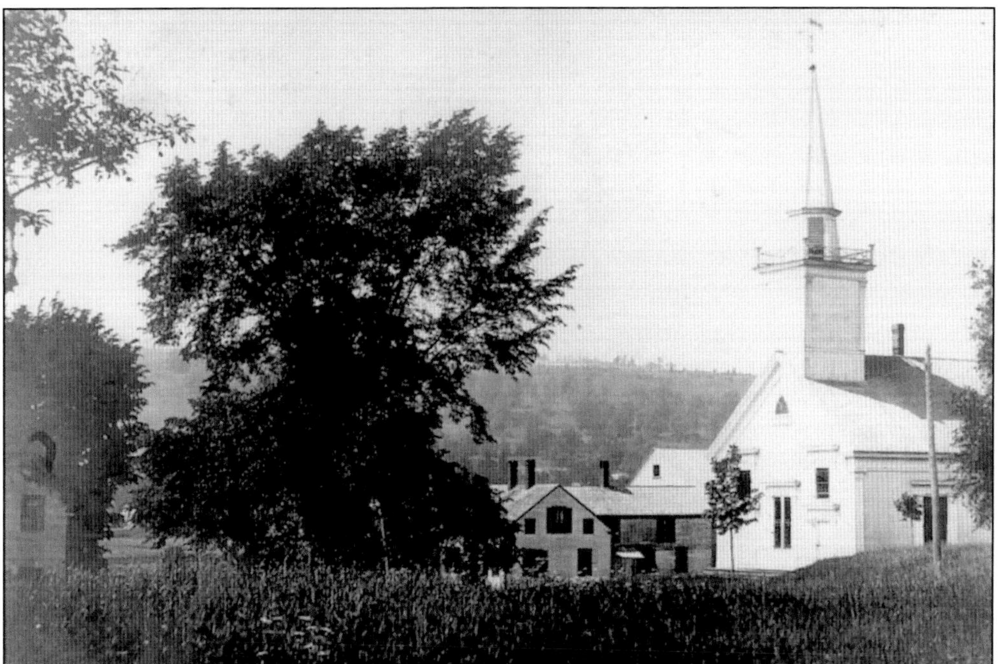

The former Appleton Union Church on East Sennebec Road pictured here exists today, not as a house of worship but as the historical society. This image was recorded from a field across the street and slightly uphill from the church, looking back toward McLain's Mills. Nothing other than the church structure remains from this scene today.

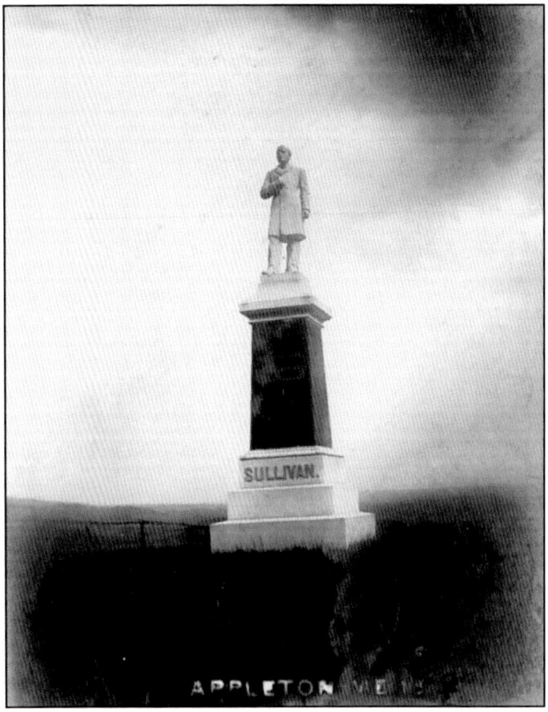

Located on the highest ground of Pine Grove Cemetery is the Daniel Sullivan monument. The father of Adalaine S. Oakes, whose mansion graces Appleton Ridge, Sullivan was an immigrant laborer who passed away in 1897 at the age of 81. Erected in 1899, this granite memorial today also carries the names of his wife, Ellen, who died in 1903, and Adalaine, who was interred in 1929.

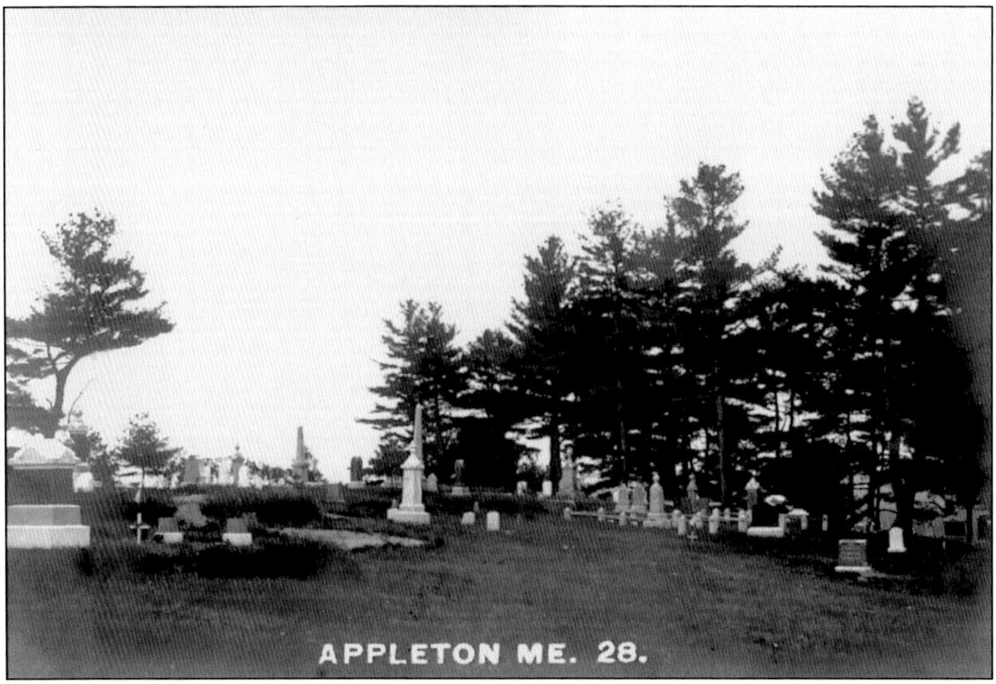

This image was recorded looking westward and slightly downhill from the Sullivan monument, near the rear of Pine Grove Cemetery. Most of the visible grave markers are easily identifiable today. Out of sight and to the right of the photograph is the location of the Sumner family crypt, shown in the next view. Next to that is the understated monument honoring those who fought in the Civil War.

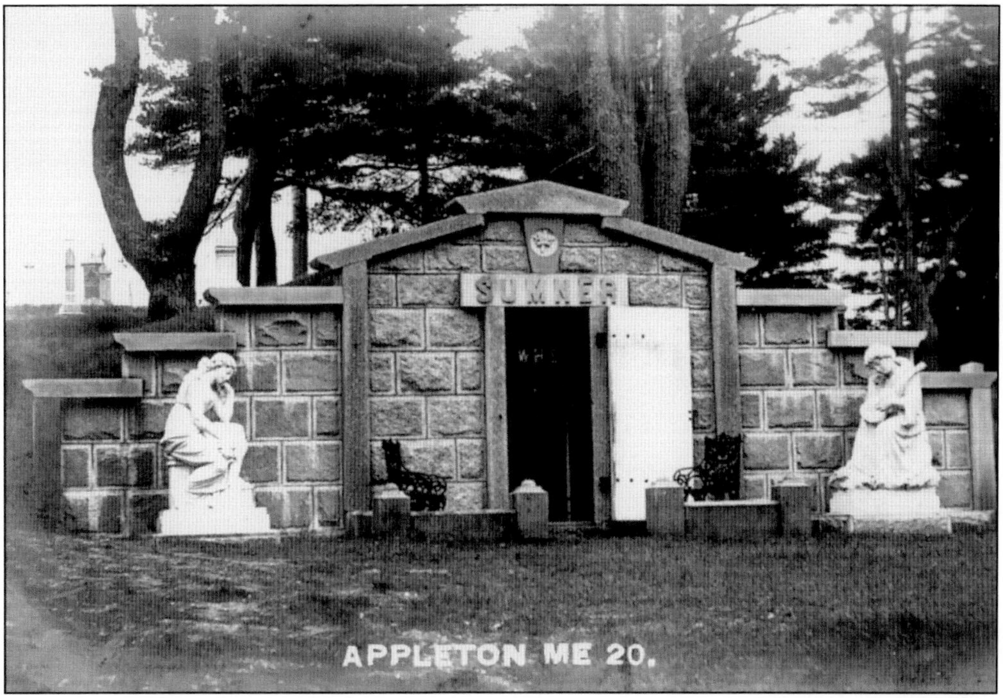

The Sumner family crypt lies at the extreme back edge of Pine Grove Cemetery, nestled in the pines overlooking the village and the ridge beyond. In this undated view, the metal door stands ajar, revealing the initials "WHS" on the iron gate within. The scene remains little changed today. The iron chairs no longer grace the entrance, and both angels have suffered some damage, but even the trees remain recognizable.

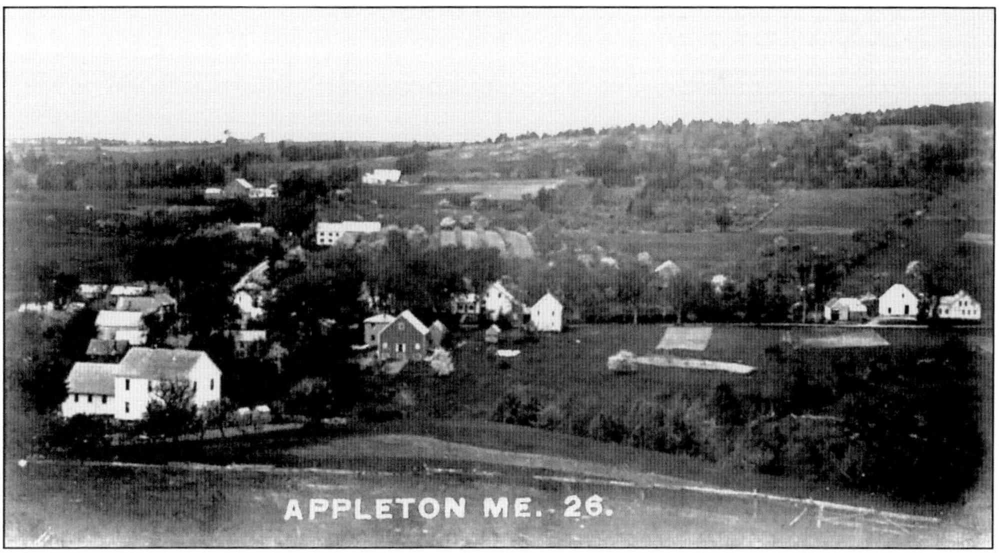

Recorded in 1906, this image was taken from just below the Sumner crypt, looking west toward the village. Most of the structures visible are no longer standing, with the exceptions of the small, partially obscured foursquare house, the general store (the roof of which is visible here), and the library building, just to the left of center. Most of this scene is now nearly completely wooded, and the modern view has been partially obstructed.

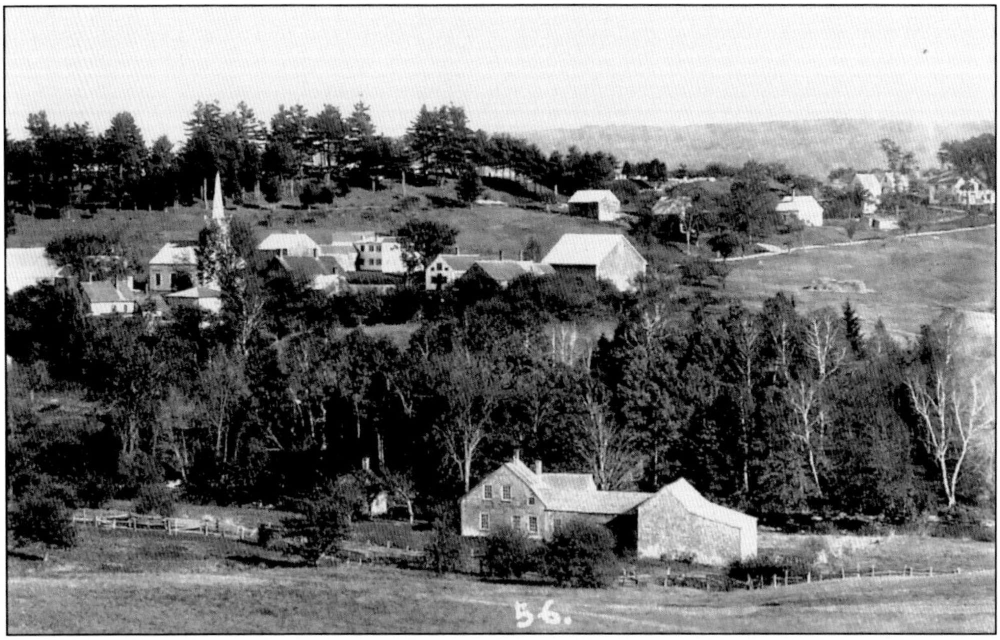

This view of East Sennebec Road was taken from just south of the village, along modern Route 105/131. Clearly visible are the steeple of the Appleton Union Church and the monuments of Pine Grove Cemetery. The field to the right of the large barn and farmhouse at the center of the photograph was the camera position for the earlier church image. The house in the immediate foreground no longer exists.

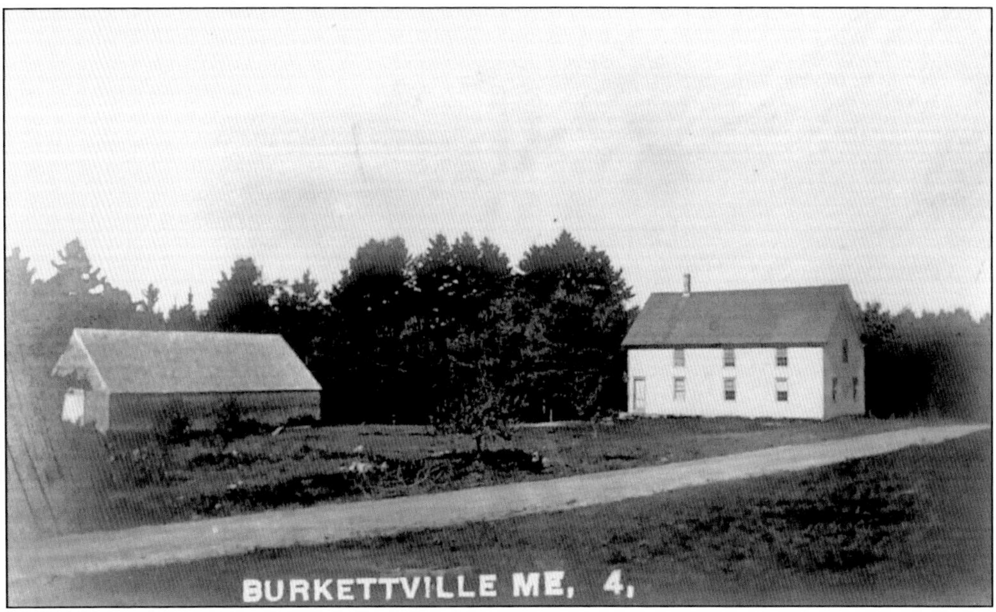

Originally named Burkett's Corner, the Burkettville section of Appleton was named for Andrew Burkett, who built two mills there. Located on modern Route 105, also known as Burkettville Road, this undated view is of the Medomak Valley Grange No. 175 building. The original structure was added onto and has nearly doubled in size since this photograph was taken. The nearby barn has since disappeared.

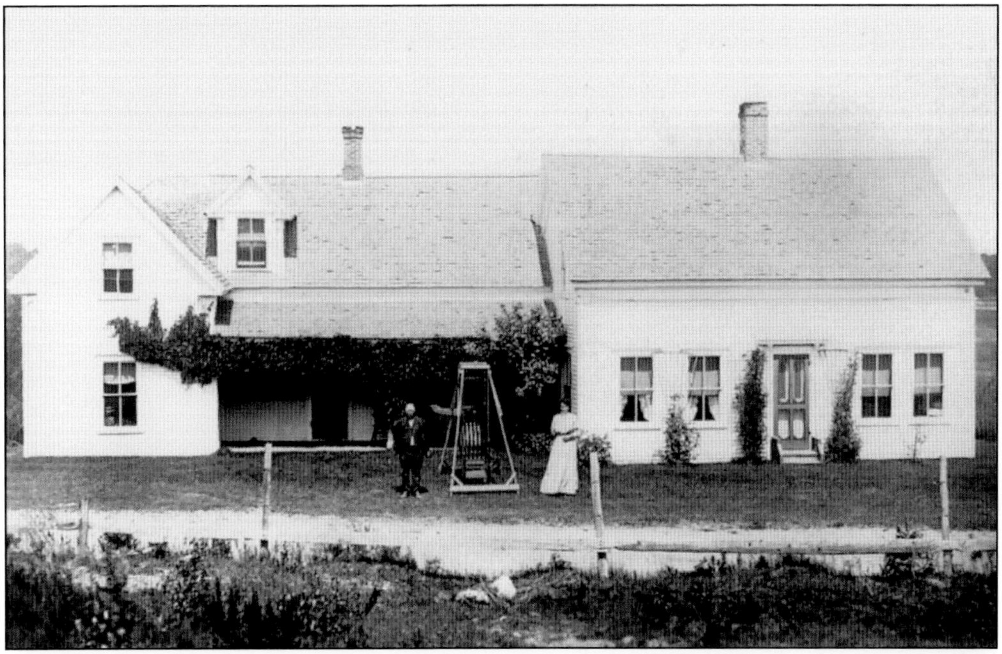

Located on Collinstown Road just south of Burkettville, the Hatch house remains standing today in wonderful and, at least outwardly, nearly original condition. Pictured standing proudly in front of their well-maintained home in this *c.* 1907 image are the original owners, Perley and Anna Hatch.

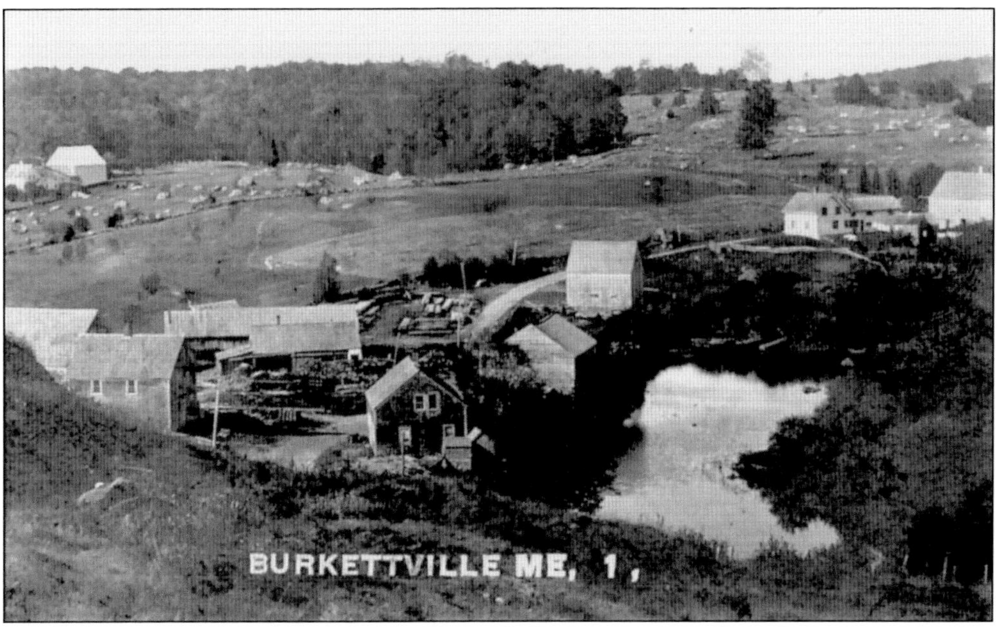

This undated view of a once bustling Burkettville has changed significantly in the intervening years. The only surviving structure is the long white farmhouse at the upper right of the photograph; everything else has long since disappeared. In the background, woodlands have reclaimed the open fields and the wide bend in the Medomak River near the sawmill has narrowed considerably.

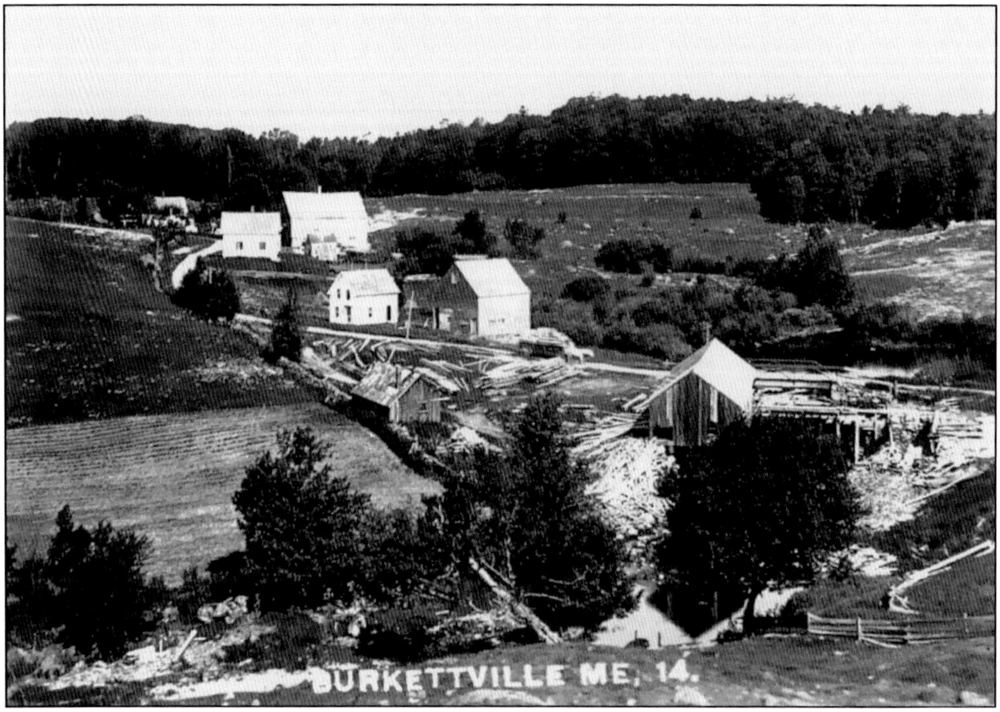

This similar view of Burkettville was taken on the side of a hill approximately one-half mile south of the previous camera location. Judging from the tree growth, this appears to be a later photograph, and shows that a portion of the mill has been removed. The white house near the top left is the same house in the previous photograph, seen here from a different perspective.

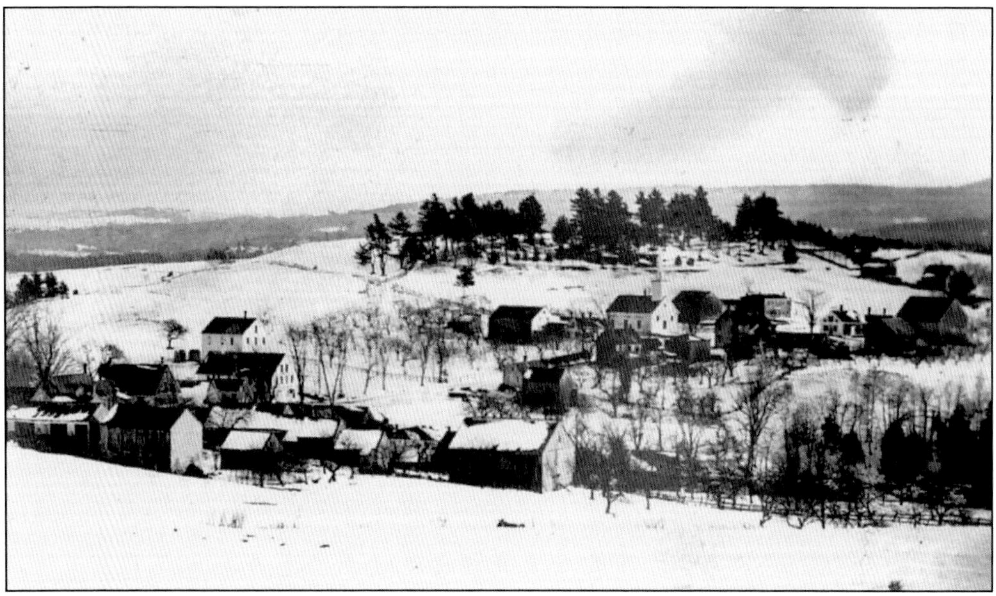

This undated wintertime view of Appleton was taken in a field up the hill from modern Route 105/131. Clearly visible are the steeple of the Union church and the monuments of Pine Grove Cemetery. Nearly all the buildings in the foreground have disappeared, as have those ascending the hill toward the church.

Three
South Liberty and Washington

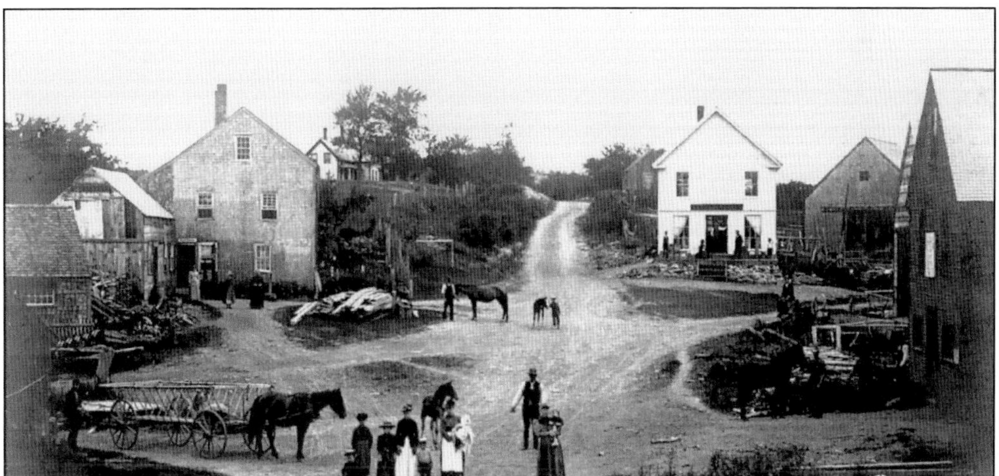

This 1903 photograph of the village of South Liberty contains no fewer than 26 people, all no doubt friends and neighbors of Frank and Bert Cunningham. The view looks toward the north along modern Route 220, with the Old County Road to the left. The white storefront to the right of center, known to older locals as "the doll house," still exists, as does the farmhouse on the hill in the distance.

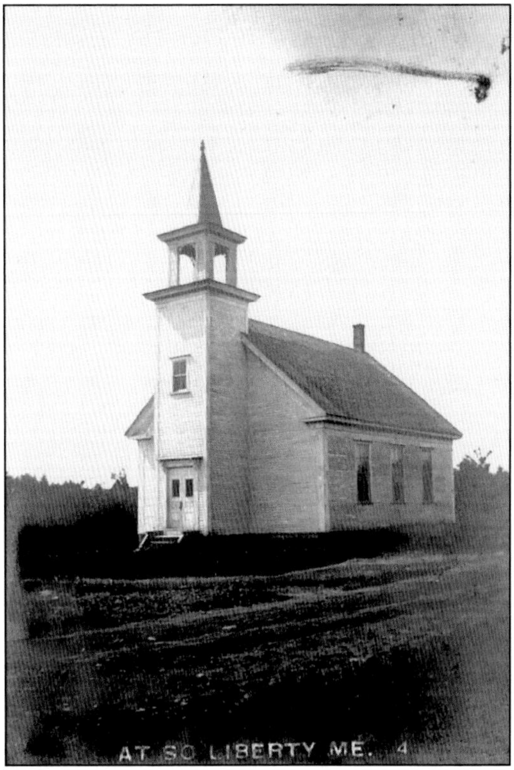

Located at the intersection of Routes 105 and 220, the former South Liberty Baptist Church building was constructed in 1898. The steeple was hit by lightning in the early 1990s and was considerably lowered as a consequence. Since replaced with a modern edifice across the street, the original structure, still owned by the congregation, now houses a youth center.

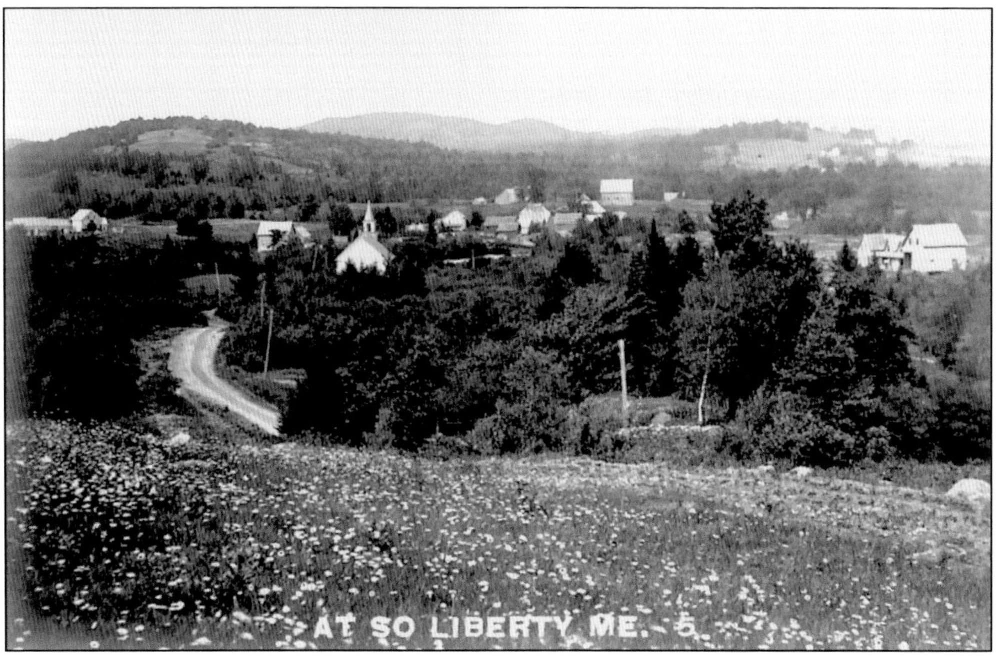

Taken from a rise along the Washington Road, this view looks northward toward South Liberty, with the hills near Liberty village off in the distance. Nearly all of the numerous houses, barns, and outbuildings visible have been lost to time. The only recognizable structure remaining is the old Baptist church building.

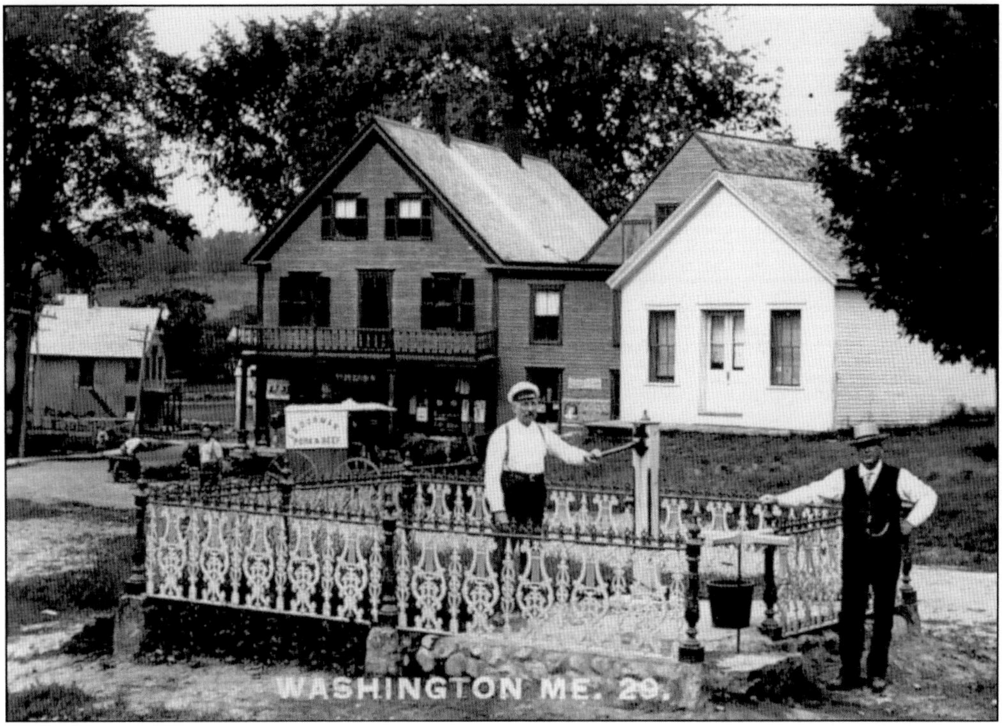

Located south of Liberty along modern Routes 105 and 220, Washington was established as a town in 1811 and was originally known as Putnam. This 1905 image of the community water pump in the village center shows Charles Lynch holding onto the pump handle. The general store and Washington post office building to the left of center was James L. Burns's, while the building to the far left belonged to Will Hatch.

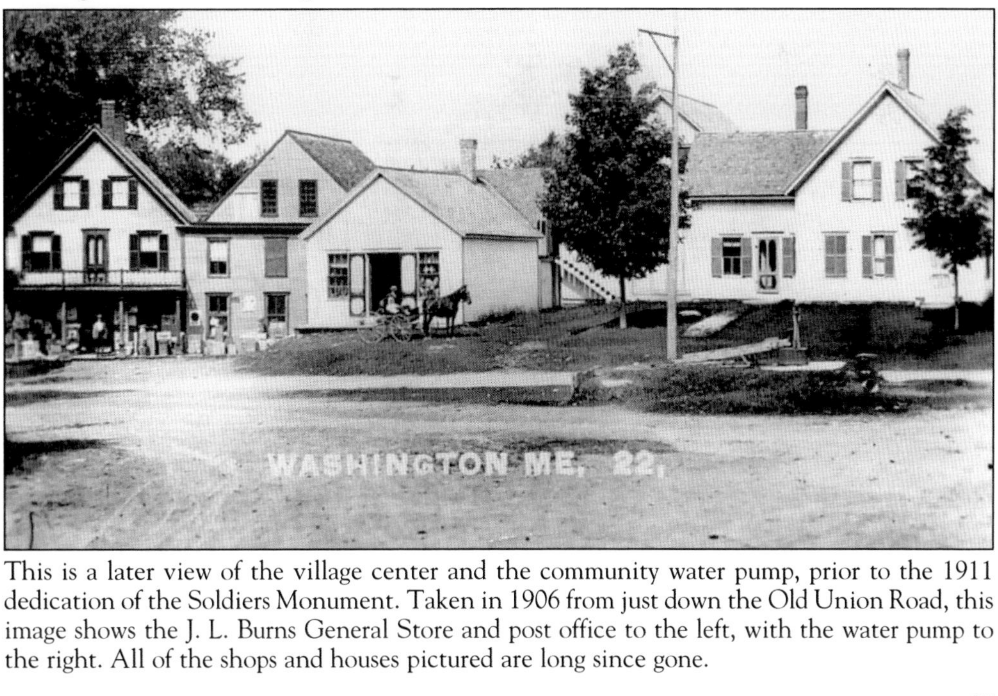

This is a later view of the village center and the community water pump, prior to the 1911 dedication of the Soldiers Monument. Taken in 1906 from just down the Old Union Road, this image shows the J. L. Burns General Store and post office to the left, with the water pump to the right. All of the shops and houses pictured are long since gone.

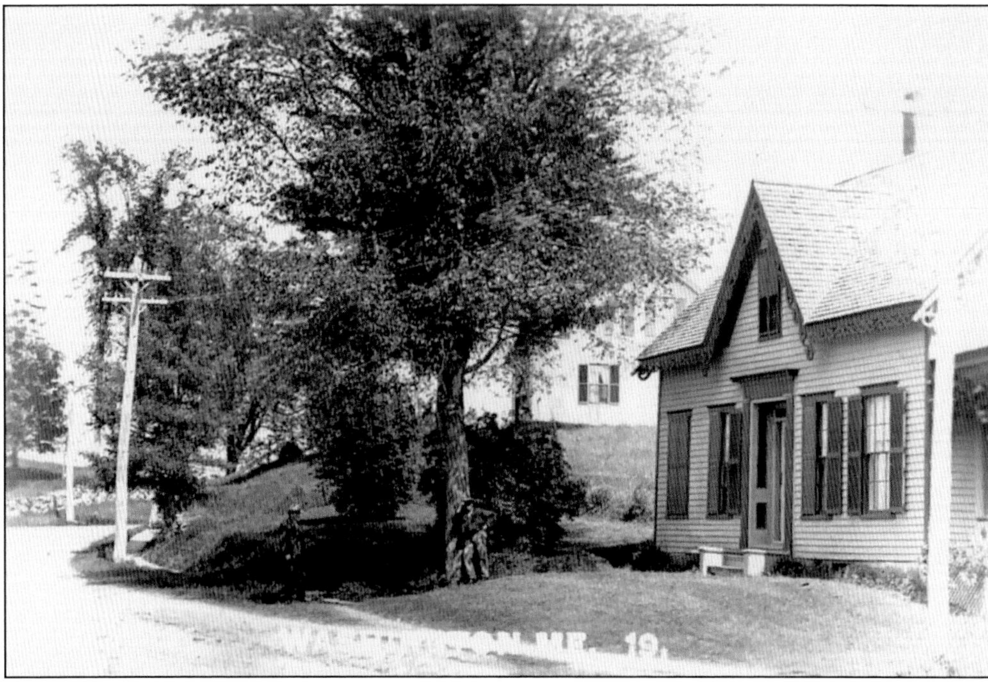

Located in the Washington village center, diagonally across the street from the Masonic Hall, the former Hiram Bliss house is one of the few originals that remain standing today. This 1904 view was photographed from the location of the community water pump, looking east down the Old Union Road.

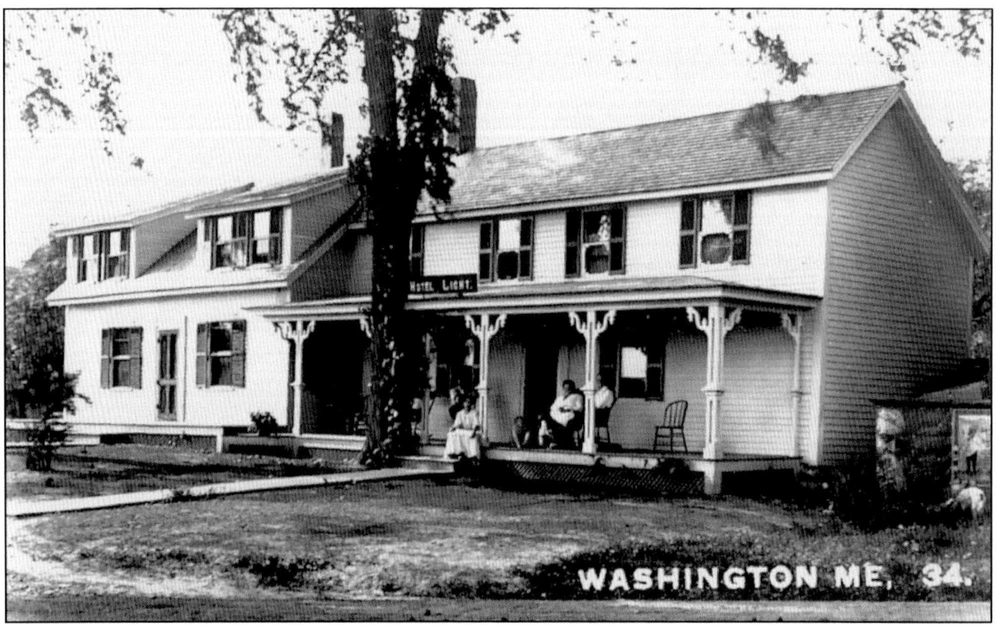

One of several hotels and boardinghouses in Washington, the Hotel Light was owned and operated by Will Light and his family. Located directly behind the J. L. Burns General Store, the hotel featured a connected livery stable and, after 1905, telephone service. Like most of the older village buildings, the hotel structure no longer exists.

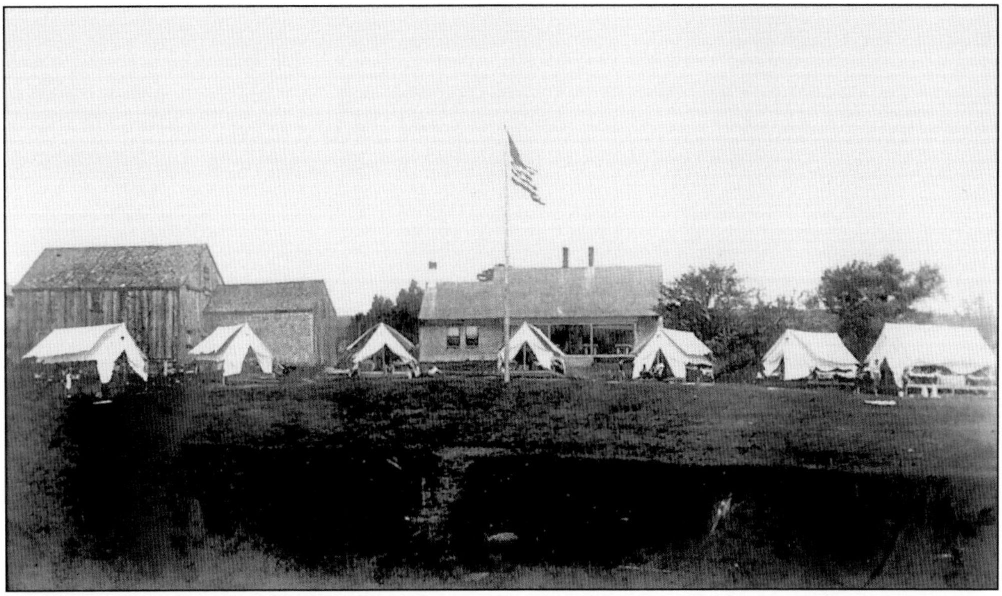

Beginning in 1904, Frank Poland brought groups of city boys to the Poland family farm on the shore of Washington Pond to experience farm and country life in a camp setting. The main lodge, visible in the center of the image, was originally a 150-year-old farmhouse of hand-hewn timbers, built by Frank Poland's great-great-grandfather. In 1906 (its third year), Medomak Camp hosted in excess of 20 campers, as pictured here.

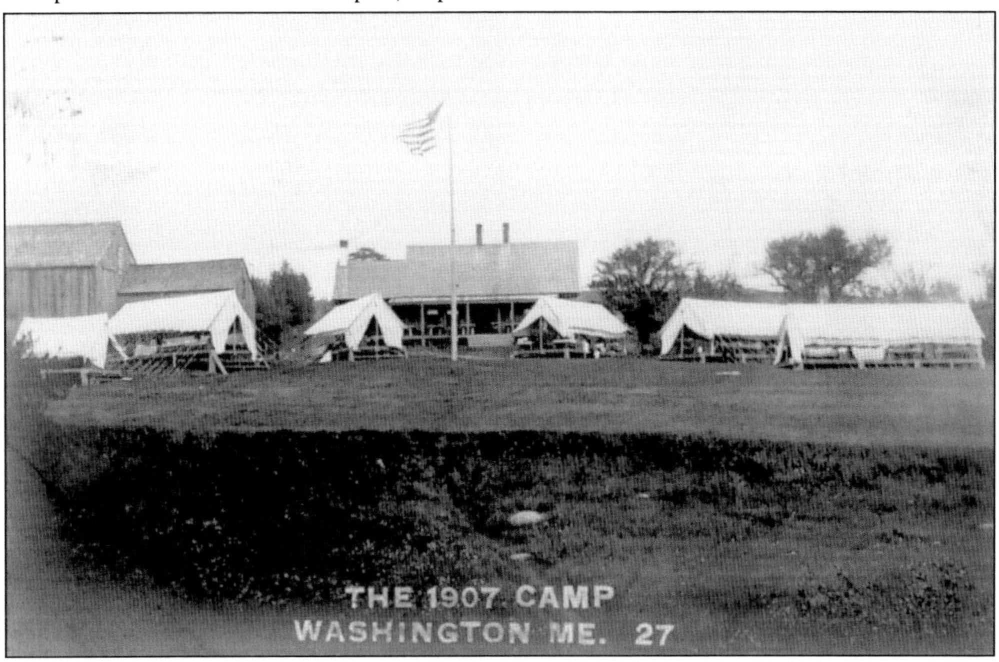

This photograph shows the 1907 enrollment at Medomak Camp, which had increased to 37 boys with "more expected." Campers traveled by way of the steamer *City of Rockland* to Bath, then by train to Winslow Mills, where they were picked up in a buckboard and brought to Washington by Will Light, owner of the Hotel Light. The camp and the more recent girls' camp are both still in operation.

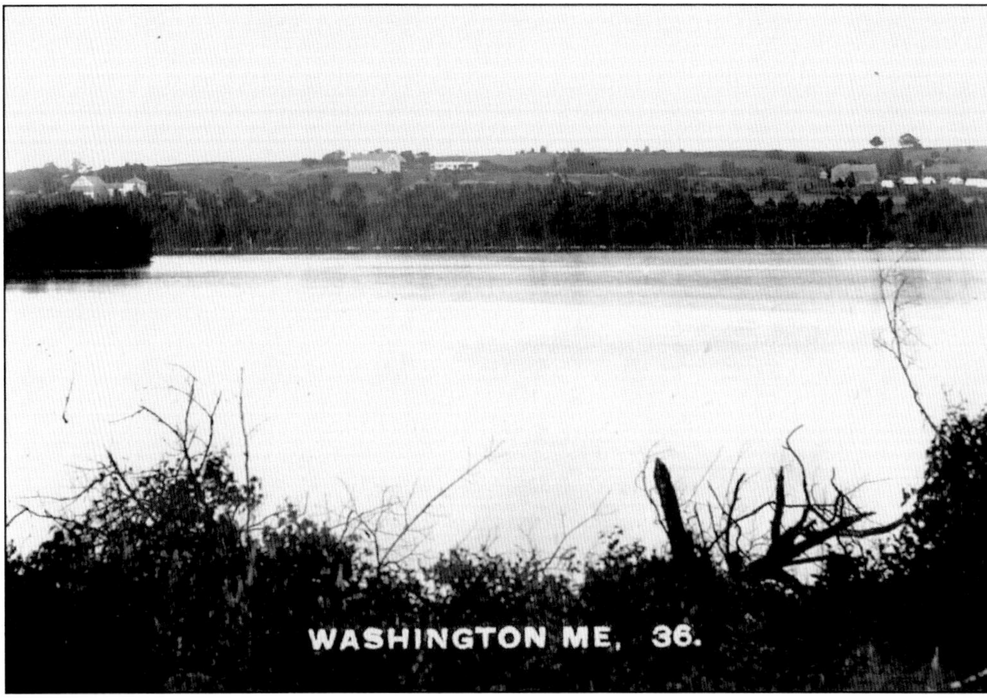

This is a 1907 view looking across Washington Pond from the Prescott Road. Visible at the far right of photograph are the white tents, lodge building, and barn of the Medomak Camp on the Poland family farm. This scene is nearly impossible to duplicate today because of the growth of the surrounding woodlands, both on the near and the distant shores.

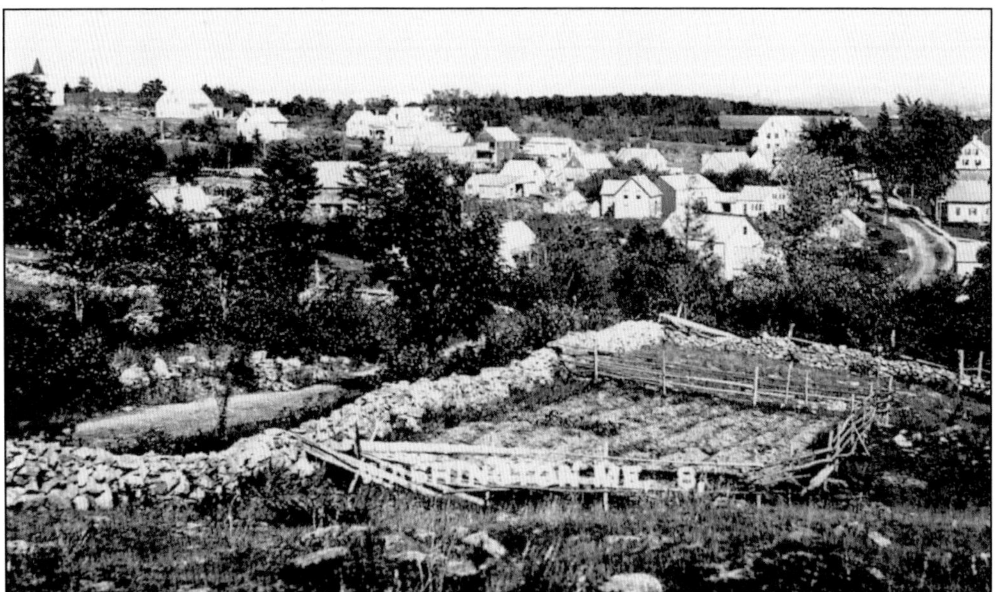

Taken from a rise on the Razorville Road, this 1903 view looks east over the village of Washington. The Old Union Road is hidden behind the trees off to the right, and modern Route 105/220 heads north toward South Liberty on the left. Very few of the many houses, barns, businesses, and outbuildings visible in this early image have survived.

The 100th anniversary of Washington's incorporation as a town brought about the largest celebration the village has ever seen. The August 8, 1911, festivities saw the dedication of the new Soldiers Monument in the village center. Inscribed with the names of 122 local Civil War veterans, the bronze tablet set in a fieldstone marker was donated by Stephen S. Bartlett and Dr. Lucero J. Gibbs of Chicopee Falls, Massachusetts, formerly of Washington.

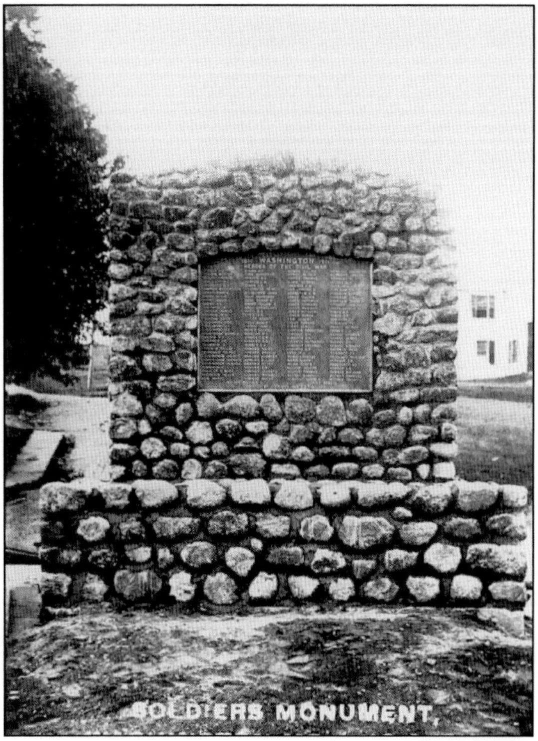

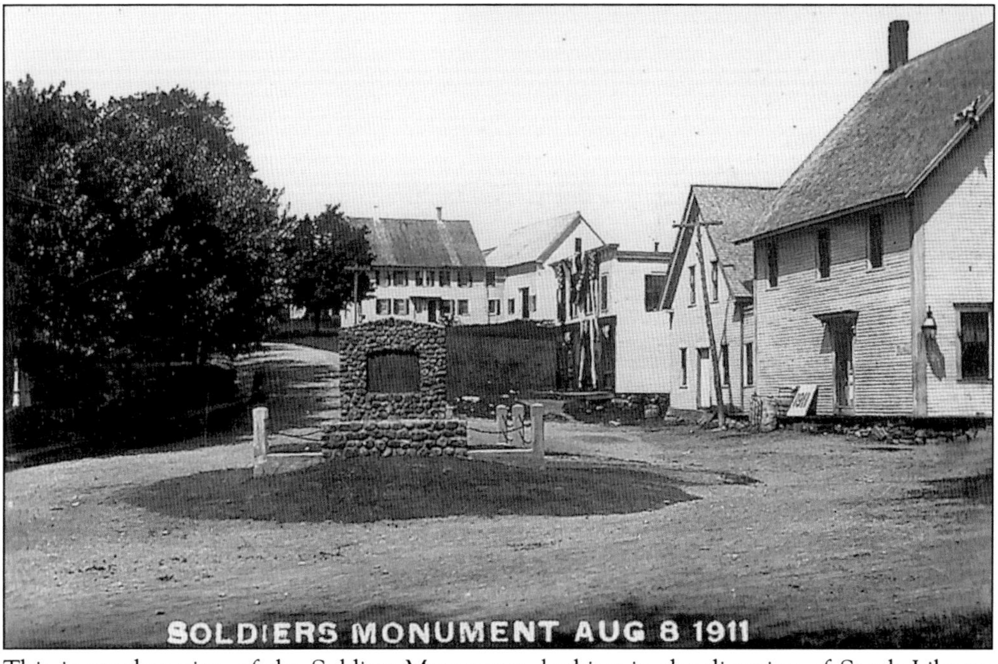

This is another view of the Soldiers Monument, looking in the direction of South Liberty. Judging by the partially removed bunting on the Masonic Hall, this photograph was taken after the festivities had concluded. Both the Masonic building and the attached structure behind it burned down in 1913. The storefront at the center of the image still exists, albeit with a new roofline, as does the large house farther up the hill.

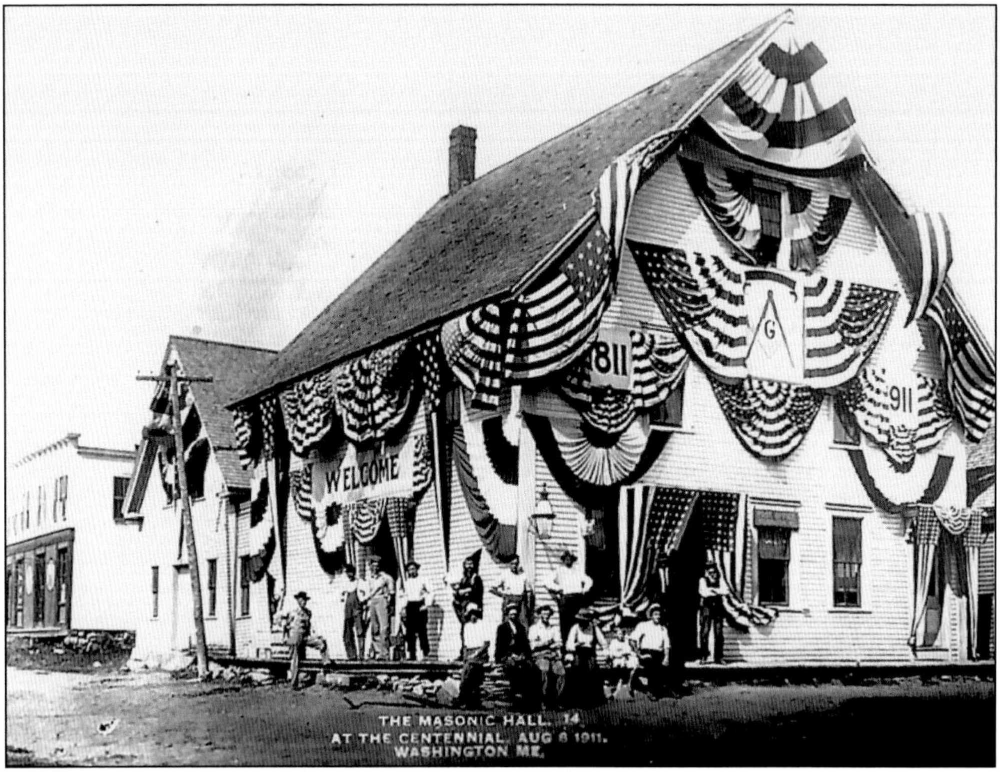

This wonderful image of the Masonic Hall draped with flags and bunting for the 1911 centennial celebration indicates the level of public spirit that was achieved. When the original hall burned in 1913, the old Congregational meetinghouse was moved from the mill section to this location as a replacement. It remains there today.

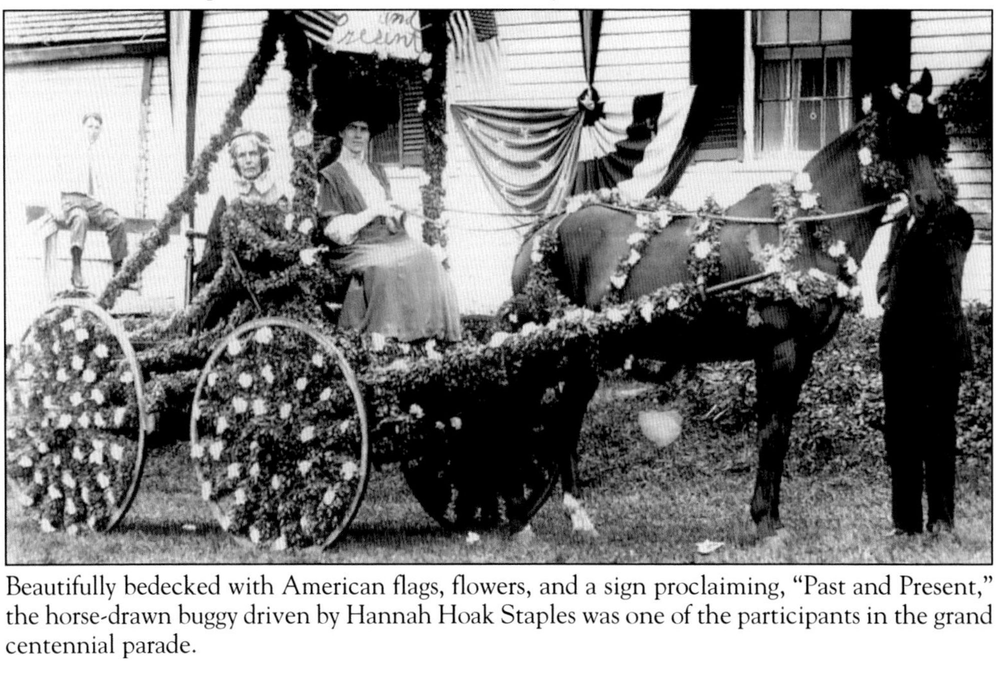
Beautifully bedecked with American flags, flowers, and a sign proclaiming, "Past and Present," the horse-drawn buggy driven by Hannah Hoak Staples was one of the participants in the grand centennial parade.

Prominent Washington attorney and historian Lindley Murray Staples can be seen here standing on the balcony outside of his law office, which is impressively decorated with American flags and bunting for the centennial celebration. Staples delivered a historical speech to the crowd assembled at the dedication of the Soldiers Monument. Located near the mills, the ground floor was occupied by the millinery and fancy goods store run by Staples's daughter, Annie L. Staples.

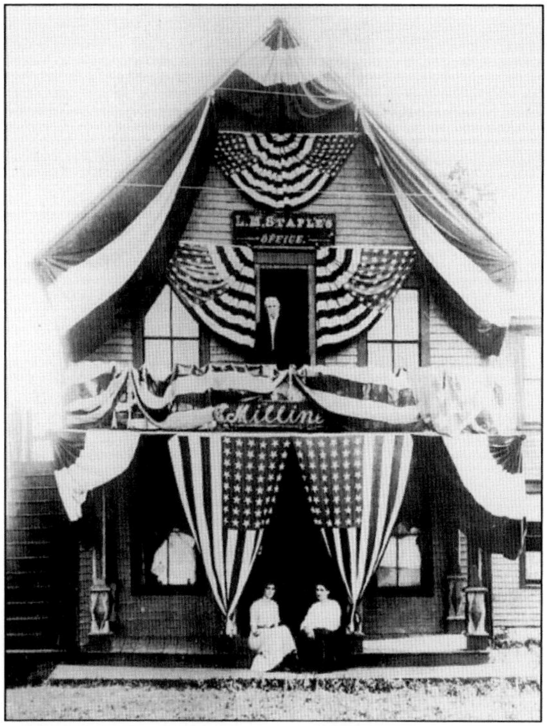

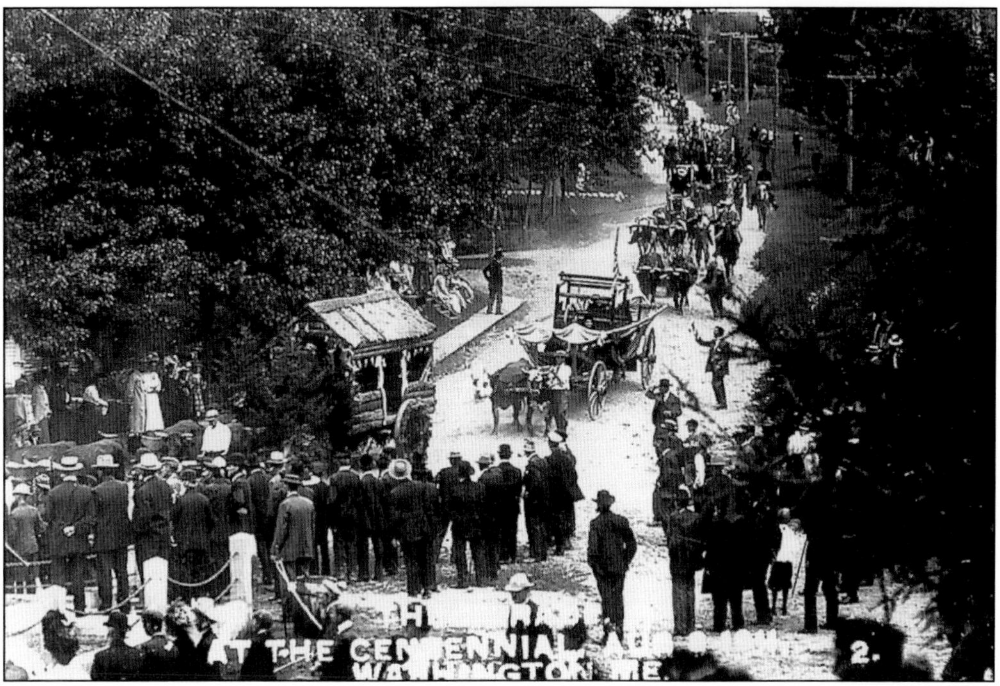

This is a view of the centennial parade as it wound its way down what is now modern Route 105/220, into the village center. The pillars around the just dedicated Soldiers Monument are visible to the left, and the Masonic Hall is just out of sight behind the trees to the right. This photograph was taken from the grassy knoll visible in the image of the Hiram Bliss house.

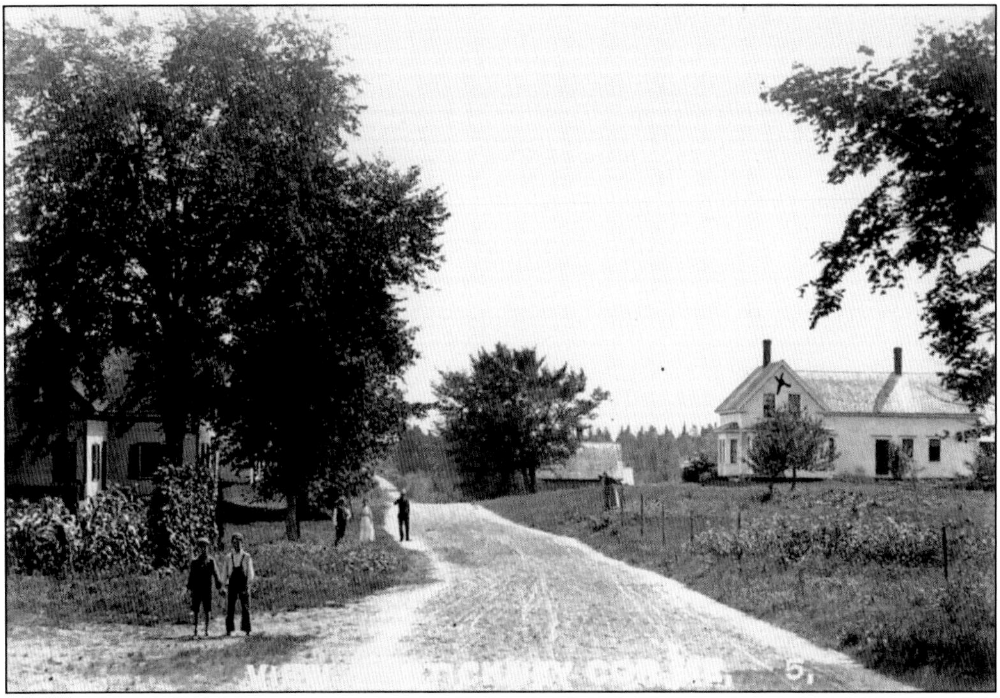

The Stickney Corner section of Washington is near the junction of modern Routes 220 and 17. This image was taken looking south toward Route 17, just past the intersection of Calderwood Road. The large white house to the right, although obscured by another building, still exists, as do the L-shaped house to the left and the building whose roof is visible at the center of the image.

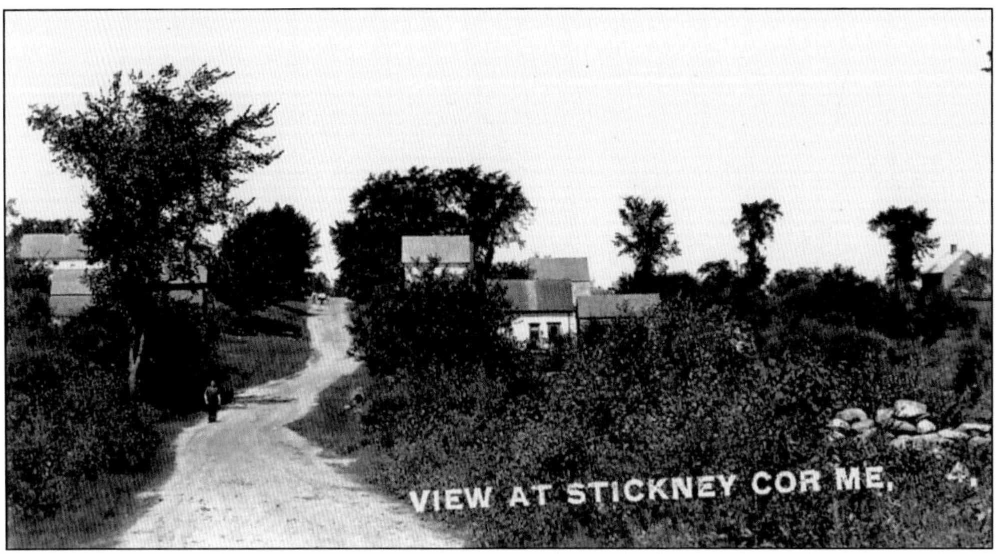

Taken from south of the previous image, this view looks back toward Washington, with the intersection of Calderwood Road at the crest of the hill. The long white structure to the left is the large building seen in the previous photograph. The small house at the center still exists, although the one just above it does not. The large house visible to the right still stands on Calderwood Road.

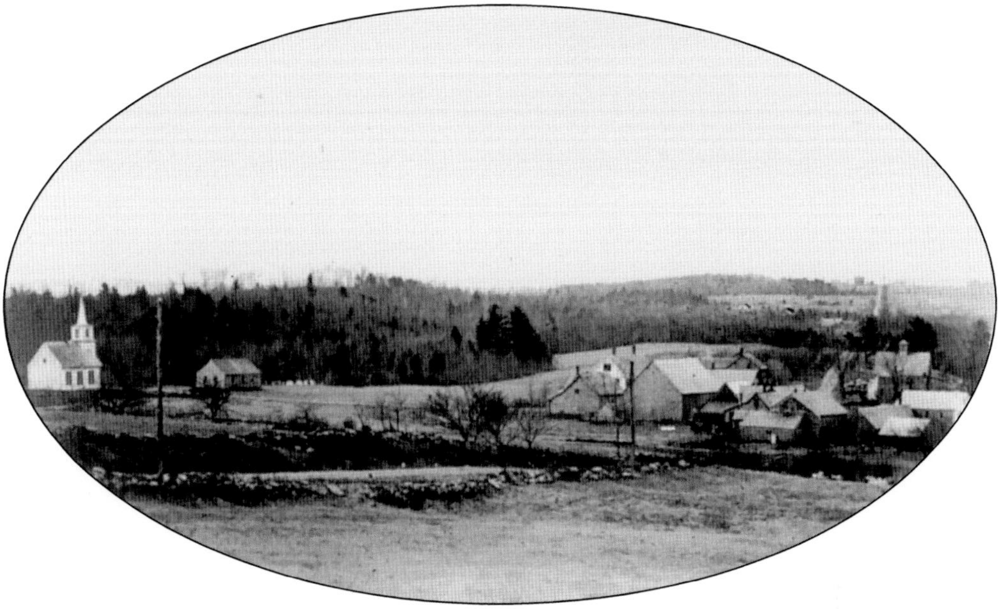

Razorville is located west of Washington proper, along modern Route 105. This early image was recorded beside the Youngs Hill Road, looking east. Visible to the left is the 1880 town hall. The building opposite the hall still exists, as does the cemetery barely visible to its rear. Also still standing are the barn visible at the center and the large house and adjoining barn at the extreme right of the image.

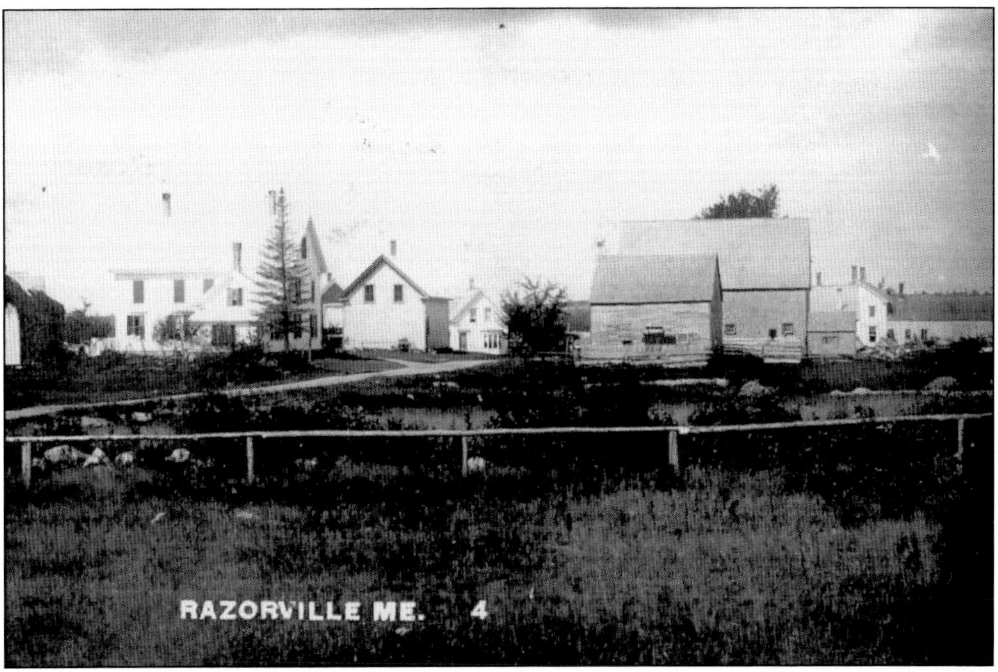

This later view was taken alongside the Razorville Road, looking west. The two houses to the left no longer exist, but the white house at the center of the image still stands at the corner of Nelson Ridge Road. The barn just to the right of center is the same one visible in the last image, less the lean-to addition. The large house at the left also appears in the earlier photograph.

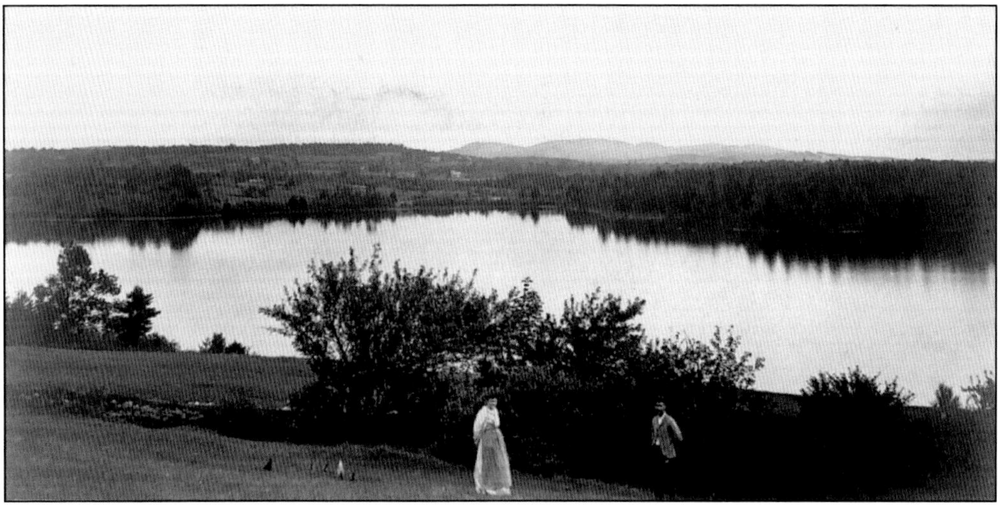

Crystal Lake is located just north of Razorville, alongside the Youngs Hill and Crystal Lake Roads. Though on private property, this vista remains largely unchanged. Today the fields astride the Prescott Road on the opposite side of the lake have grown back into woodlands, but the contour of the shoreline is unmistakable. There is no indication as to who the young couple pictured may have been.

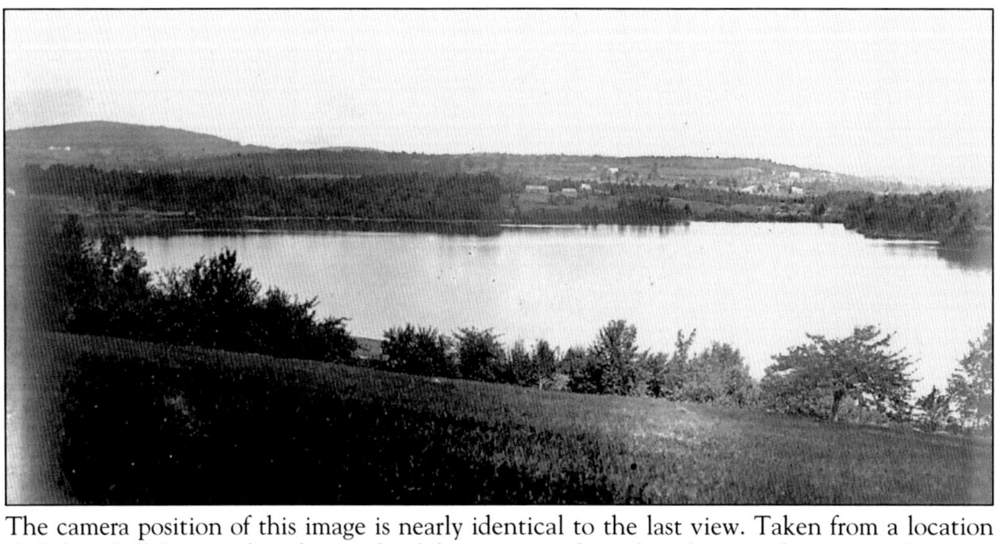

The camera position of this image is nearly identical to the last view. Taken from a location slightly uphill from and to the north of the previous shot, this photograph captures the same scenes on the far shore. A close examination reveals that the long building near the center of the photograph has the same open door and window as the previous image, indicating that these two pictures were most likely exposed close together.

Four

Jefferson and Points South

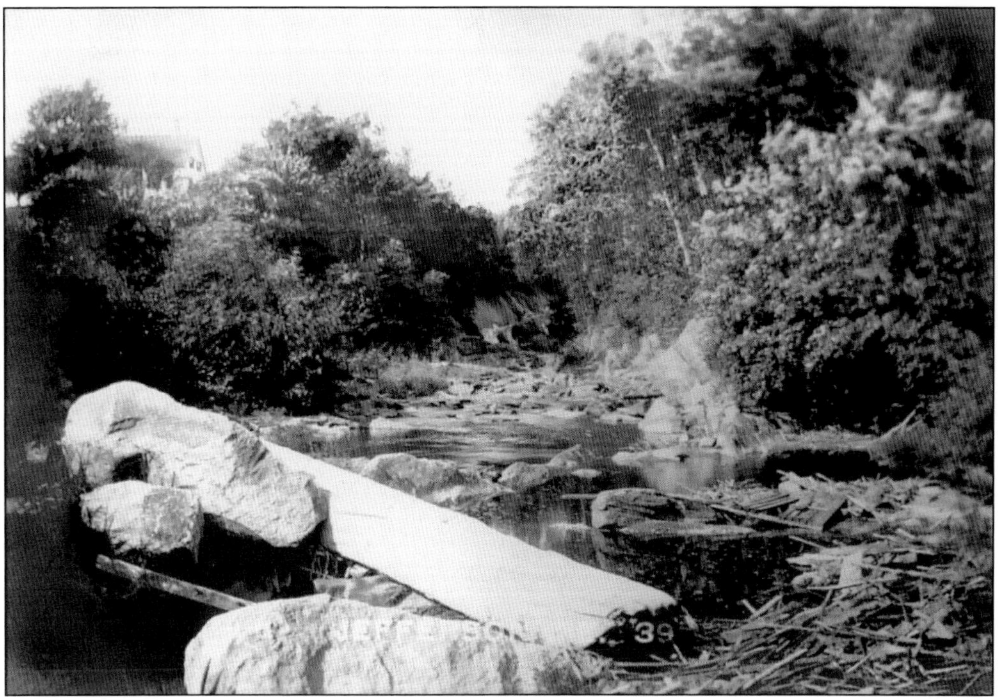

This is an undated view of the East Branch Stream below the dam. The camera location of this photograph cannot be determined exactly, but a portion of the scene toward the rear of the image resembles that visible from the Goose Hill Bridge today. The present existence of the house visible on the hill to the left is in question and may hold the key to positively identifying this view.

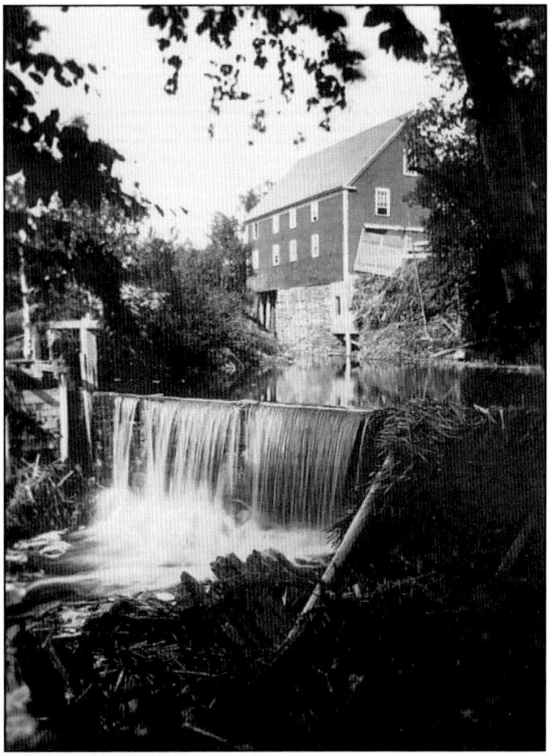

Taken just south of the bridge across the East Branch Stream on Goose Hill Road in North Jefferson, this undated image is of the backside of the Charles Davis Mill and the falls. Engaged in the milling of long lumber and the manufacture of barrel staves, the Davis Mill, one of three mills along this stretch, burned *c.* 1910.

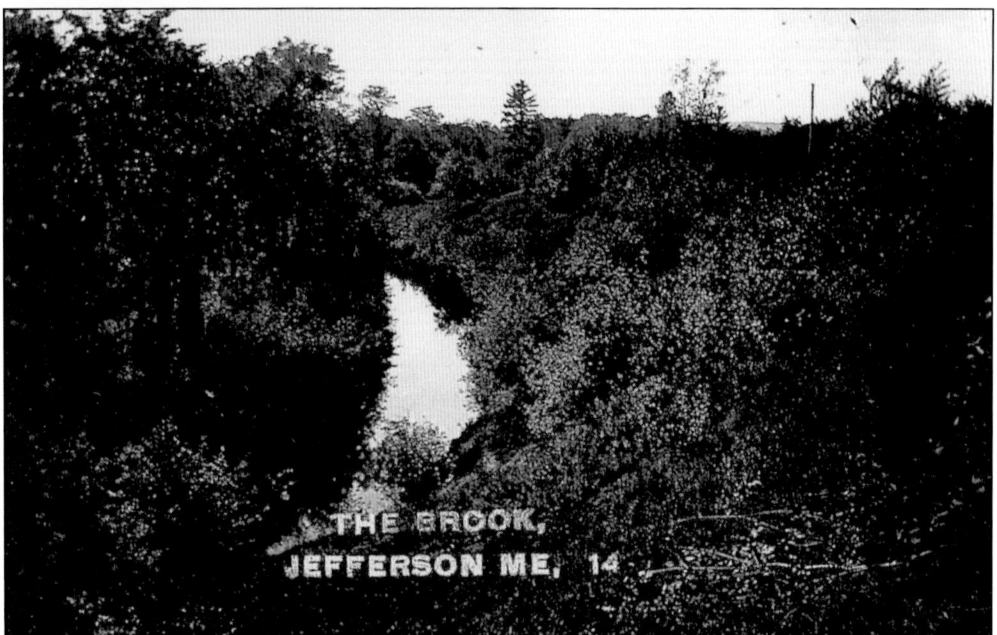

Labeled "The Brook," this image apparently shows the upper reaches of either the Davis Stream or the East Branch Stream above the Davis Mill. As with the previous photograph, the exact location of the original camera position is impossible to determine, which prevents a positive identification of the image.

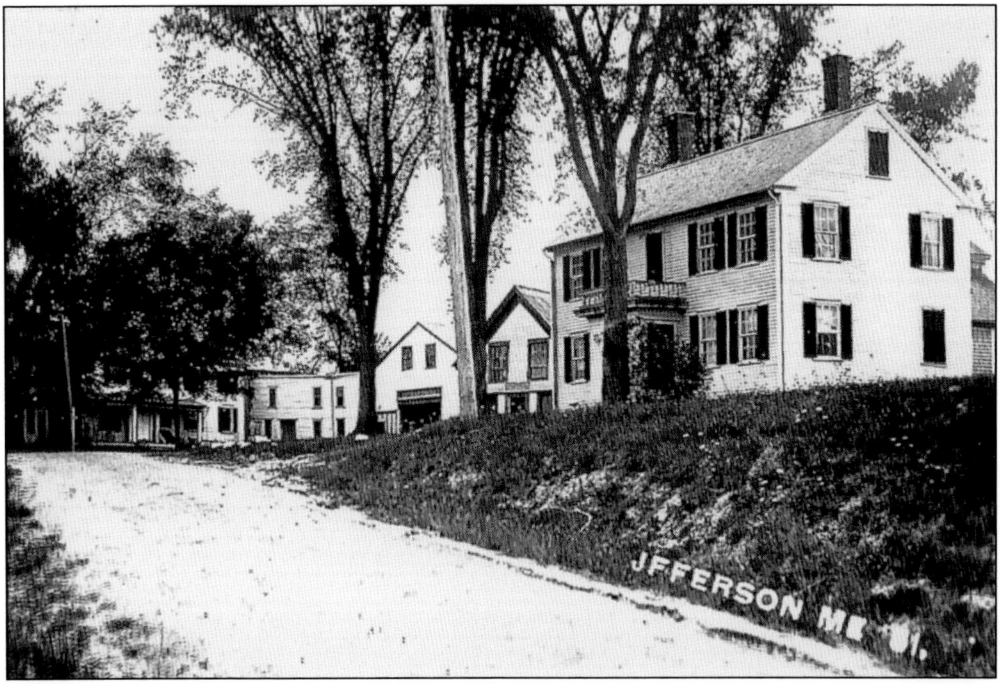

Modern Route 126, also known as the Washington Road, is in the foreground of this 1911 image, and the large white house to the right still exists today. The small shop to the left of the house is now a two-car garage, and Valley Road passes just to its left. The balance of the buildings visible have since disappeared.

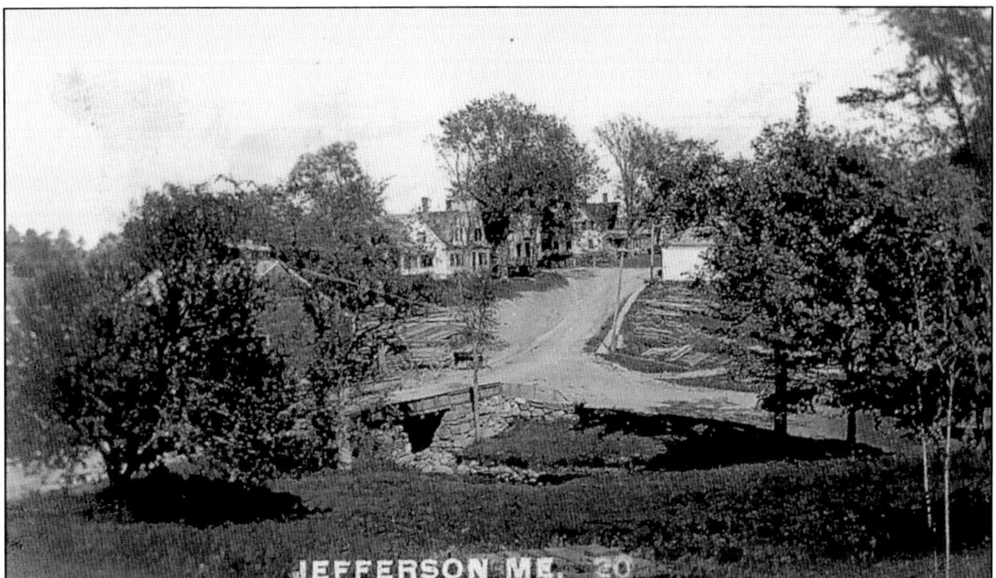

This 1905 image was taken at the corner of the Washington Road and Village Street, looking east. The former Joseph Y. Meserve lumber mill, one of the largest in Jefferson, is visible just behind the bridge. The original building burned several years ago, and a new cabinet shop now occupies the site. The white house at the center of the image still exists, as does the twin-peaked house closest to the mill.

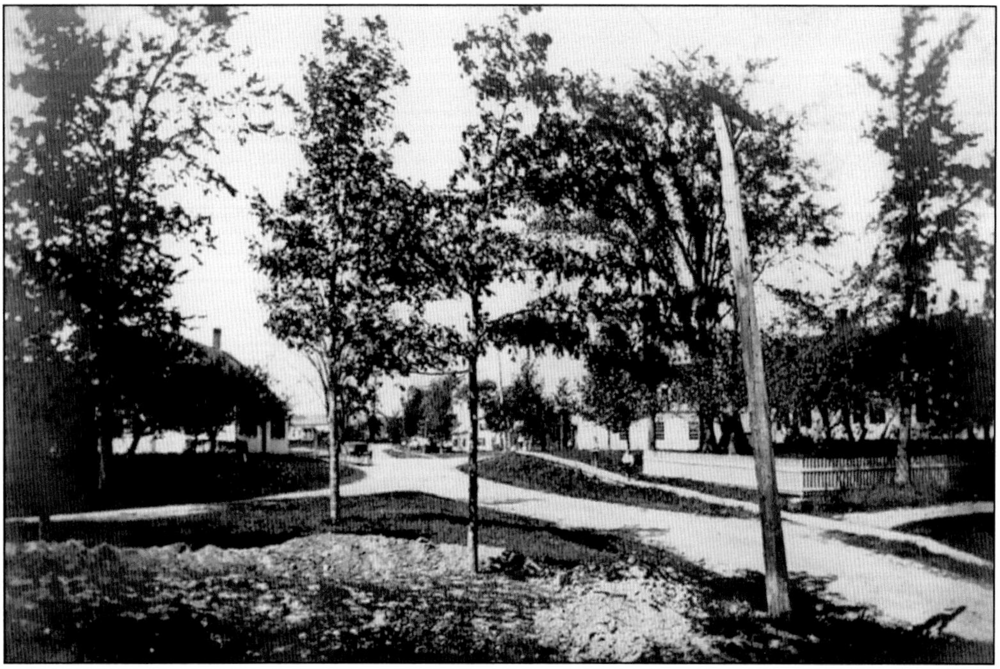

This 1906 view was recorded up the hill from the last image along Village Street, looking west. The white building barely visible just beyond the picket fence is the Christian Endeavor Hall, seen in the next photograph. The house on the far left no longer exists, but the one just to its right is still standing at the corner of the Mountain Road, as is the one at the center of the image.

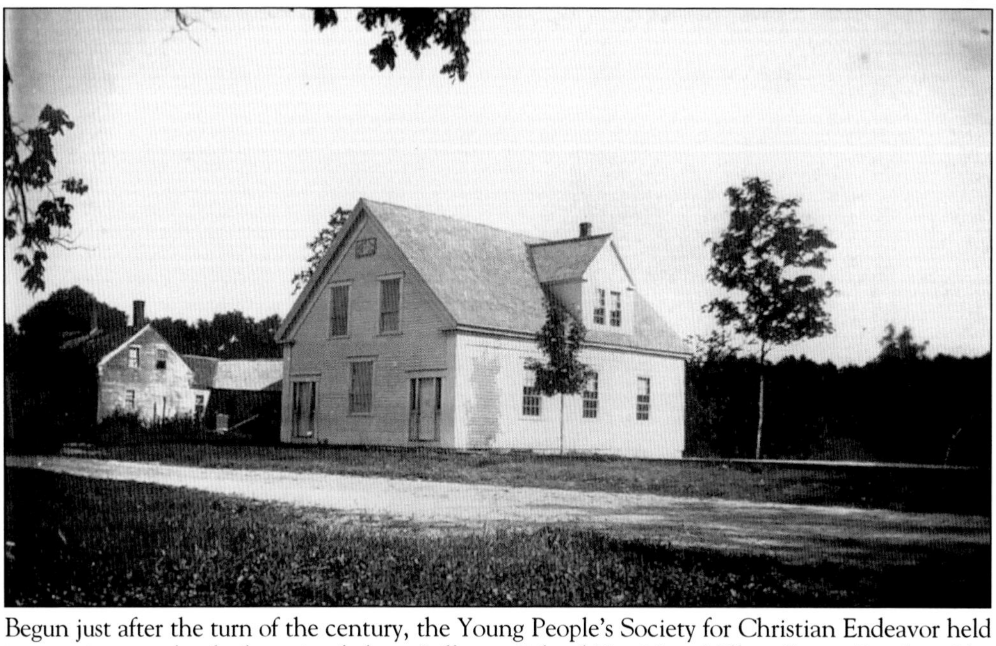

Begun just after the turn of the century, the Young People's Society for Christian Endeavor held its meetings in what had previously been Jefferson School No. 15 on Village Street. Purchased by the community, with the title held by the First Baptist Church, the structure has since passed into private hands and is known locally as the Christian Endeavor Hall. The sign, barely visible in the front peak, reads, "Lakeside Lodge A.O.U.W [Ancient Order of United Workmen.]"

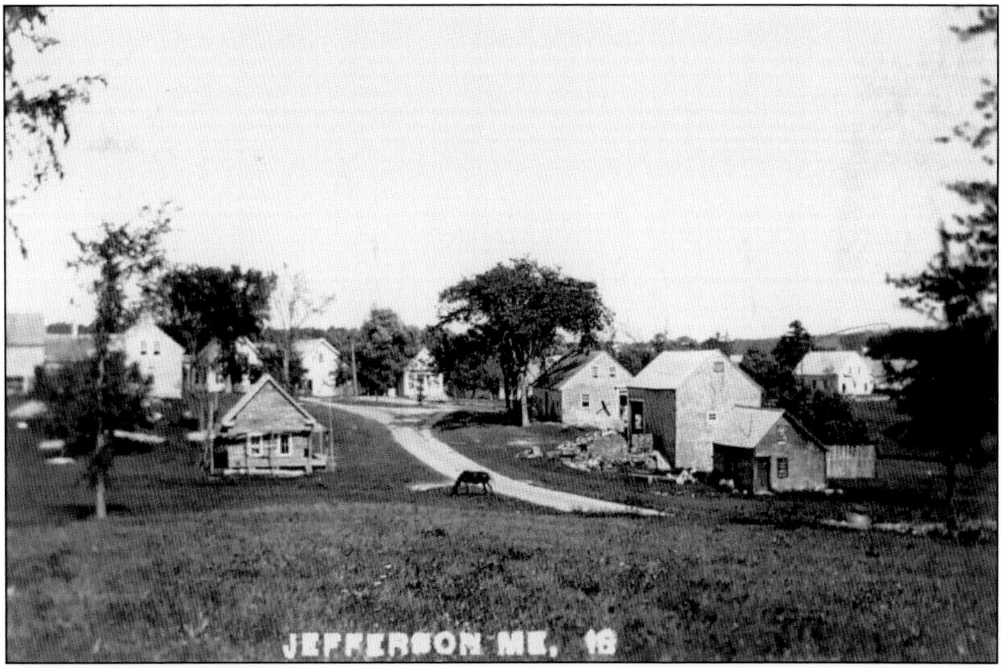

The camera position for this 1906 view was diagonally across the street from the current tennis courts. Looking back along Village Street, the Christian Endeavor Hall can be seen to the far right, with the Mountain Road heading off to the left in the distance. The small house in the center and the large barn next to it still exist, as do the large house and attached barn at the extreme left.

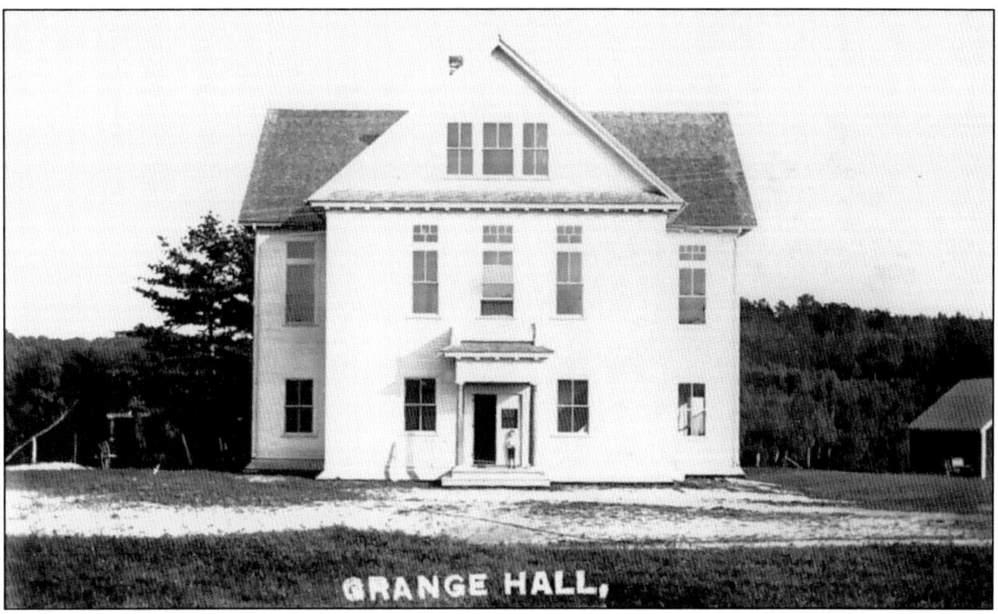

Located on the left-hand side of Route 126, heading south toward the lake, this view of the Willow Grange No. 366 appears little changed today. The group was organized at the village of Jefferson in 1901. The hall was constructed in 1905, the year before this photograph was taken. This wonderfully preserved hall was one of three Granges that were active in town into the 1970s.

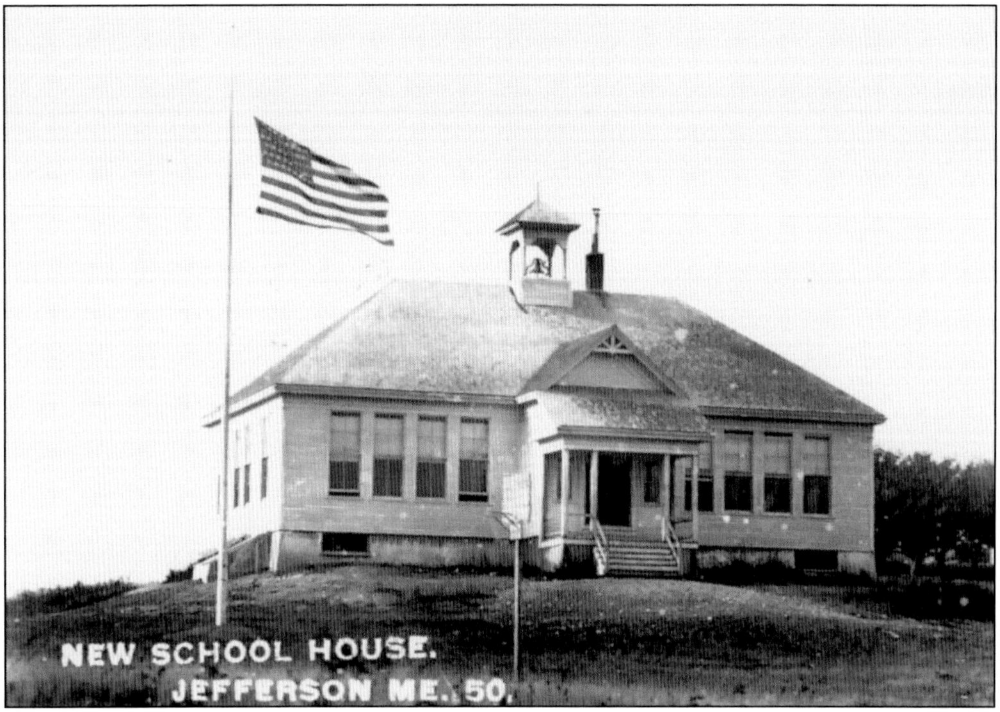

In 1911, the town of Jefferson voted to construct a new schoolhouse. Consisting of two classrooms and a recitation room, this new Jefferson Village School cost $2,800. Located across the street from the Willow Grange, the schoolhouse still exists today, albeit much enlarged. It is three times longer now and has lost the distinctive belfry. Only the building's entryway and roofline serve to recall its humble beginnings.

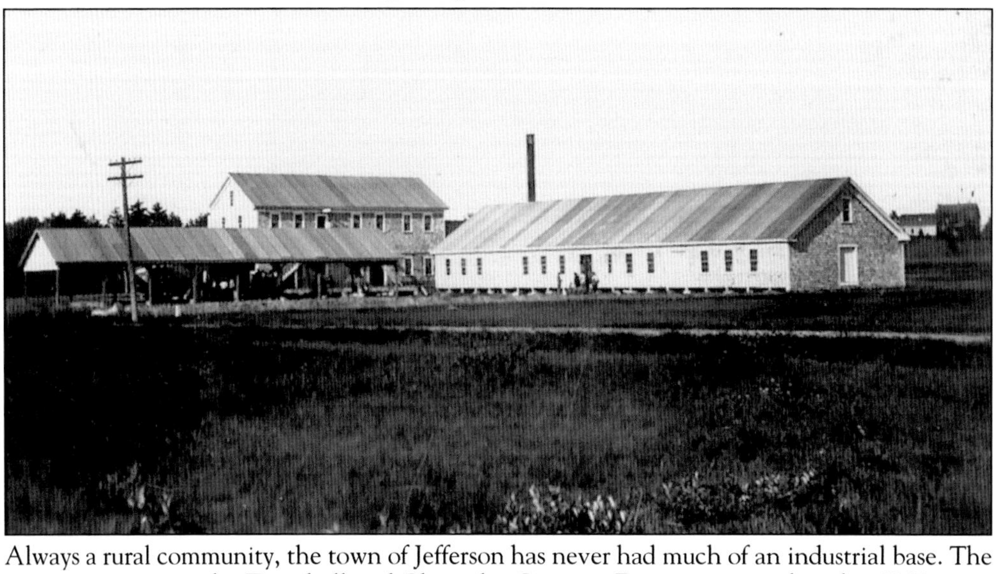

Always a rural community, the town of Jefferson has never had much of an industrial base. The one exception was the Twitchell and Champlin Canning Factory, pictured in this 1908 view. Located next to the Village School and across the street from the Masonic lodge, the operation lasted approximately 10 years. At its height, the canning factory employed about 50 people and packed corn, beans, and blueberries in season.

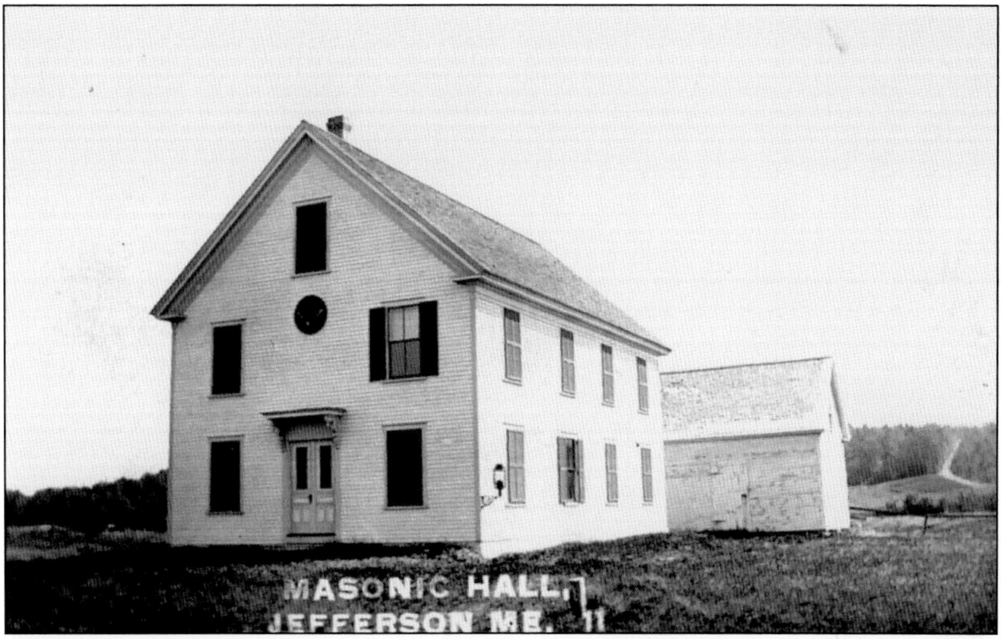

Organized in 1867, the Masonic Riverside Lodge No. 135 is located opposite the site of the former canning plant, at the corner of Seeger Road. Meeting the first Wednesday of each month, this lodge continues to be active today. The shedlike structure to the rear of the building no longer exists, and several of the windows have been sheathed over, but by and large, the view today is very similar to this 1906 photograph.

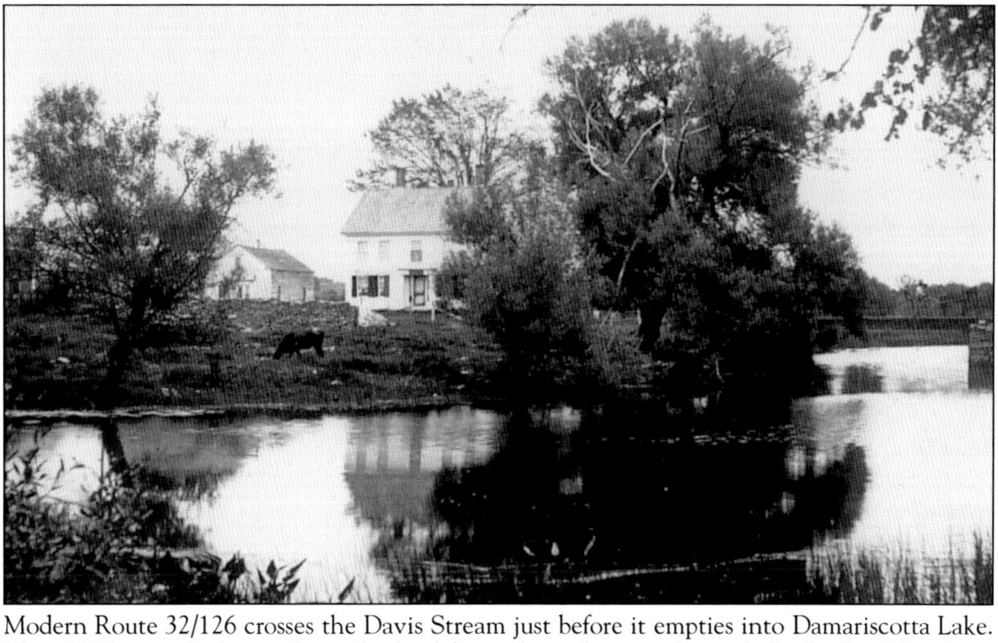

Modern Route 32/126 crosses the Davis Stream just before it empties into Damariscotta Lake. This 1905 view looks south, with the lake a short distance beyond the bridge. The large building to the left of the bridge still exists as a private residence, while the small barn has disappeared. This photograph was taken from a location behind the house on the corner of the Washington Road.

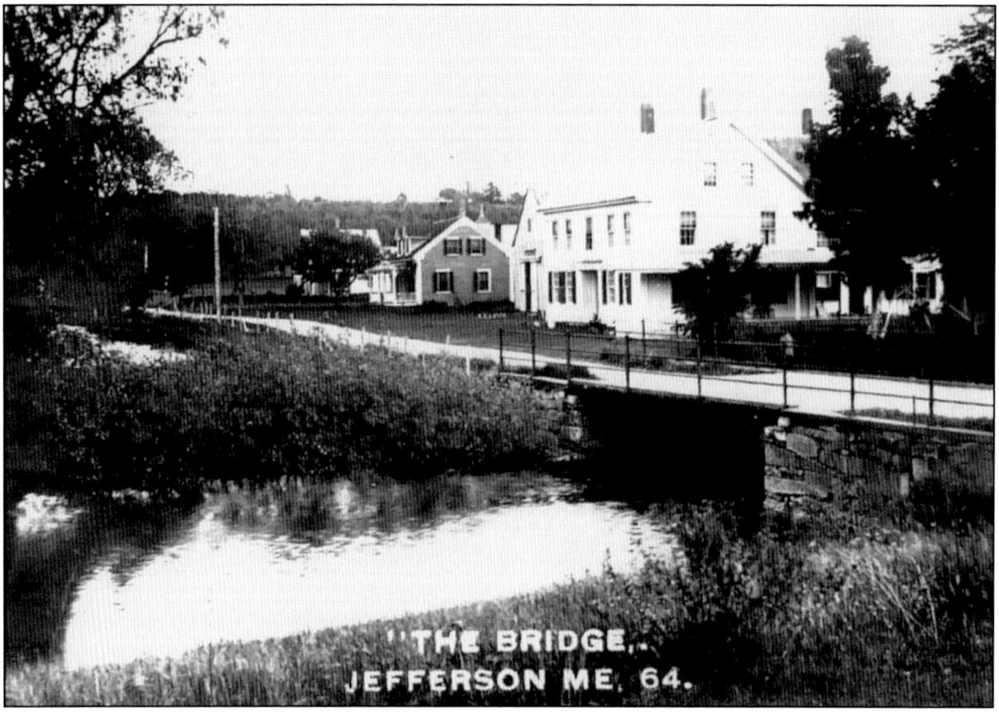

Another view of "the Bridge," this 1911 image was recorded closer to the span, just back from the intersection of the Washington and Waldoboro Roads. The large white house to the left is the same one visible in the previous photograph. The gray house with the two dormers and the large front porch at the center of the image still exists, although the barn next to it has been replaced.

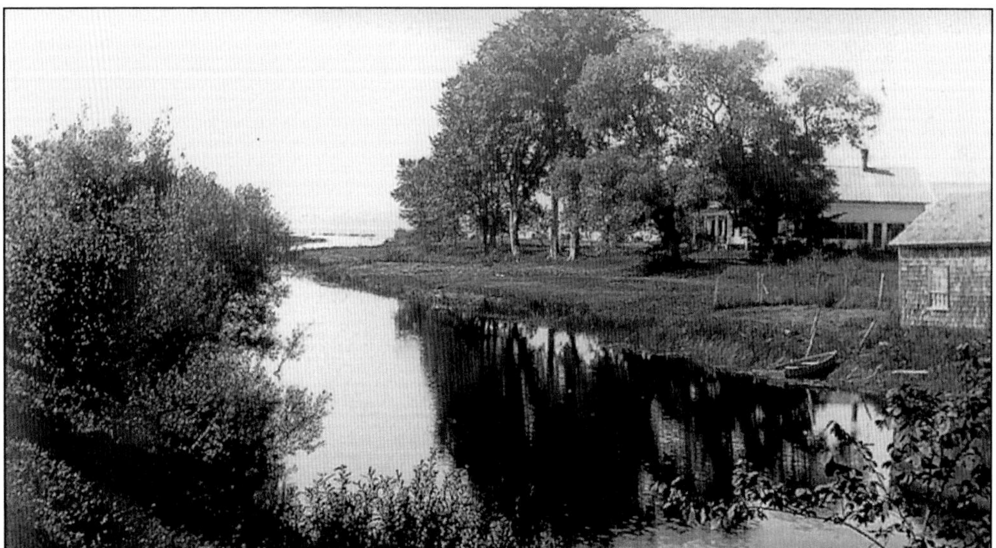

This undated image was taken from just east of the bridge along the Waldoboro Road, looking downstream toward Damariscotta Lake. The white house seen in the previous two images stands just out of sight to the left. The large house partially obscured by trees on the far shore still exists today, but the small barn at the extreme right does not.

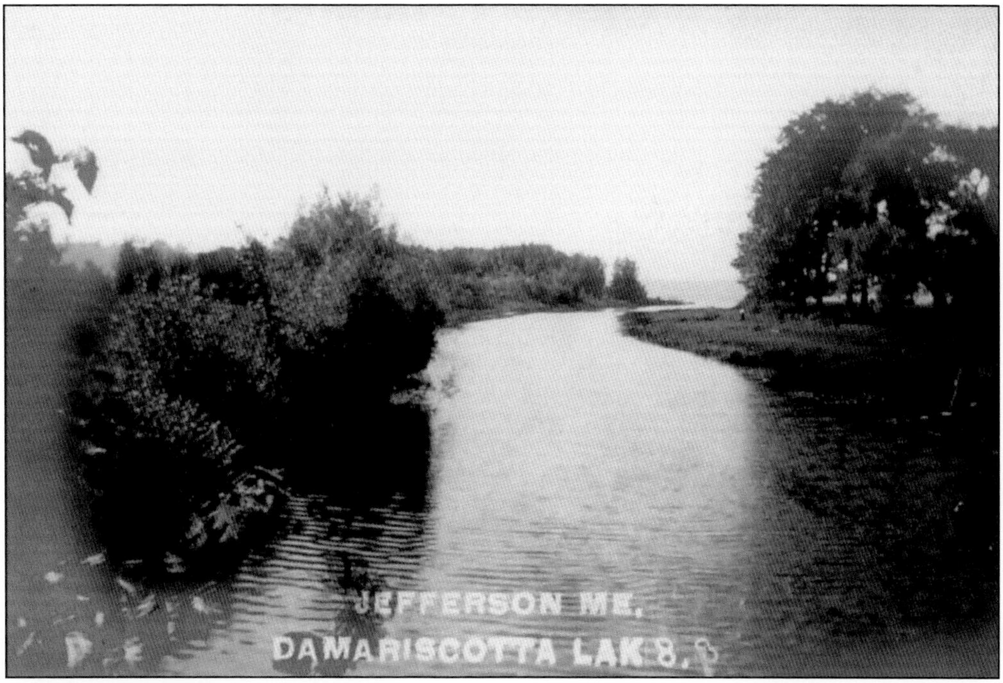

A nearly identical view to the previous one, this image, also undated, was taken from atop the bridge itself, looking downstream. Barely visible in the trees to the right is the front porch of the house seen in the last photograph. The rowboat seen on the bank to the far right also appears in both views.

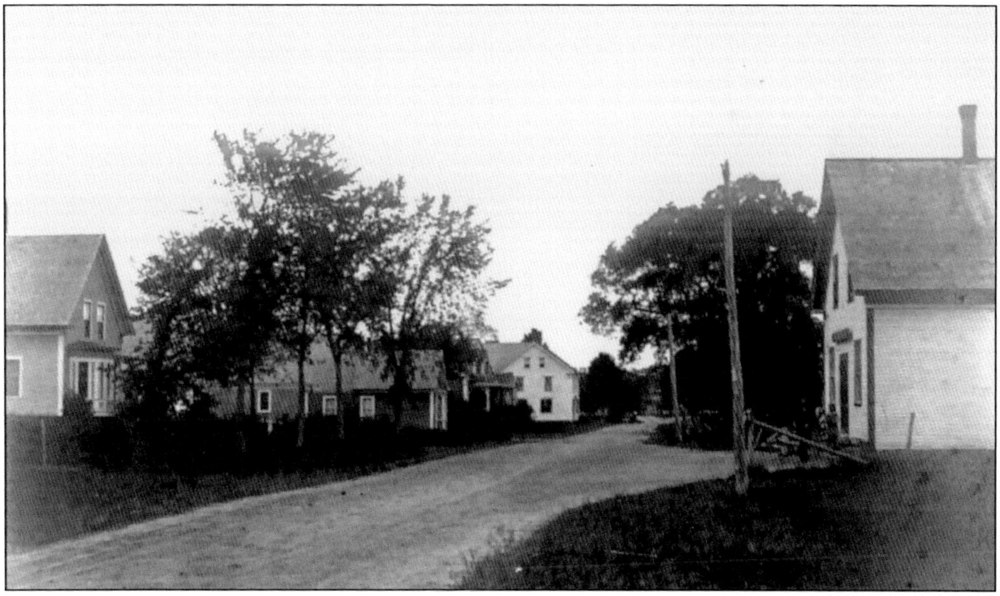

This image was taken from in front of the present-day Jefferson Market, looking toward the west. The white house visible at the center of the photograph is the one next to "the Bridge." The house on the left still exists, as does the house with the large front porch farther down the street. The store to the extreme right has since been assimilated into the current, block-long market building.

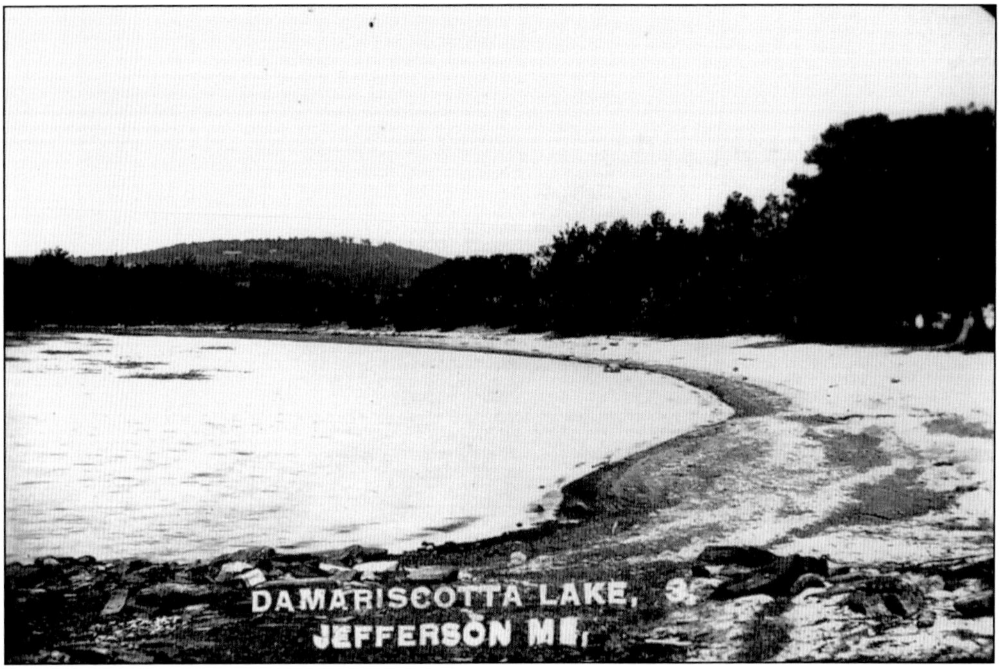

This is an undated view of Crescent Beach, looking toward the west. Now a part of Damariscotta Lake State Park, the beach has long been a favorite holiday spot. In years past, cottages and cabins once dotted the beach, and a large sycamore tree, a local landmark long since deceased, graced the waterfront.

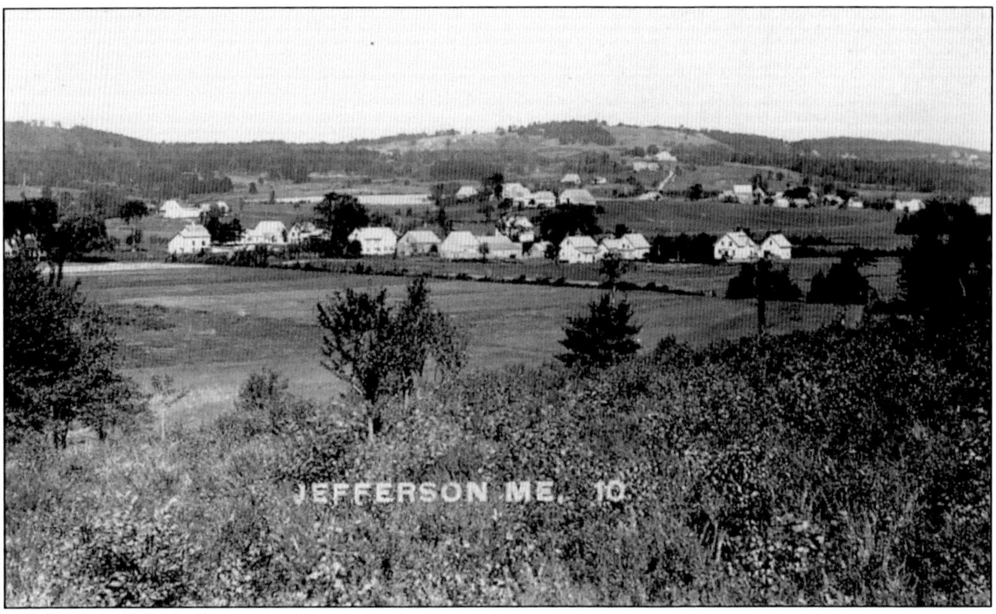

Taken from the hillside east of Crescent Beach, this image looks back at the Waldoboro Road. The rear of the Masonic lodge is at the center of the photograph, along the Washington Road. The white house next to "the Bridge" is to the left of center, and the tall trees mark the location of the bridge itself. The store and attached barn to the right are the present-day location of Jefferson Market.

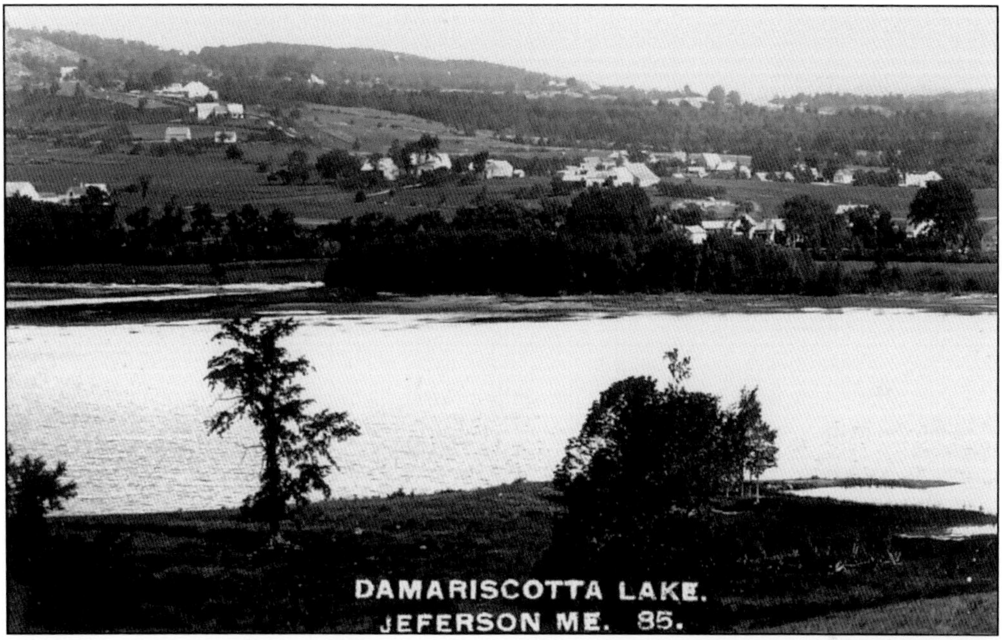

This view looks toward the northwest from a small peninsula just to the south of Crescent Beach, along the East Pond Road. The Davis Stream enters Damariscotta Lake to the left behind the tree line, and the large tree to the right marks the position of "the Bridge" on the Waldoboro Road. Lookout Hill and the houses along the Mountain Road can be seen rising to the left in the distance.

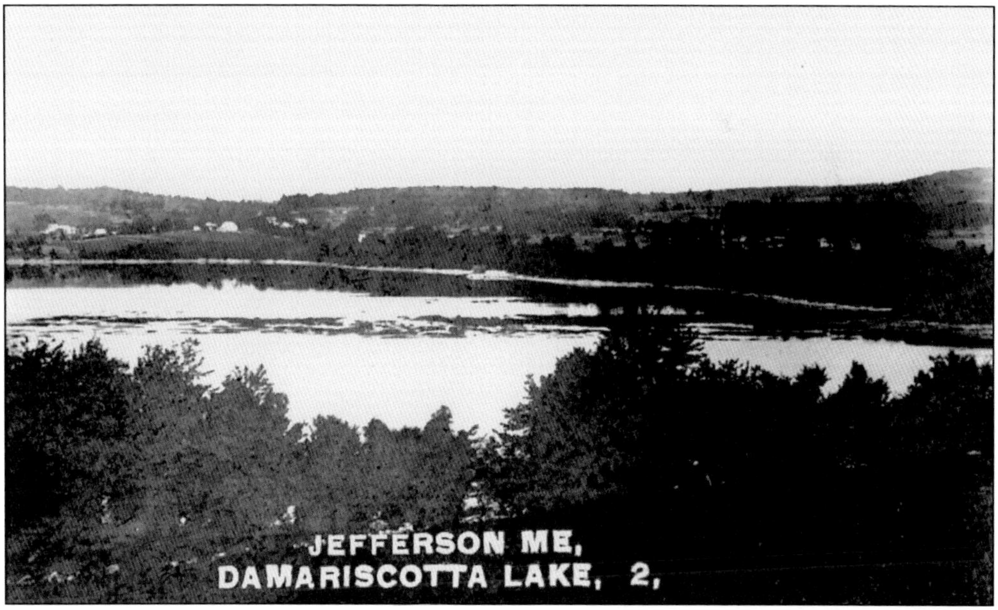

This very early image was taken from the same peninsula as the last photograph. Looking in a more westerly direction, the shadowing on the water is pickerel weed, marking the location of the influx of the Davis Stream into the lake. Barely visible just above this line is the mansion of Dr. Jackson and its massive barn, which sits across the road from the house. On the horizon, the western edge of Lookout Hill rises to the right.

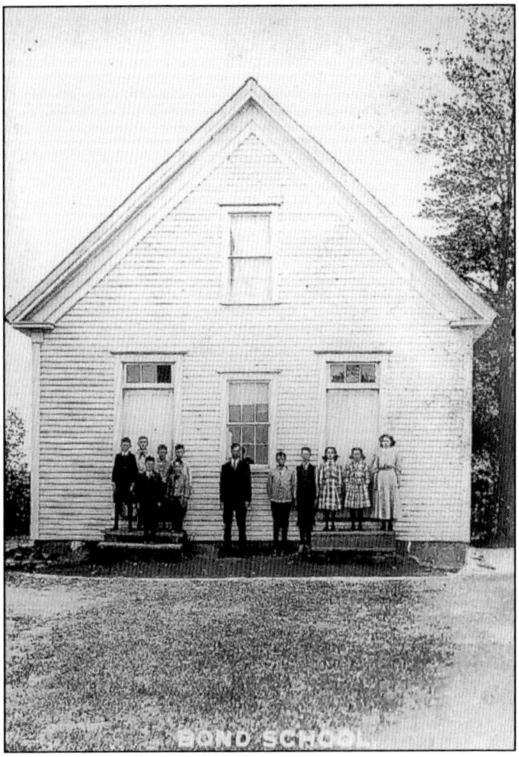

In 1900, there were 350 students registered in Jefferson, and they attended a total of 12 schoolhouses. One of those was the Bond School, pictured here in this undated photograph. In this view, 11 students of various ages and their teacher can be seen, none of whom are identified. Located on the East Pond Road approximately one and a half miles south of the intersection with the Waldoboro Road, the structure still exists today as a private residence.

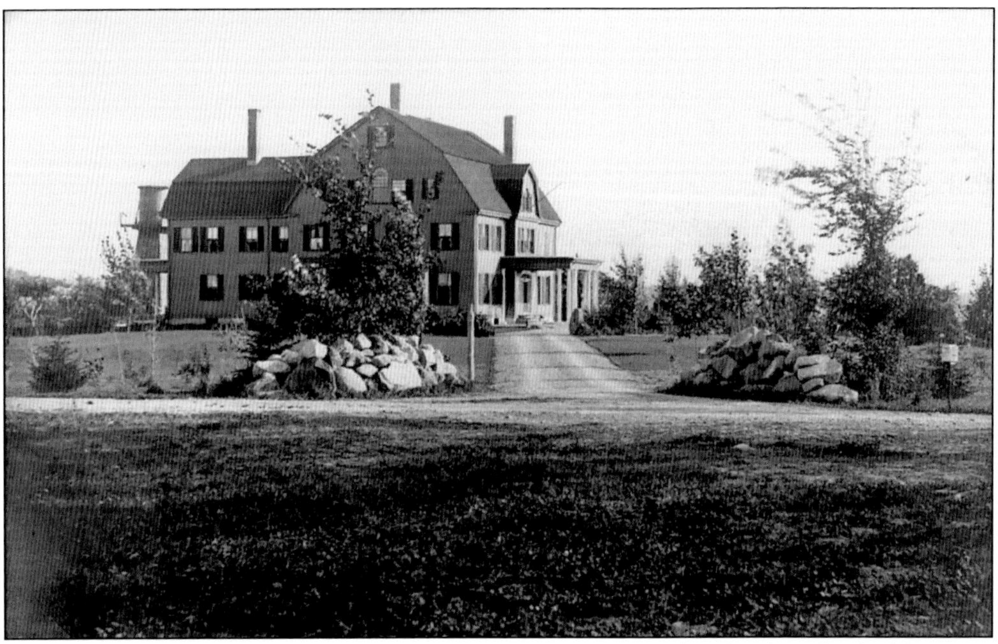

This photograph of Dr. F. W. Jackson's mansion was taken shortly after the building was constructed in 1905. The view can be seen today from modern Route 32/126. Located on a 1,000-acre lot, the home was described by newspaper accounts as "one of the finest country homes in Maine." The tower seen to the rear of the main house was for water storage. The water was pumped from a well and gravity fed to the expansive gardens.

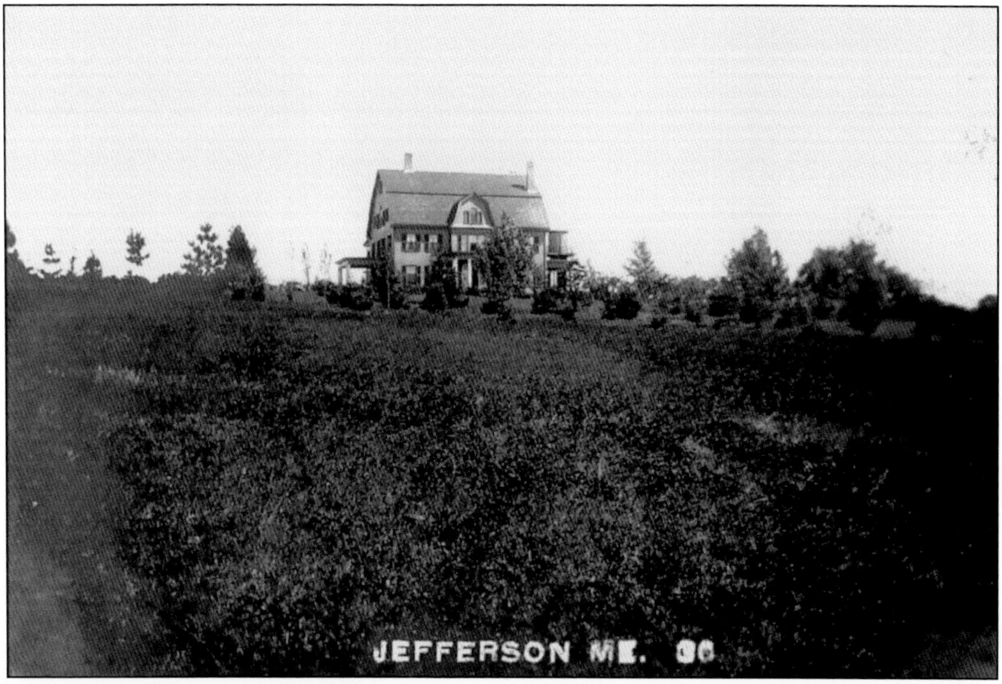

In a view looking east and uphill toward the front portico of the house, Damariscotta Lake is to the right and the road is toward the left. Judging by the tree growth and the shadowing, this photograph was most likely captured at the same day and time as the last view.

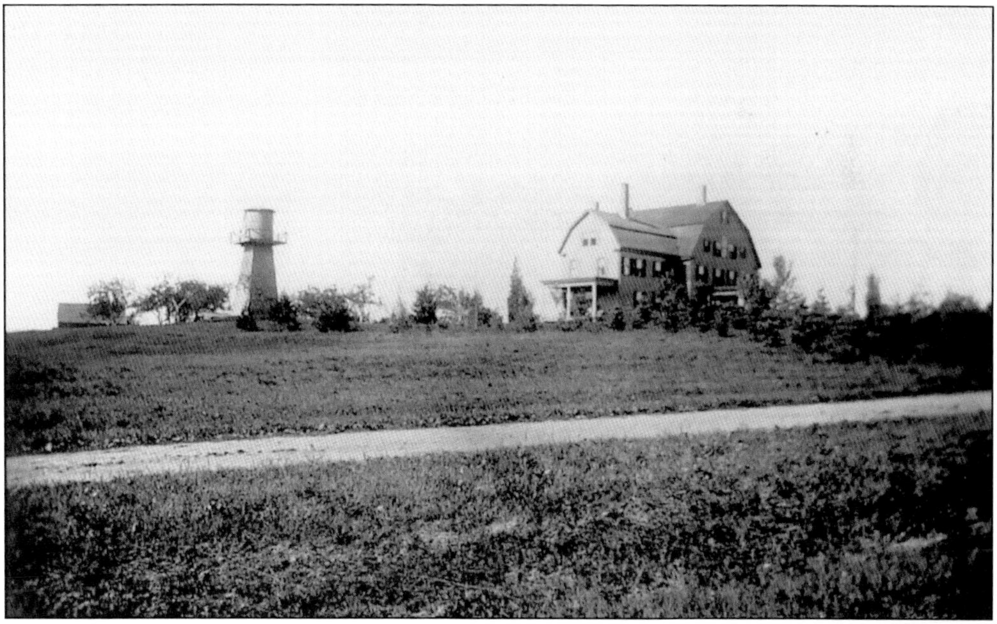

This third image of the Jackson mansion, like the previous two, appears to be part of a series. With modern Route 32/126 passing in the foreground, this view looking westward captures the rear wing, as well as the water tower. Appearing at the base of the tower, the small roof to the left most likely covered the pump house. The roof in the distance to the left cannot be identified.

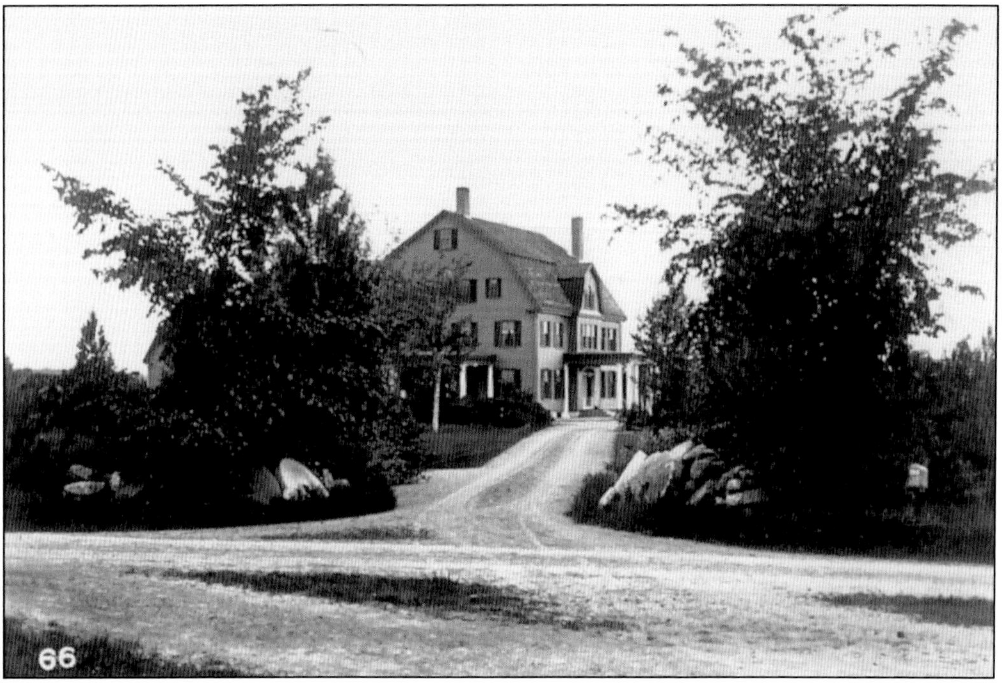

Taken from a position across the road, this later, undated image reveals some changes around the Jackson home. Visible behind the house and beyond the trees to the left of the driveway, the edge of a barnlike structure can be seen. Also apparent and seen today are the millstones on either side of the driveway entrance. These stones can also be seen in the yard in two of the earlier views.

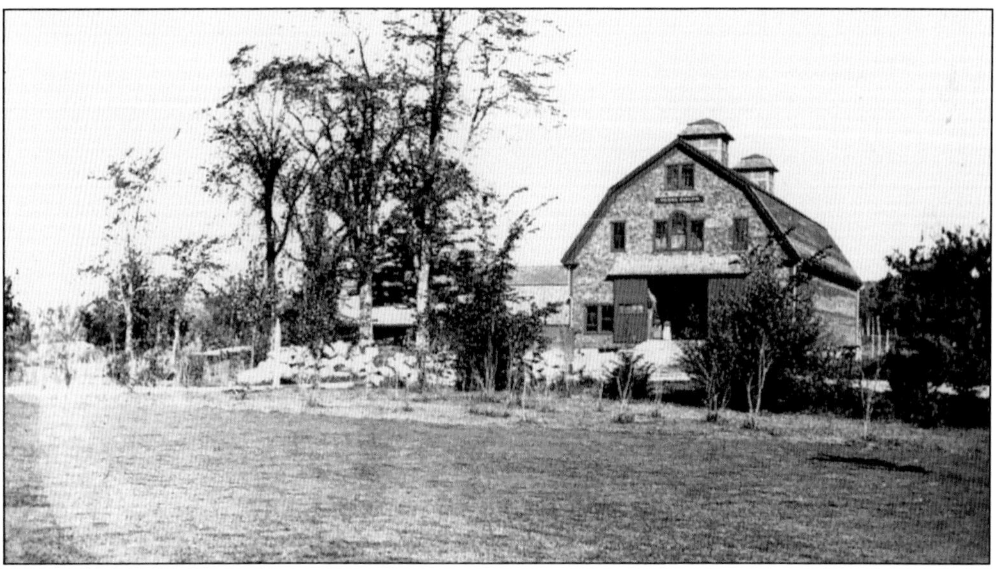

Taken across the road from the mansion, this undated photograph shows the immense barn that was a part of Dr. Jackson's estate. The barn sports the name Sunny Fields on the front facade, and this image reveals an unidentified woman standing in the open doorway, as well as the second-floor loft loaded with loose hay. This building remains standing today as part of Bond Brothers Lumber.

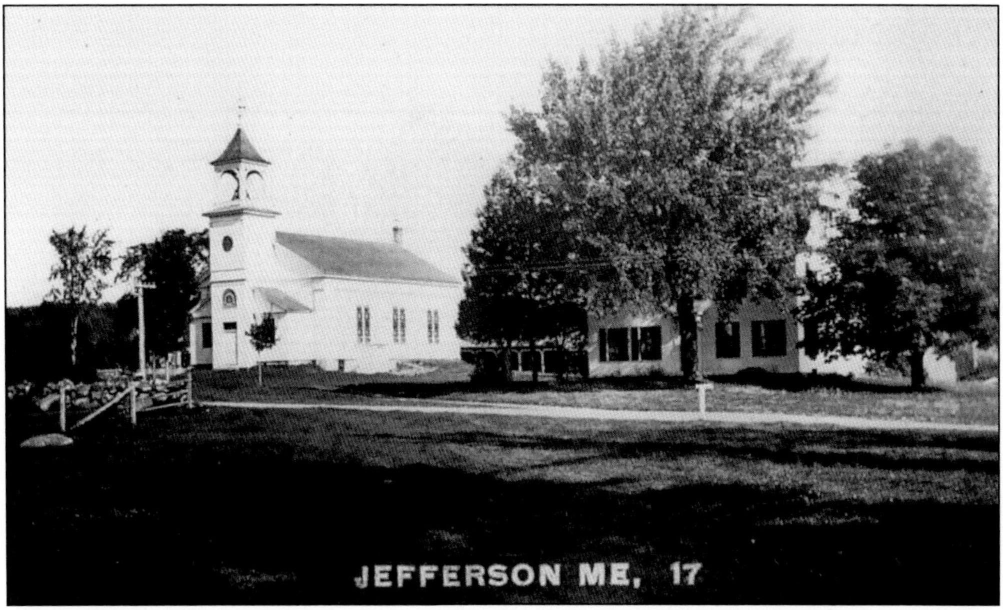

Built in 1807 as a meetinghouse and located on modern Route 32/126, the First Baptist Church has been remodeled and updated several times over the years. In October 1922, the steeple was damaged by a lightning strike and was subsequently repaired. The white house seen to the right of the church in this 1906 view still exists, although the carriage house located behind the church does not.

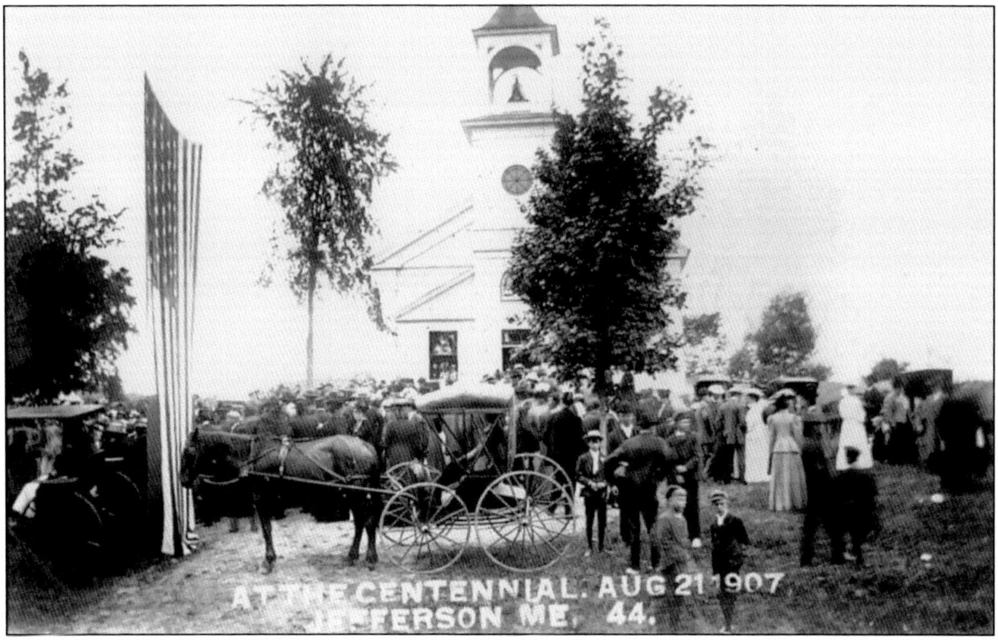

On August 21, 1907, the town of Jefferson celebrated the 100th anniversary of its incorporation. The festivities included a parade with 16 floats and several marching bands. A speaker's platform and bandstand were set up on the front lawn of the First Baptist Church, where a memorial bronze tablet was dedicated. Pictured here is the large crowd assembled in front of the church for the ceremonies.

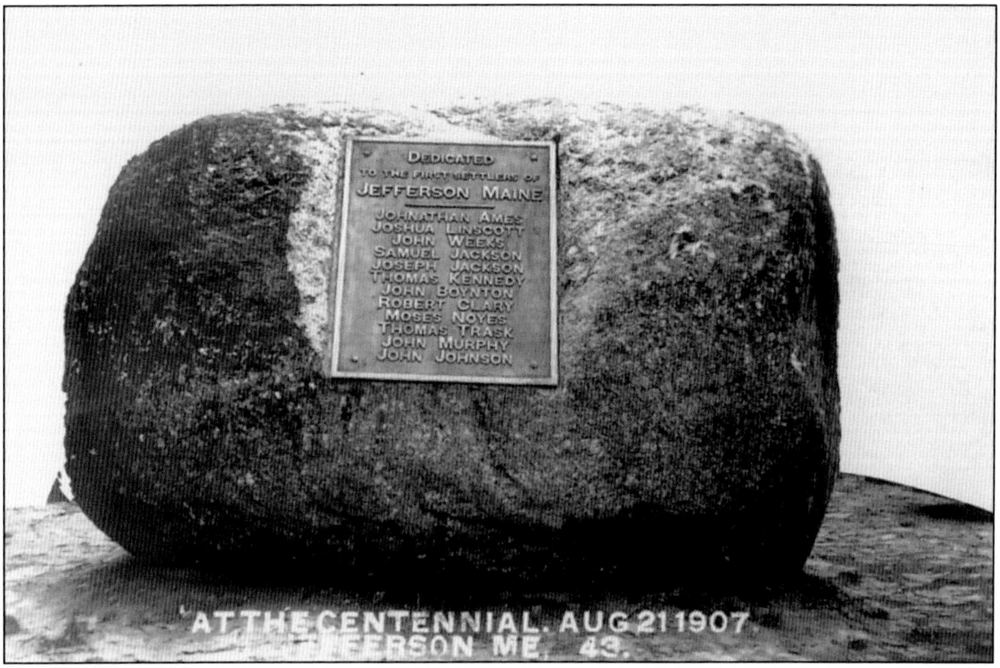

On August 12, nine days prior to the centennial celebration, a 20-yoke team of oxen pulled a 20-ton stone from lakeside land owned by Myrick Weeks and placed it on a foundation in front of the First Baptist Church. A bronze tablet bearing the names of 12 of the first settlers of Jefferson was affixed to the stone, which was dedicated on August 21, 1907.

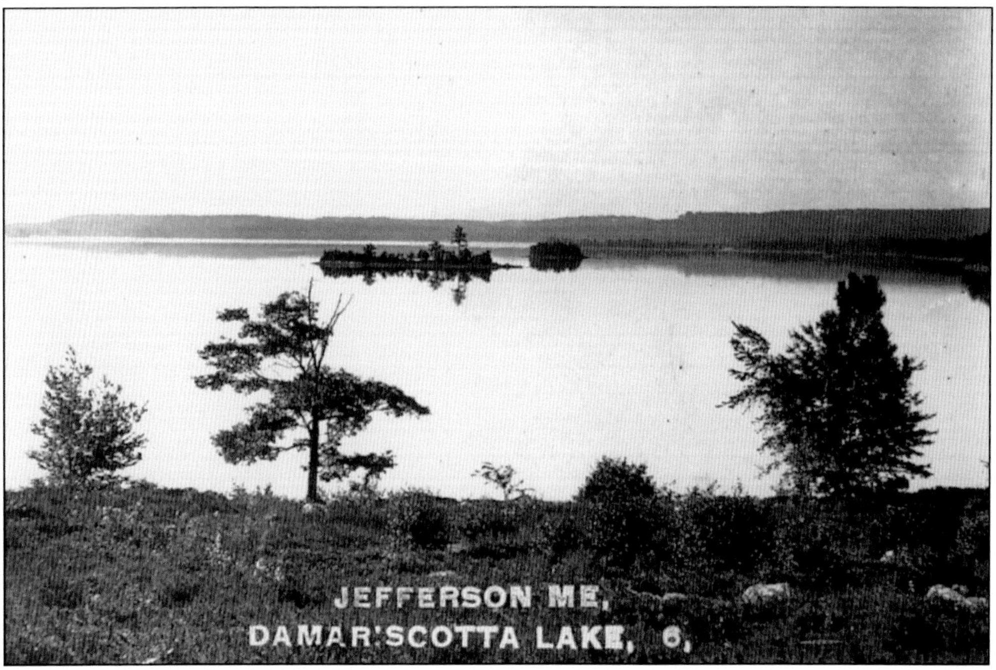

This undated photograph, looking south across Damariscotta Lake, was taken a short distance west of the First Baptist Church. On private land, but still visible and little changed today, this view of the two small islands can be seen from modern Route 32/126.

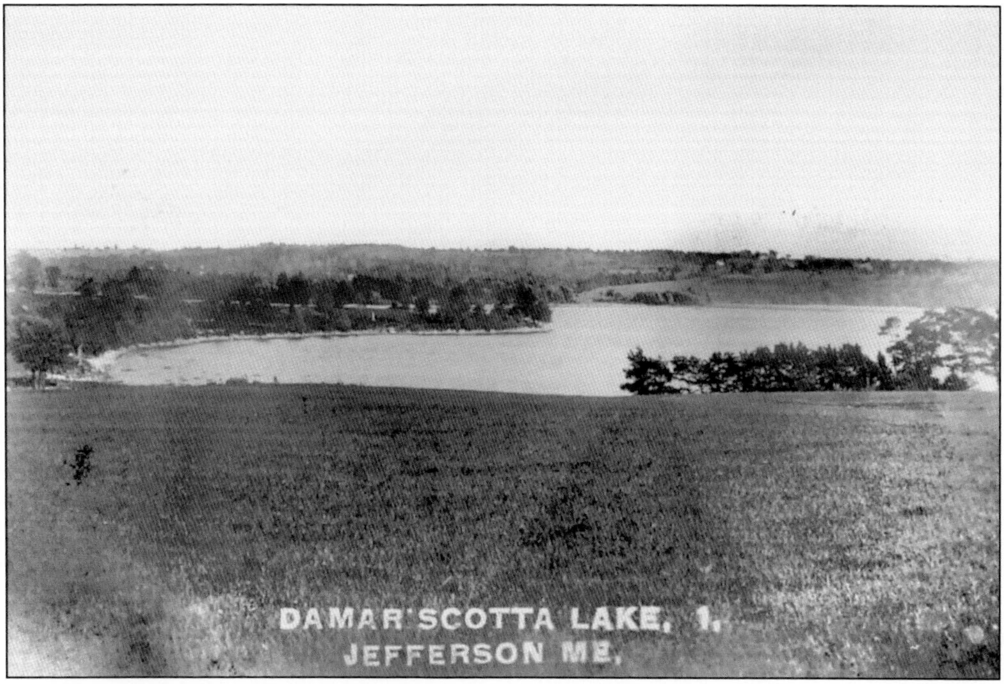

Another undated photograph of the lake, this one was taken looking east from in front of the former Weeks homestead—now the Damariscotta Lake Farm. As with the previous image, this view has changed little and was taken on what is now private property but can still be seen from modern Route 126. In the distance is the eastern shore of the lake, and Crescent Beach is out of sight to the left.

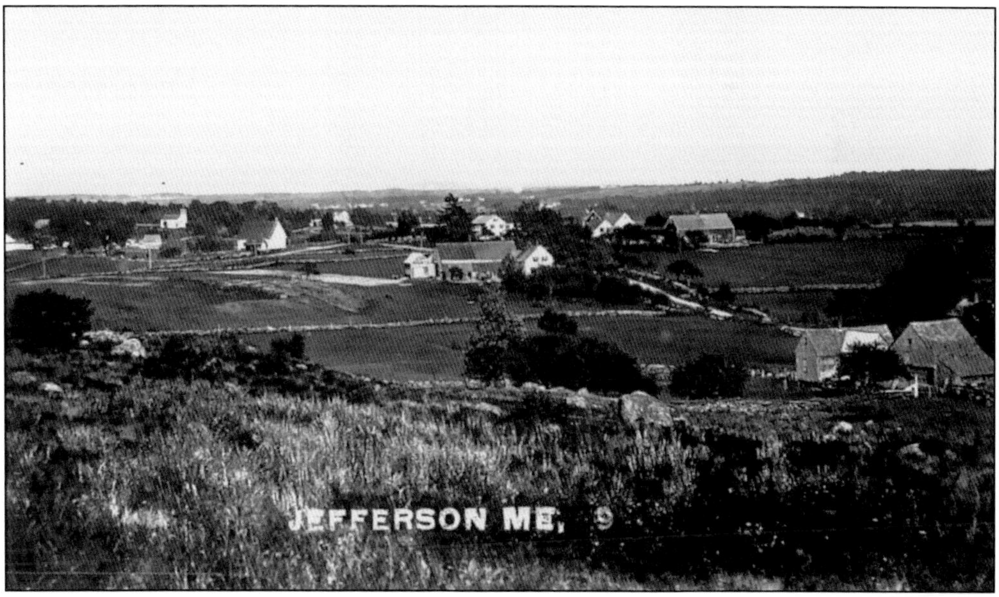

This 1906 image was taken along the western shore of the lake, just past the intersection of Routes 126 and 213. The house and barn at the center of the photograph still exist, as does the house just beyond it. To the left of center can be seen the Old Town Hall and Hearse House, located at the corner of the Gardiner Road. The First Baptist Church is also visible in the distance.

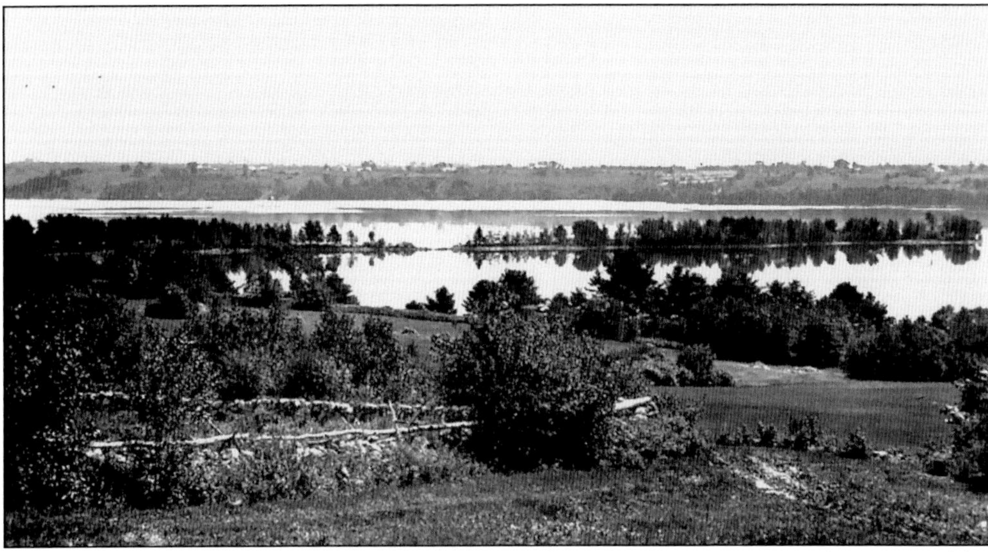

Located along the western shore of Damariscotta Lake, Wavus Point, seen at the center of this 1911 photograph, has long been the location of summer camps for children. In 1922, Delbert and Emma Andrews established Wawenock Camp for girls and, a year later, started Camp Damariscotta for boys. Although no longer owned by the Andrews family, the Wavus camps continue to operate today.

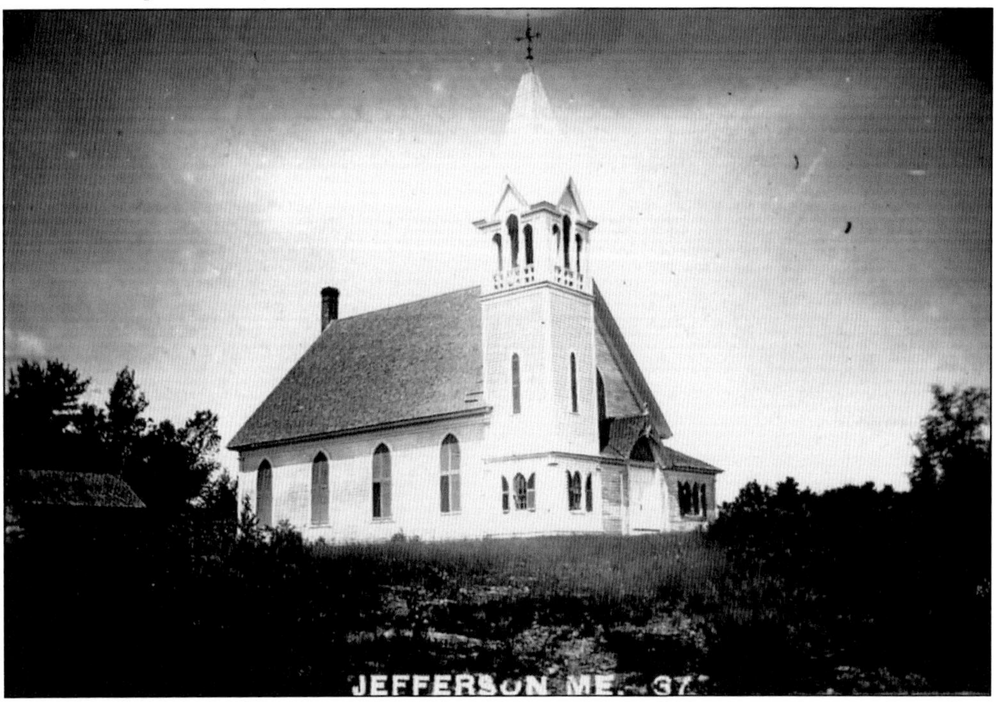

The Second Baptist Church is located along the Bunker Hill Road, also known as modern Route 213, about five miles past the Gardiner Road. Looking much the same today, this wonderfully preserved edifice was built in 1889 and sits on a hillside overlooking Damariscotta Lake. The small structure to the left no longer exists, but the Ladies' Aid Social Hall, a center of social activity for the area, stands just out of sight.

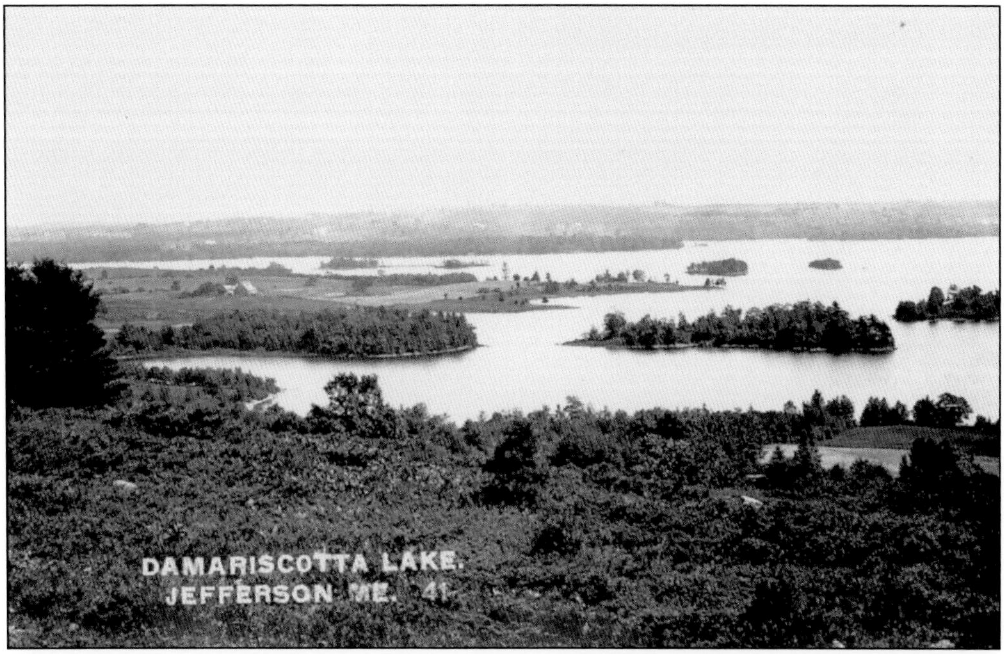

This undated view of the lake was taken just to the south and across the street from the Second Baptist Church, looking toward the east. The fields on the peninsula at the center of the photograph have since grown back into woods, but the shoreline is unmistakable. Off in the distance, near the opposite shore, is Morang Cove, and Muscongus Bay lies to the right.

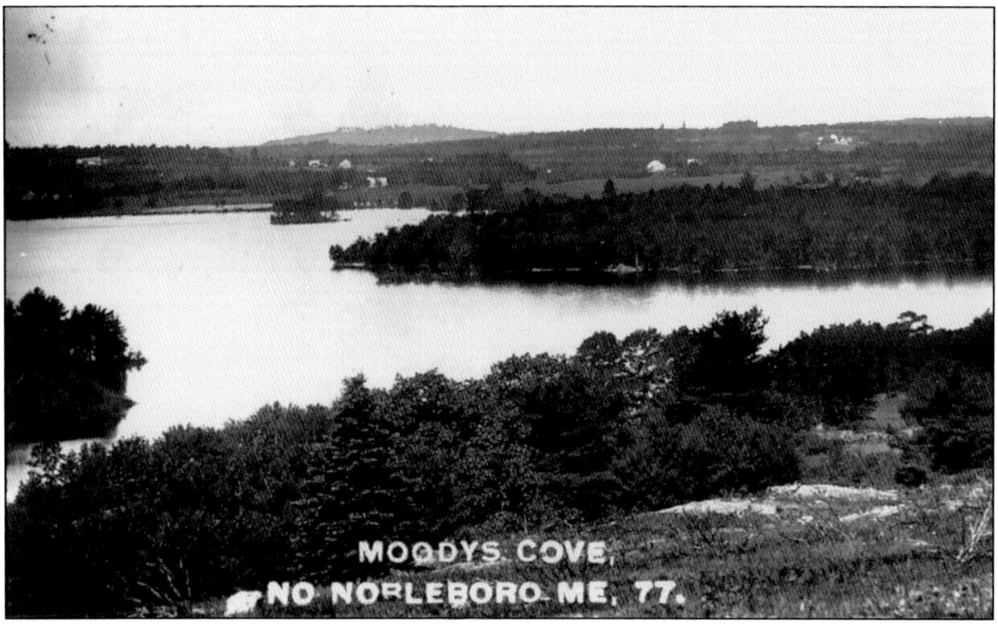

North Nobleboro lies on the eastern shore of Damariscotta Lake, south and east of Jefferson. This undated view of the lake was taken from a small peninsula off the East Pond Road, looking west. Moody's Cove, today known as Morang Cove, lies in the right foreground, with the Narrows disappearing to the right in the distance. On the far shore is the Bunker Hill section of Jefferson.

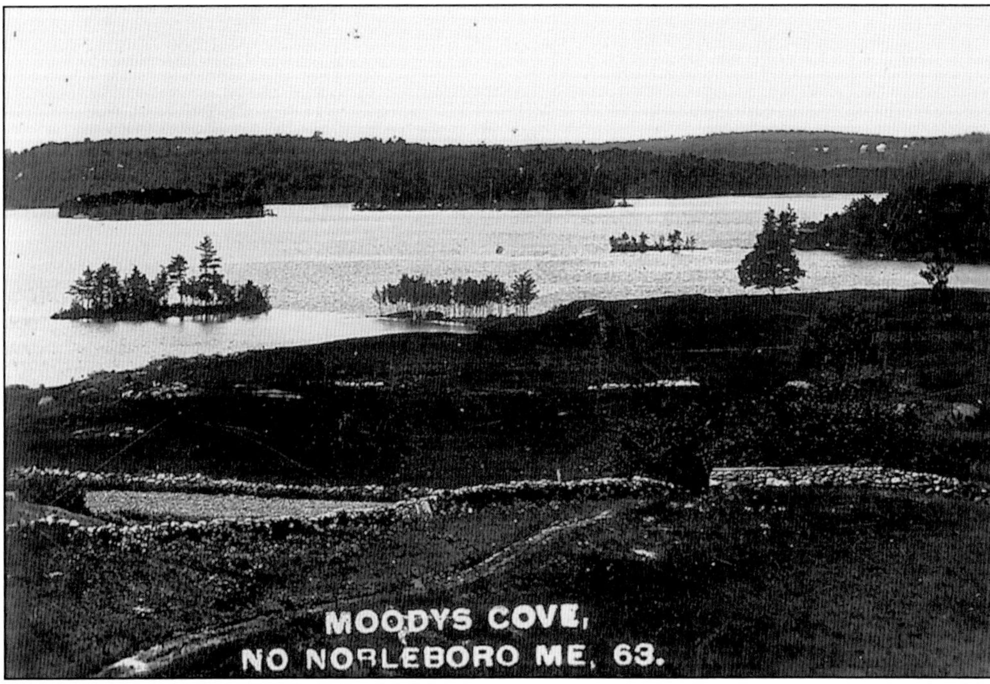

This photograph of North Nobleboro was taken from a location very close to that of the last view but looks in a more southwesterly direction. The tree line on the far shore is the West Neck section of Nobleboro, and to the left of the two large islands in the distance, just out of sight, lies Deep Cove. Woodlands in the foreground have obscured the modern view of this image.

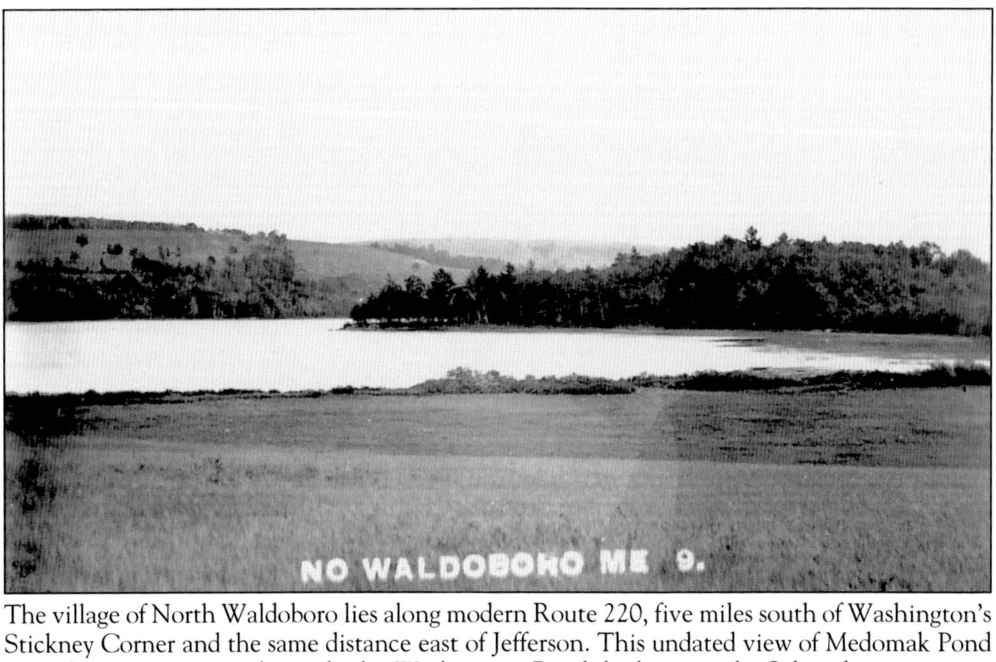

The village of North Waldoboro lies along modern Route 220, five miles south of Washington's Stickney Corner and the same distance east of Jefferson. This undated view of Medomak Pond was taken in a pasture alongside the Washington Road, looking north. Other than extensive tree growth on the far hillside, the view remains little changed today.

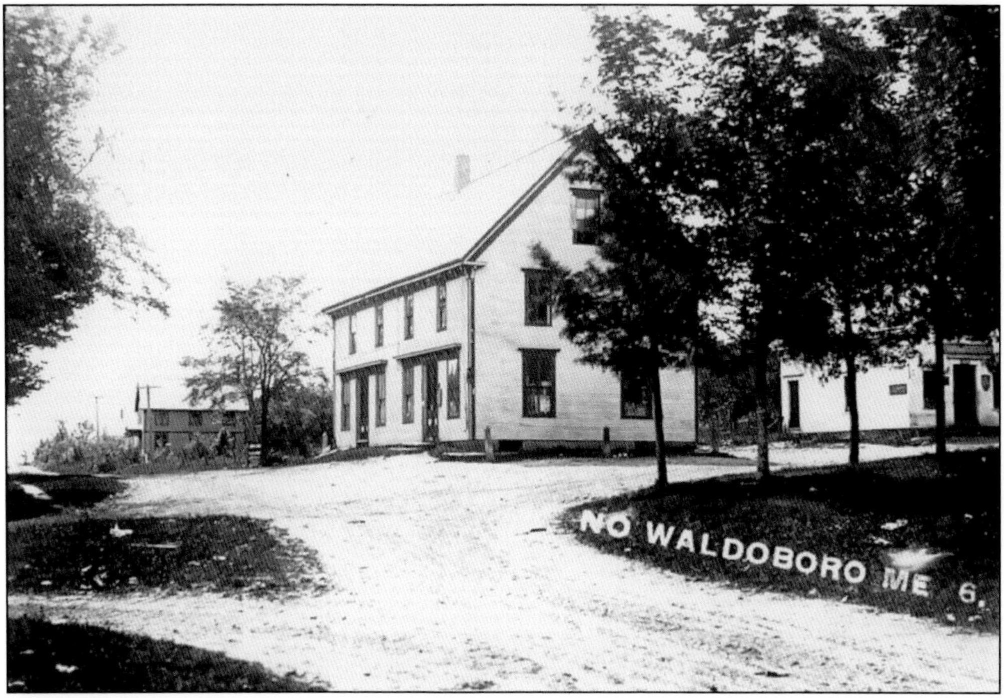

This 1907 image was taken at the intersection of the Washington and Old Augusta Roads, looking south toward Waldoboro. Formerly the Burnheimer grain store and later a general store, this structure still exists today as a private residence. Neither the building in the distance to the left (the former Community Hall) nor the one to the right (a dry goods store) exists today.

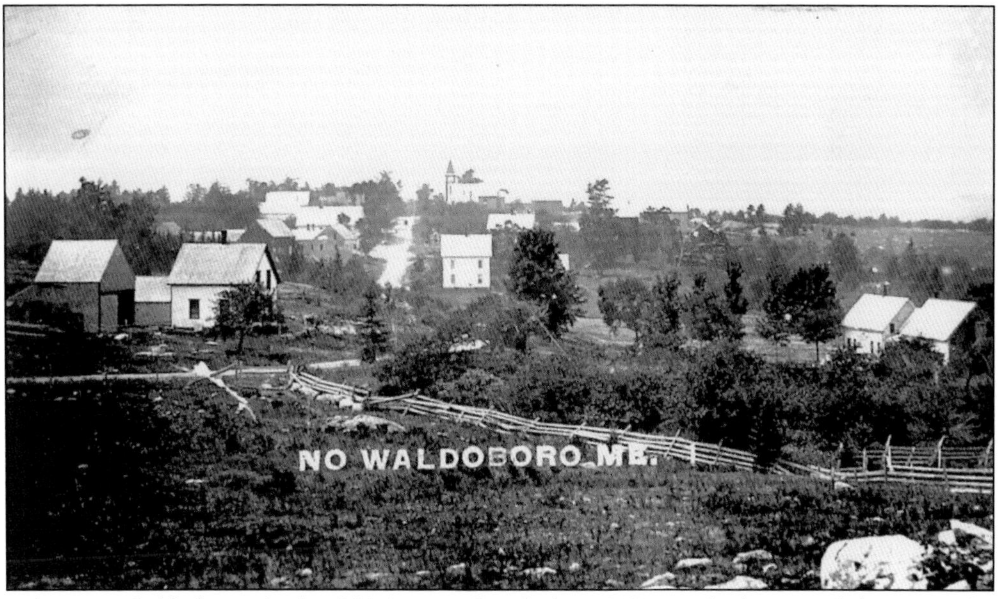

Taken in a field alongside the Old Augusta Road, this 1907 view looks toward the west. The house and barn to the left, as well as the house to the far right, no longer exist. The white house at the center of the image, known by locals today as the "red roof inn" because of its distinctive new metal roof, stands just downhill from the intersection with Route 220.

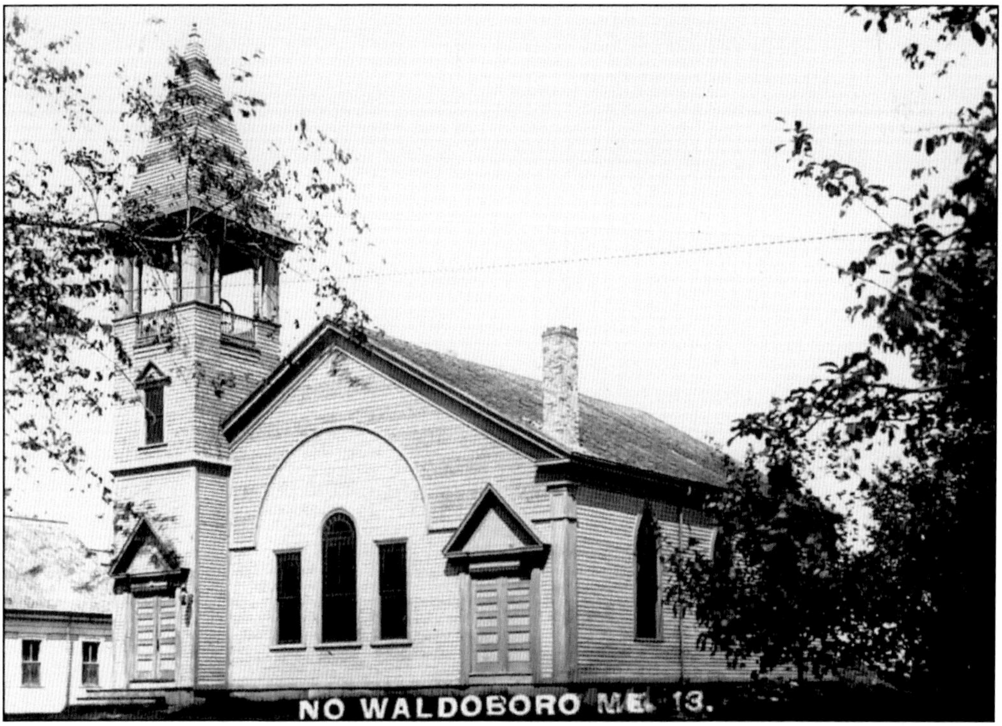

The North Waldoboro Methodist Episcopal Church was organized in 1843, and the building itself—seen in the distance in the previous view—was erected in 1850. While this 1906 image captures an imposing edifice, by the time the structure was torn down in 1990, it had become a hazard. The parsonage building, built in 1936, was moved to the Flanders Corner Road, where it exists today as a private residence.

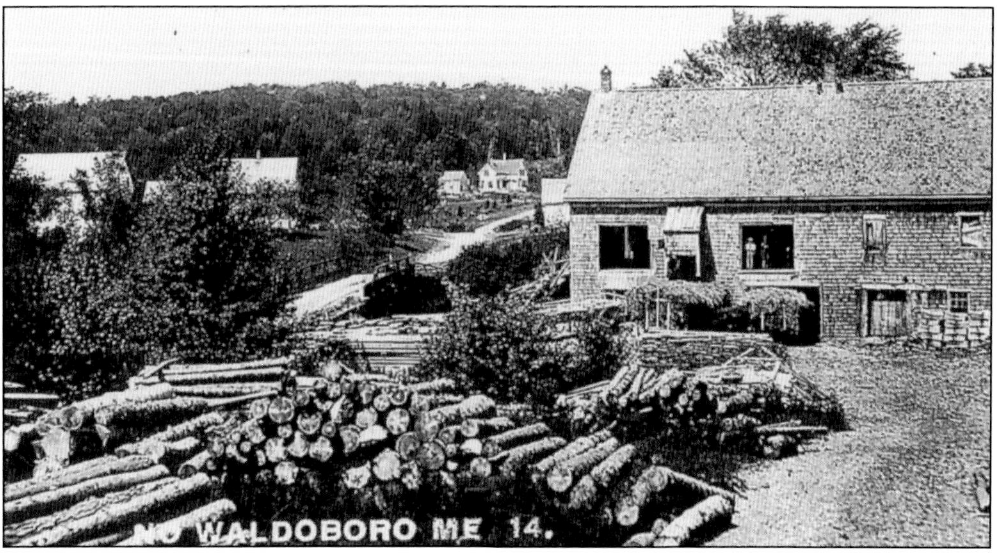

The Miller sawmill was located west of the village of North Waldoboro along the Old Augusta Road, astride the Medomak River. It was once engaged in the production of long lumber and shingles. Only scattered foundation stones can be seen today. Seen in the distance at the center of this photograph, the white house is the only structure from this 1910 image that still exists.

Five

SETTLEMENTS TO THE WEST

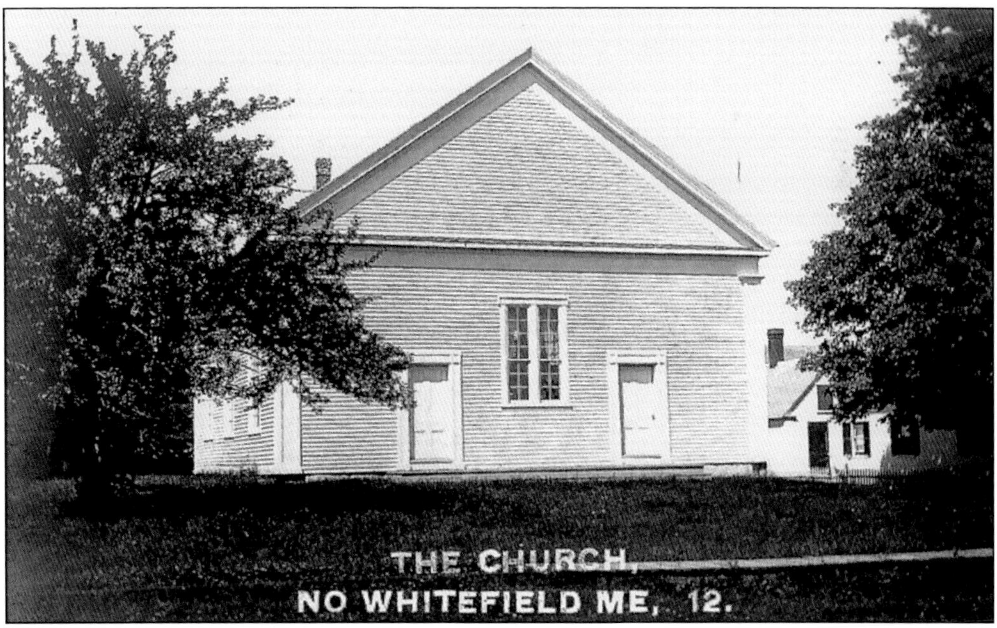

The village of North Whitefield, a portion of the town of Whitefield, lies about eight miles west of Jefferson on the western end of Pleasant Pond, also known as Clary Lake. Seen in this 1906 view, the North Whitefield Baptist Church stood just west of the village, along modern Route 126. The church building no longer exists, having burned in the 1970s.

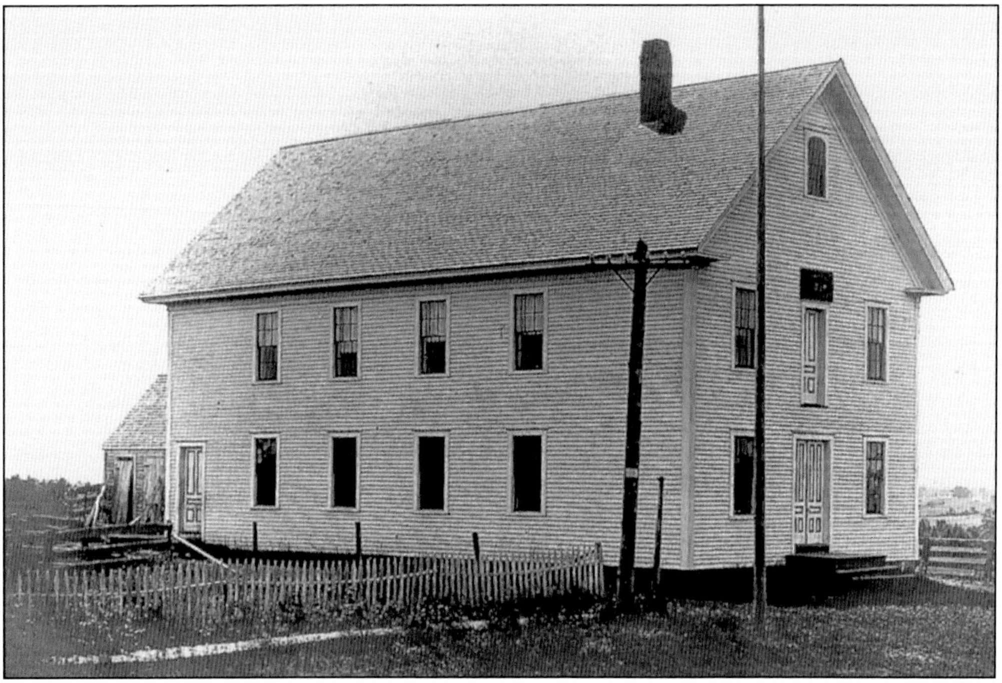

Located diagonally across the road from the Baptist church at the corner of Arlington Lane and modern Route 126, this structure was originally built as a Grand Army of the Republic hall. Sometime during the 1920s, upon the passing of the majority of Civil War veterans, it became the local high school. Still later, it became known as Arlington Grange Hall No. 528, a purpose it continues to serve today.

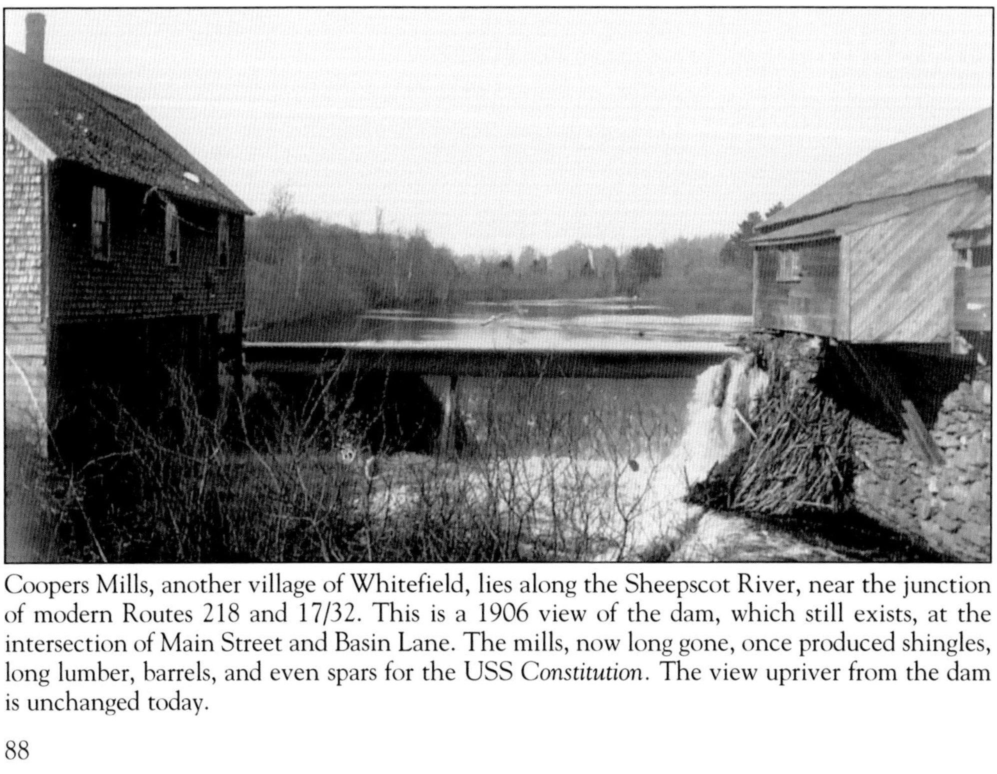

Coopers Mills, another village of Whitefield, lies along the Sheepscot River, near the junction of modern Routes 218 and 17/32. This is a 1906 view of the dam, which still exists, at the intersection of Main Street and Basin Lane. The mills, now long gone, once produced shingles, long lumber, barrels, and even spars for the USS *Constitution*. The view upriver from the dam is unchanged today.

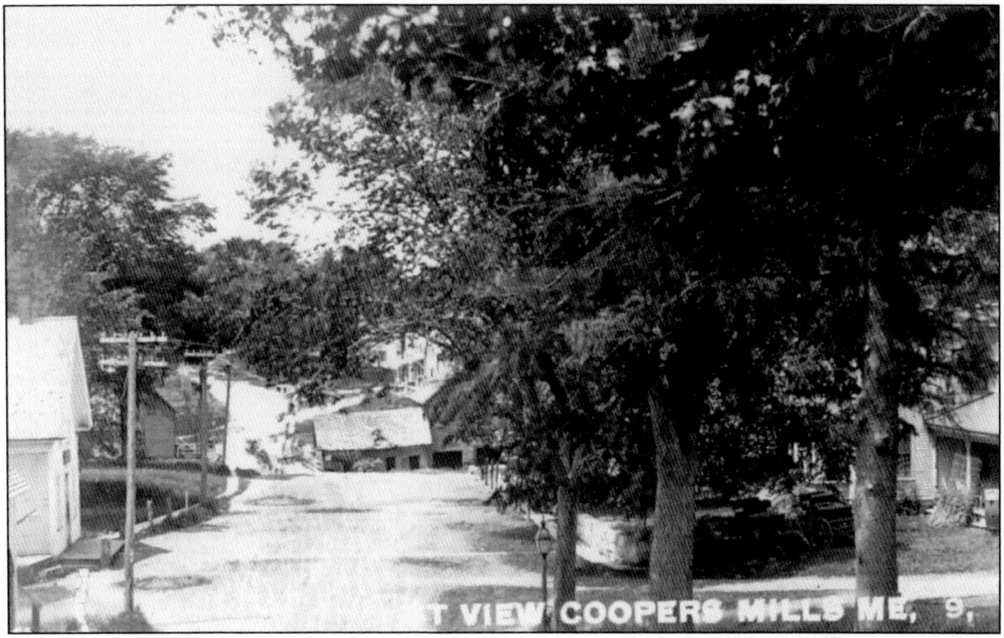

This 1906 view of Coopers Mills was taken east of and uphill from the dam location on Main Street. The building just to the left of center is one of the mills seen in the previous image. The house at the far right, less the stone wall, still exists, while the storefront to the left is gone. One of the distant houses, near the intersection of the Coopers Mills Road, also still stands.

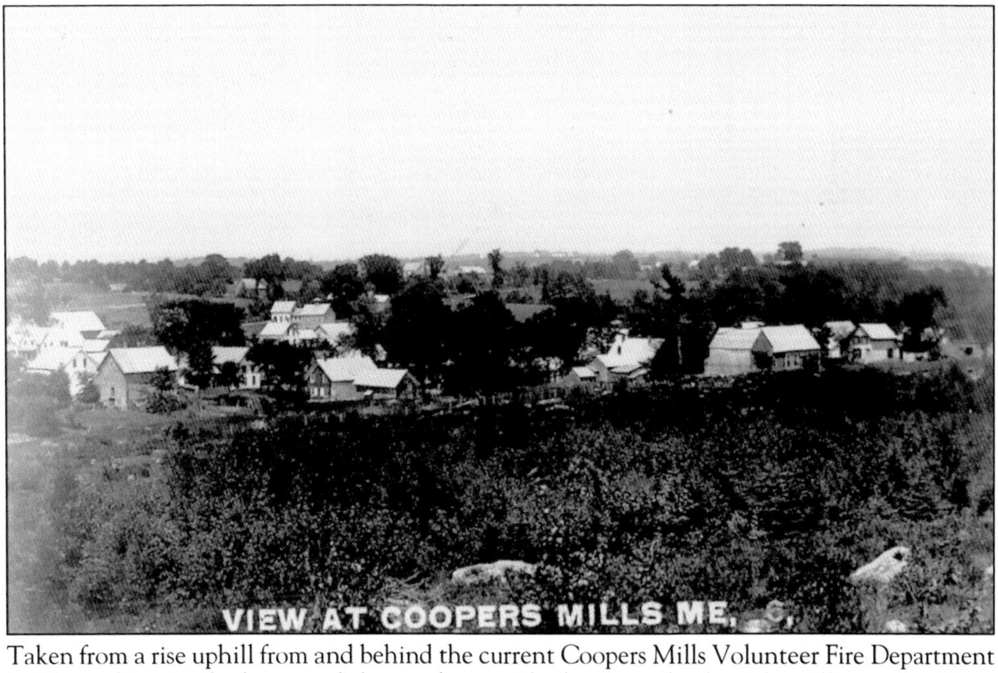

Taken from a rise uphill from and behind the current Coopers Mills Volunteer Fire Department building, this view looks toward the northwest. The house at the far right still exists on Main Street, while the current fire station is the building just to its left. In the distance, the large farmhouse visible to the left of center still stands on a hill on the Coopers Mills Road.

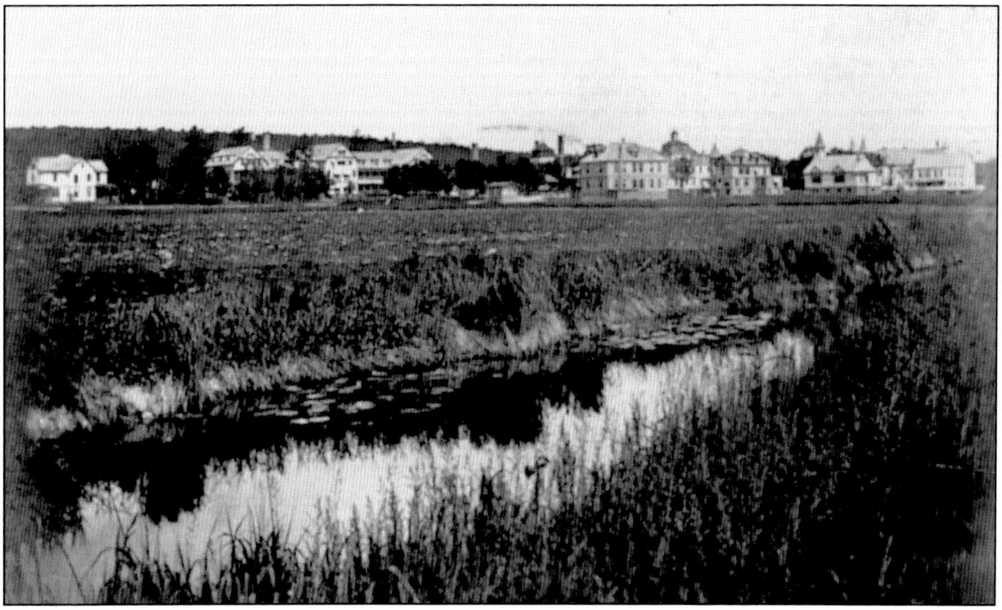

Originally called the National Asylum for Disabled Volunteer Soldiers, the veterans' facility in the town of Chelsea opened in November 1866. Known as Togus (from the foreshortened American Indian name *Worromontogus*), it is America's oldest soldiers' home. Once served by a narrow-gauge railroad and electric trolley line, Togus became a Veterans Administration facility in 1930. Continually modernized and much changed today, the facility continues to provide full-service medical care to veterans.

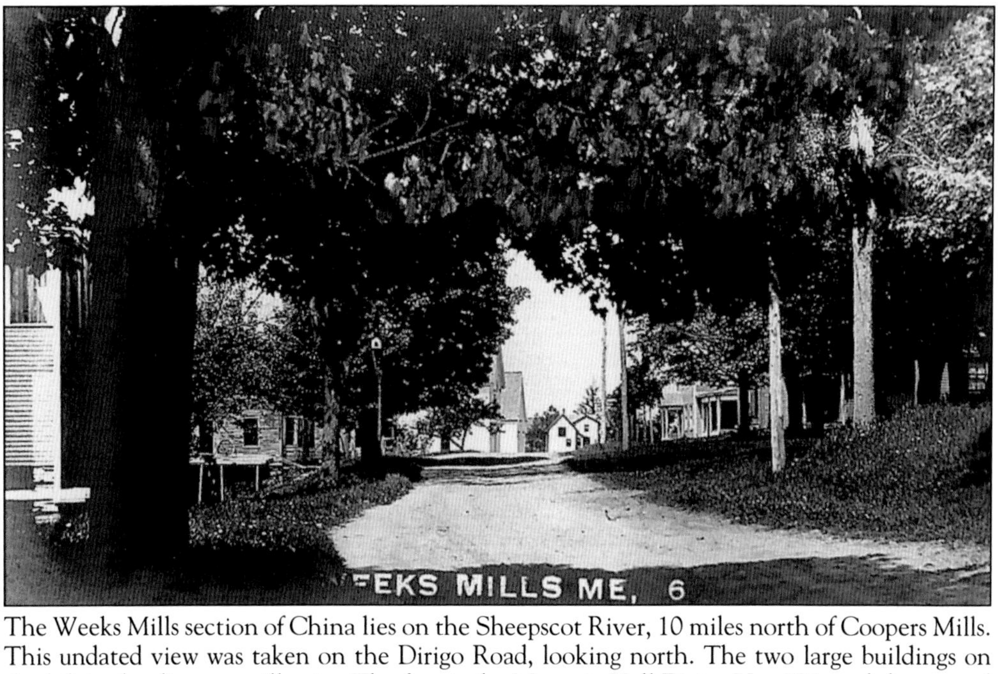

The Weeks Mills section of China lies on the Sheepscot River, 10 miles north of Coopers Mills. This undated view was taken on the Dirigo Road, looking north. The two large buildings on the left in the distance still exist. The first is the Masonic Hall Dirigo No. 104, and the second is the Advent Christian Church. Only two of the houses partially obscured to the right still stand; the rest have disappeared.

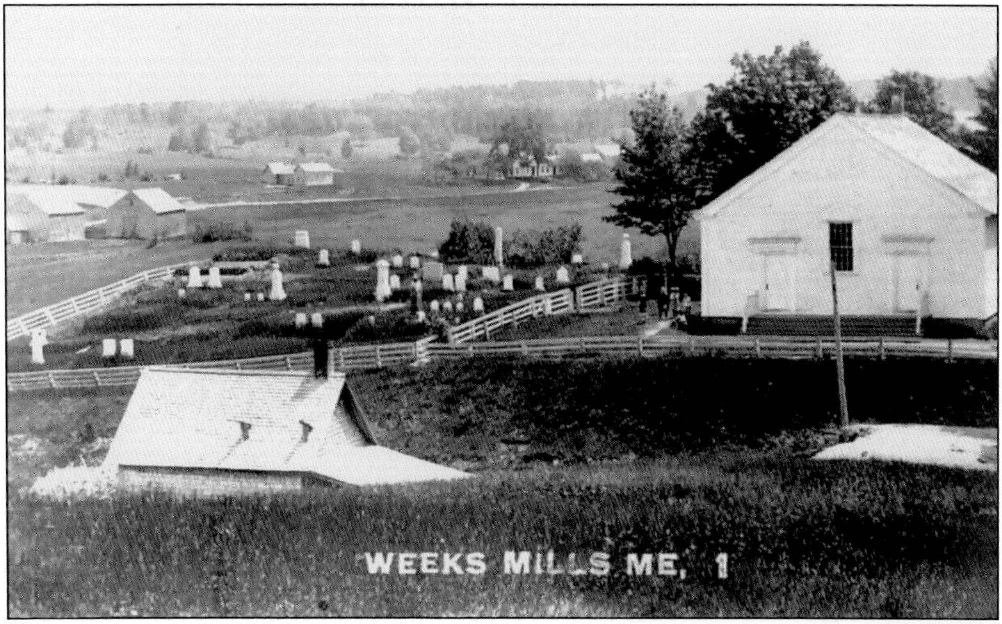

This 1913 image of the Weeks Mills Baptist Church is interesting for two reasons. The first is the youngster seen standing on his head to the left of the church. The second is the open grave seen to the left and rear of the cemetery. An examination of the markers reveals that the grave belongs to Charles H. Stuart (1888–1913) described on the stone as "My Boy."

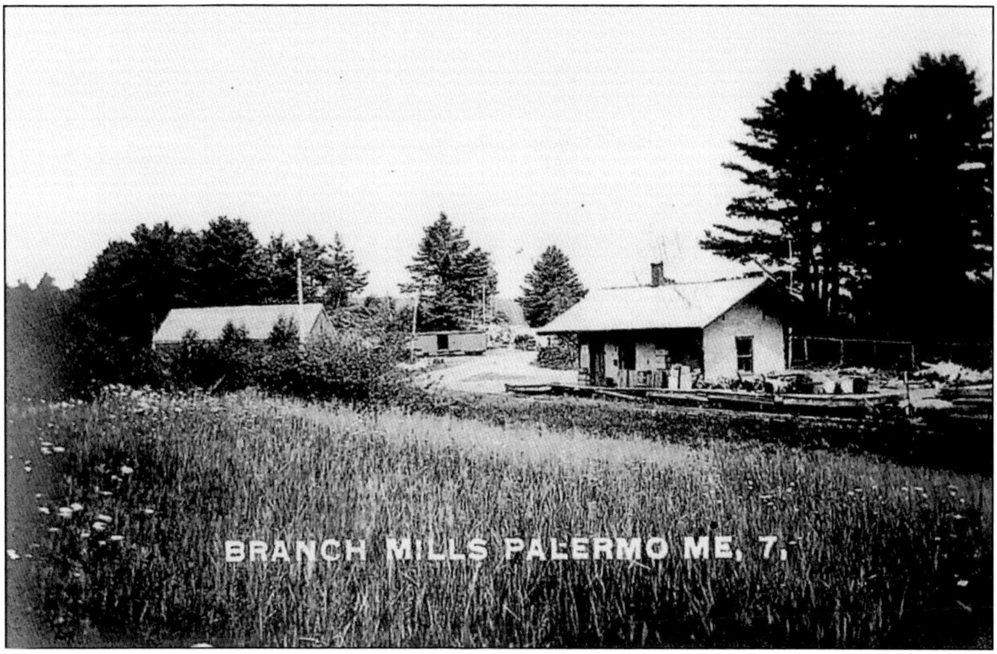

Palermo lies about 7 miles northeast of Weeks Mills and 10 miles west of Liberty. The Wiscasset, Waterville, and Farmington Railway was a two-foot-gauge railroad that ran from Wiscasset to Albion, passing through Palermo. The former freight house, pictured in this 1906 image, exists today as a private residence on the Bill Auld Road and is visible from modern Route 3. The railroad ceased operations in 1933 and was scrapped.

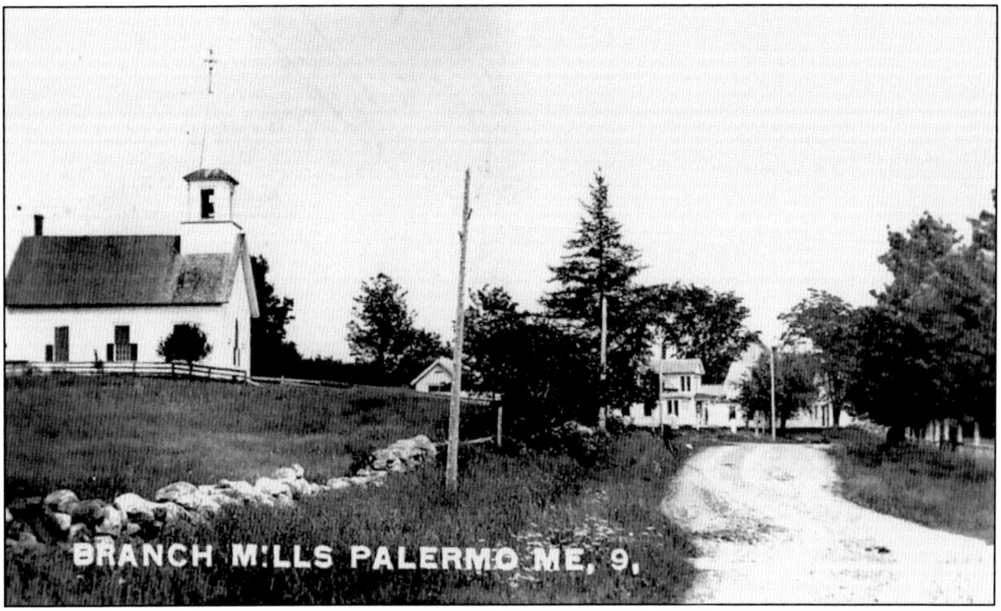

This undated image was taken on the Branch Mills Road, looking toward the east. The Branch Mills Union Church was built in 1861 and still stands on the corner of the Parmenter Hill Road today. The steeple has been lowered, but otherwise the building appears unchanged today. The large house visible to the right of center still exists, although the one just beyond does not.

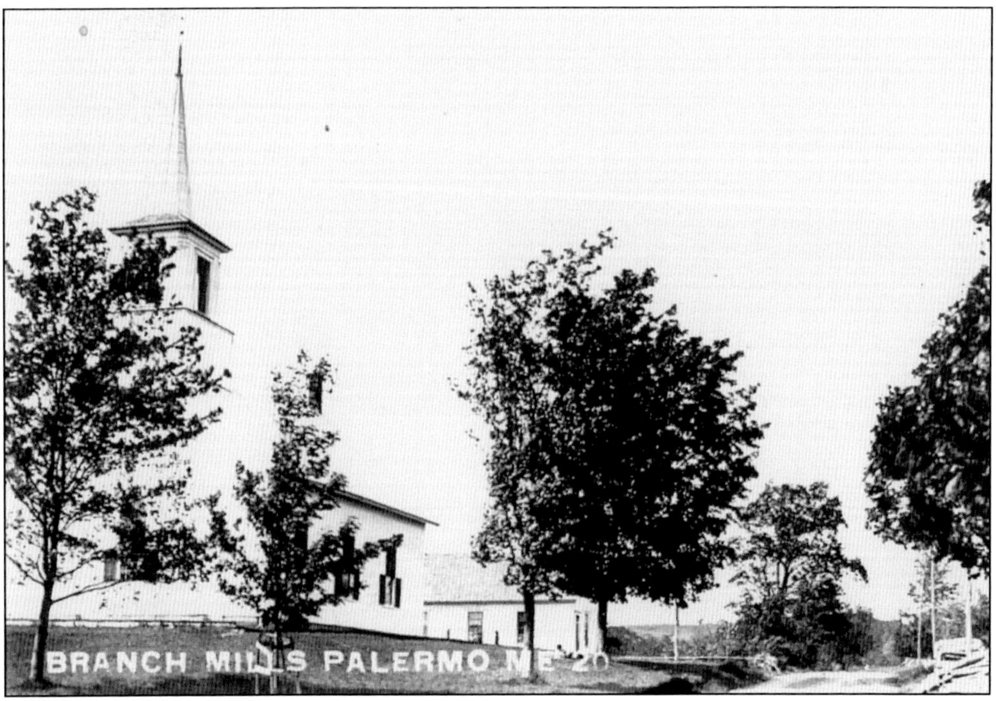

Looking north up the Parmenter Hill Road, this is another undated view of the 1861 Branch Mills Union Church. The white building to the rear of the church no longer exists. The large house visible in the previous image stands to the right, just out of sight.

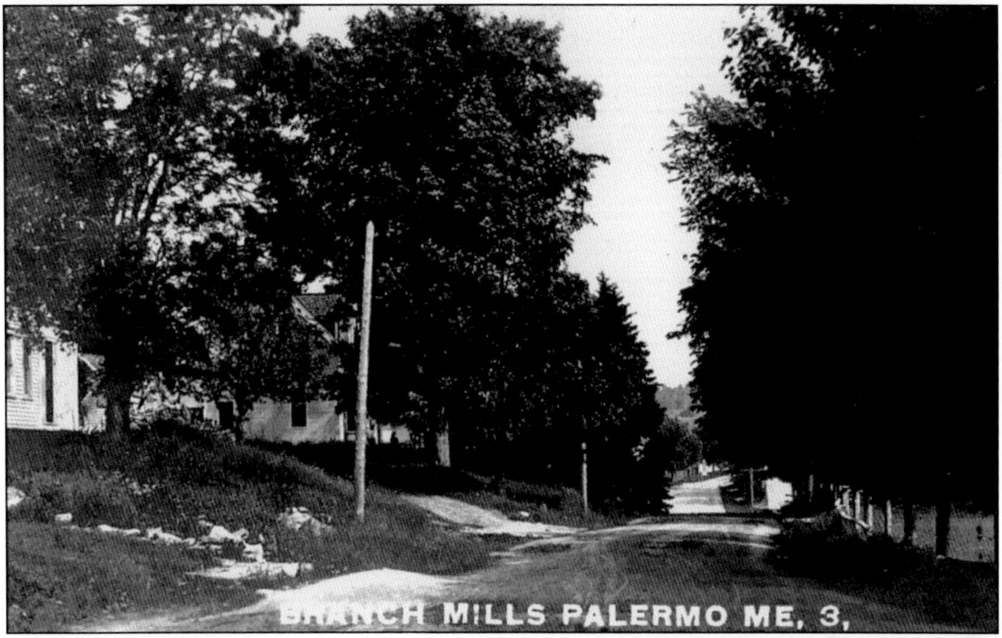

This 1906 view of Branch Mills was taken from just past the church, looking southeast. The house to the left no longer exists. The house with the gingerbread trim, farther downhill, still stands today. Located on the left at the bottom of the hill, just to the right of center, is the mill, with Branch Pond to the left and the West Branch of the Sheepscot River to the right.

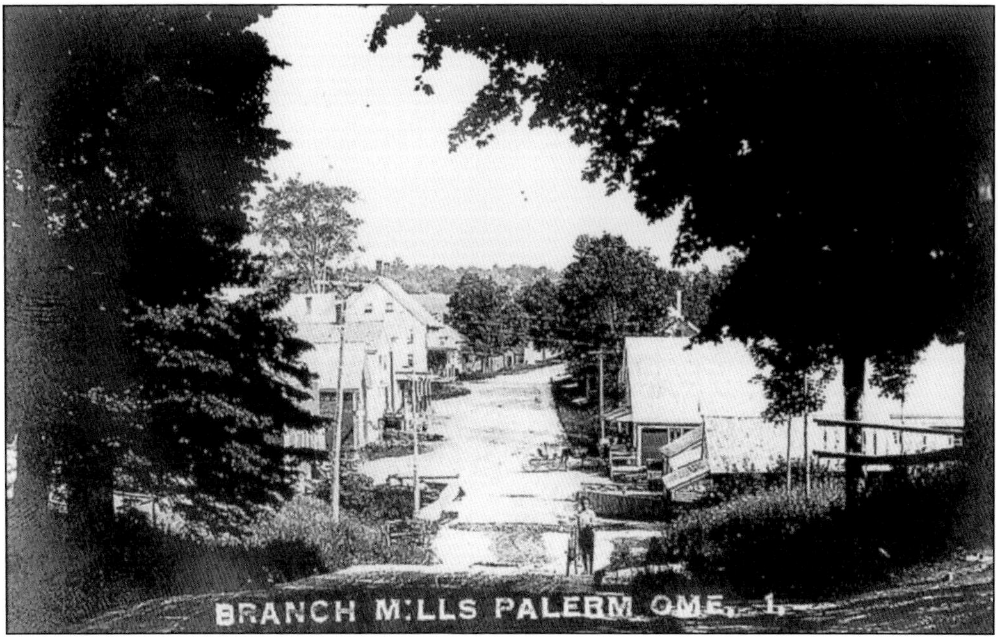

Taken just downhill from the previous photograph, this 1906 image gives an overview of the buildings along the length of the Branch Mills Road. A 1908 fire, which started in the J. R. B. Dinsmore gristmill, swept along the left side of this scene and down Water Street to the right. It destroyed the bridge and numerous houses and businesses, including the Grange Hall and Shuman Hotel. The loss was estimated to be $50,000.

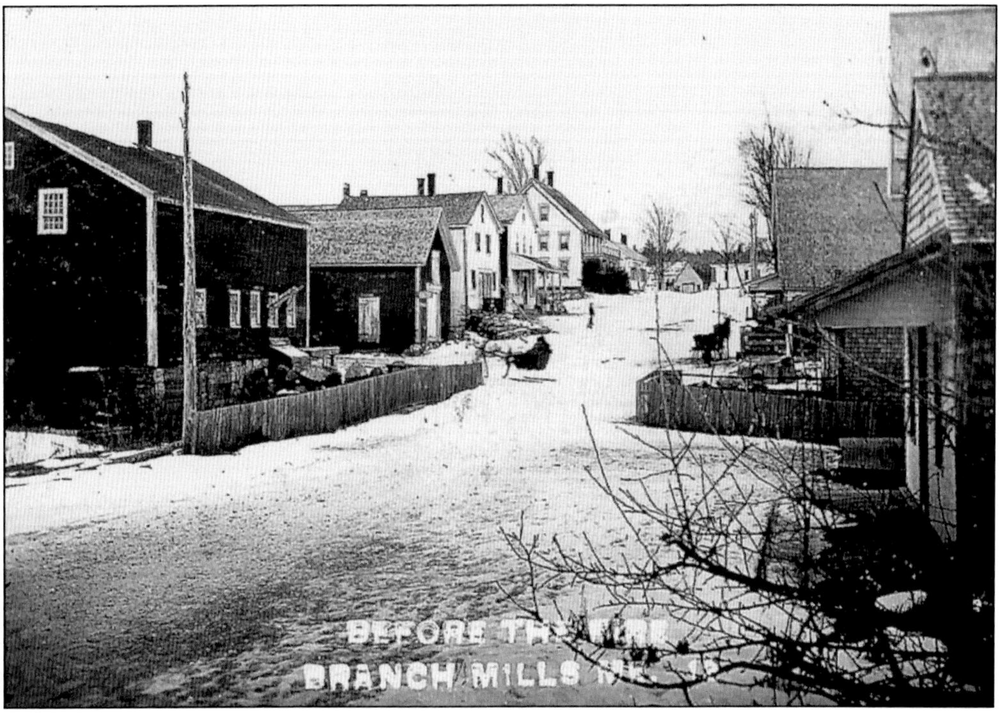

An undated wintertime photograph of Branch Mills, this image was taken diagonally opposite the J. R. B. Dinsmore gristmill, prior to the 1908 fire. Nearly everything visible in this view burned. The bridge over the Sheepscot River, sided with the wooden fence, is visible in the foreground. Barely visible in the background, at the intersection of the North Palermo Road, is the monument honoring the first settlers of China and Palermo, dedicated in 1903.

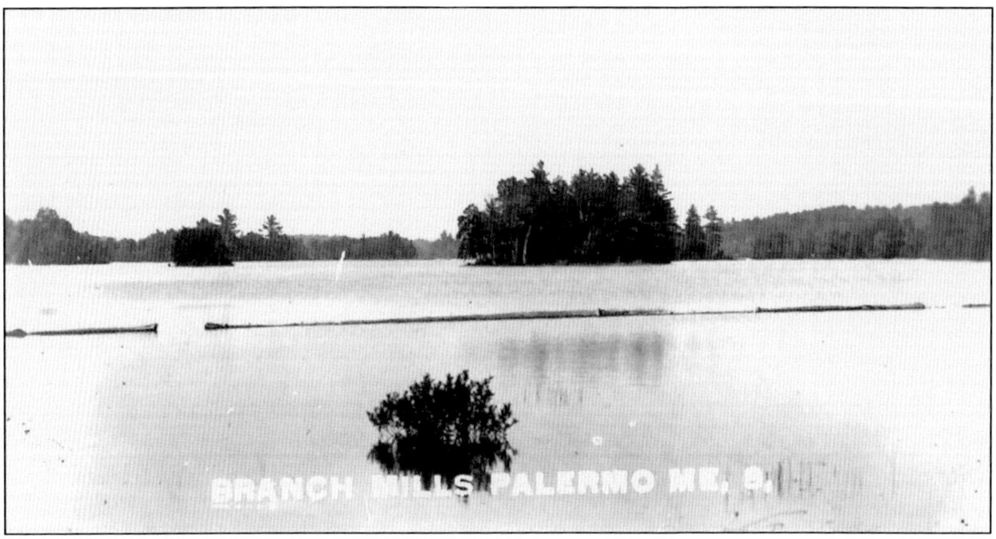

Looking toward the northeast, this undated view of Branch Pond was taken from the dam behind the mill. After the devastating fire, a new Dinsmore Grain Company gristmill was built on the site and still stands today. The floating logs seen in the foreground were lashed together and anchored to opposing shores. They were meant to capture or deflect driftwood and debris before it reached the mill.

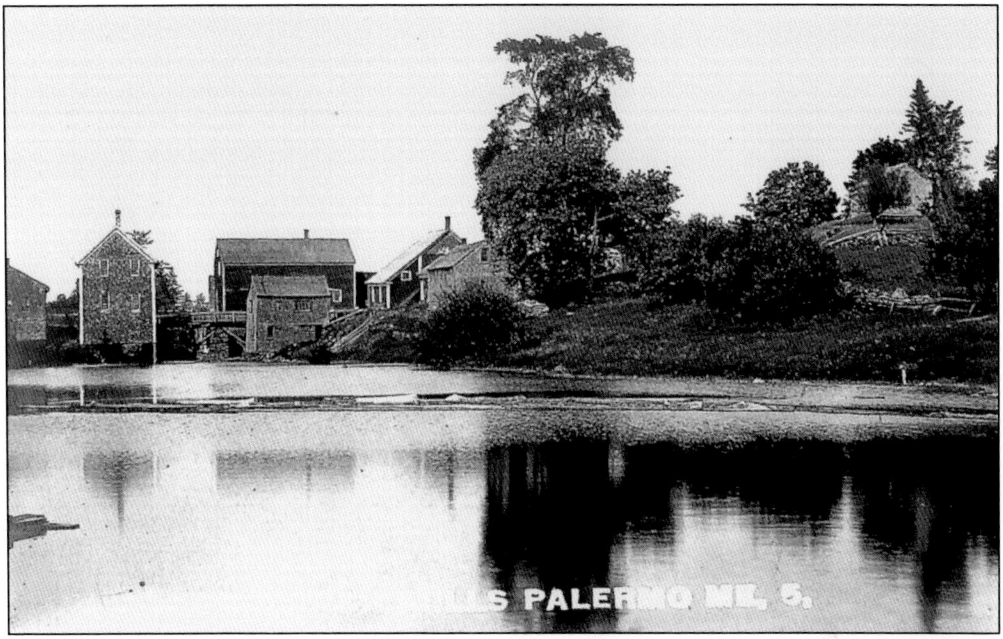

This 1906 view was taken at the site of the former stave mill, downstream from the Dinsmore mill and along Water Street. Looking northeast, the long building to the left of center is the street side of the Dinsmore mill. The bridge is visible just to its left, and the falls over the dam can be seen behind that. The log barrier in midstream served the same purpose as the previous one.

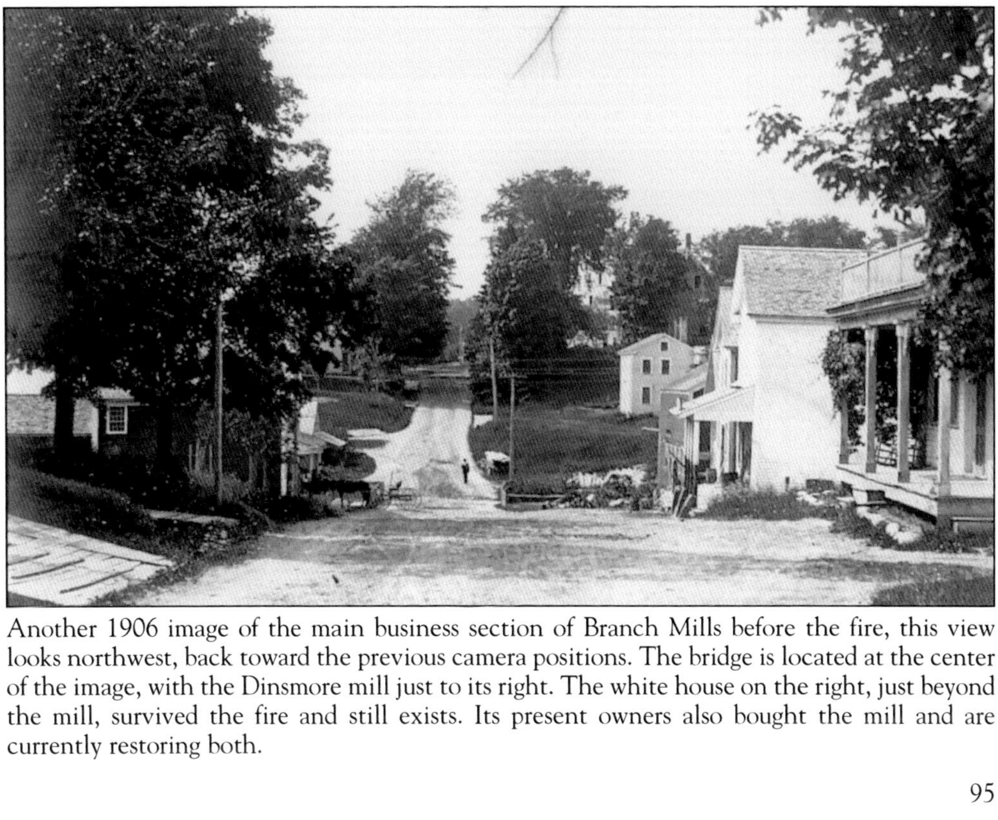

Another 1906 image of the main business section of Branch Mills before the fire, this view looks northwest, back toward the previous camera positions. The bridge is located at the center of the image, with the Dinsmore mill just to its right. The white house on the right, just beyond the mill, survived the fire and still exists. Its present owners also bought the mill and are currently restoring both.

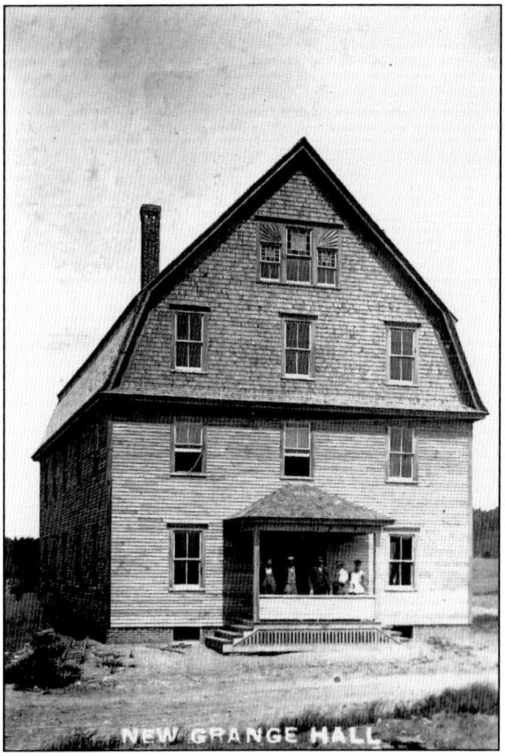

Built in 1909, the new Branch Mills Grange Hall replaced the one lost in the 1908 fire. Taken near the camera position of the last image, the Grange Hall still exists today as an antique store. This image shows five unidentified men standing on the front porch. Three of them are obviously tradesmen, and it appears that the finishing touches are just being put on the hall.

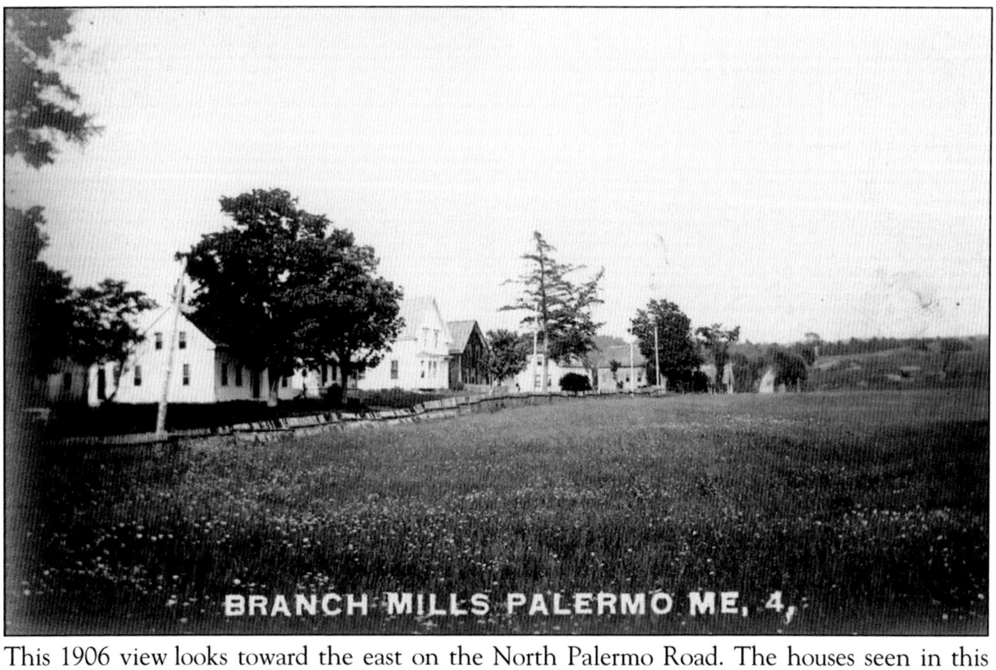

This 1906 view looks toward the east on the North Palermo Road. The houses seen in this photograph were lost in the fire. The first three can be identified, from left to right, as the Cain house, owned by Earl Adams; George Crommett's home; and the William Darby house. The camera position for this image was what it is today the site of the Palermo Volunteer Fire Department. The monument to the first settlers stands out of sight to the left.

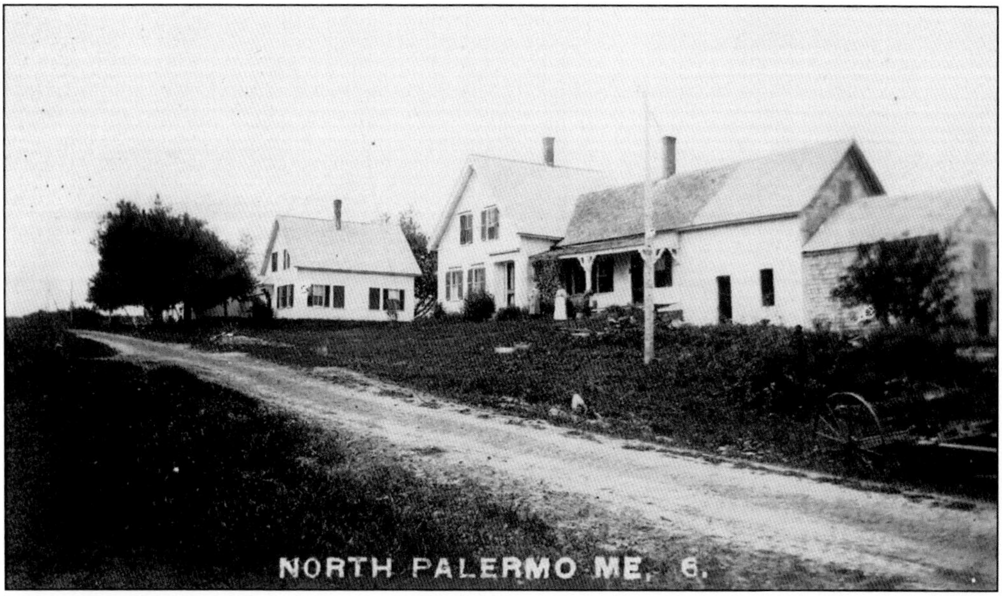

This undated image of two homes—both farmhouses, judging by the attached barns and hay rake alongside the road—was taken in North Palermo. While either one or both of the houses may exist today, their location has yet to be identified. Interesting to note are the two women posing in front of the house to the right, and the fact that telephone lines have been strung along the road.

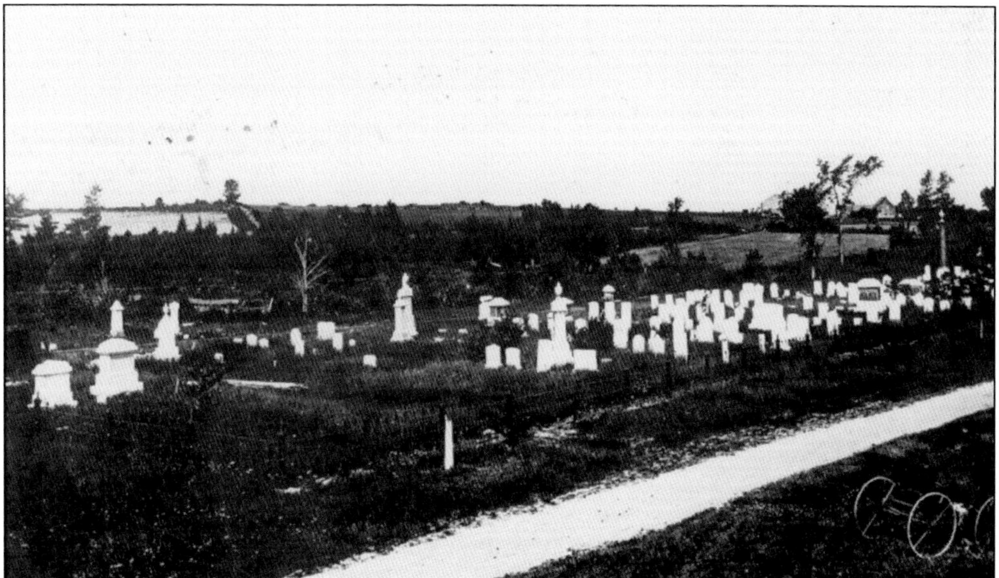

The North Palermo Cemetery is located alongside the Level Hill Road. This 1906 view was taken looking southwest. The original wrought-iron fence still surrounds the cemetery, and many of the older gravestones can be identified today. Interesting to note are the granite columns visible alongside the road, which were used for hitching horses and are still in place. Especially noteworthy is the buggy of photographer F. W. Cunningham.

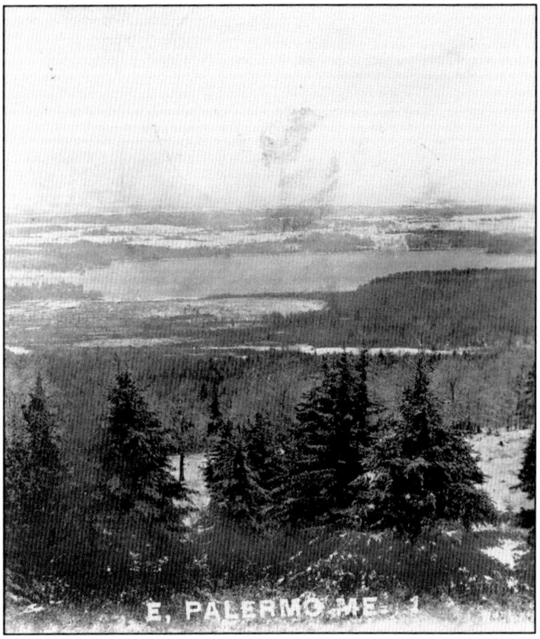

This is a 1905 early-winter image of Sheepscot Pond, taken from alongside the Banton Road in East Palermo. Looking toward the northwest, Deadwater Slough can be seen on the near shore, and the meandering of Colby Brook is identifiable to the extreme left of the bog. The camera position for this photograph is now overgrown, and this view is unattainable today.

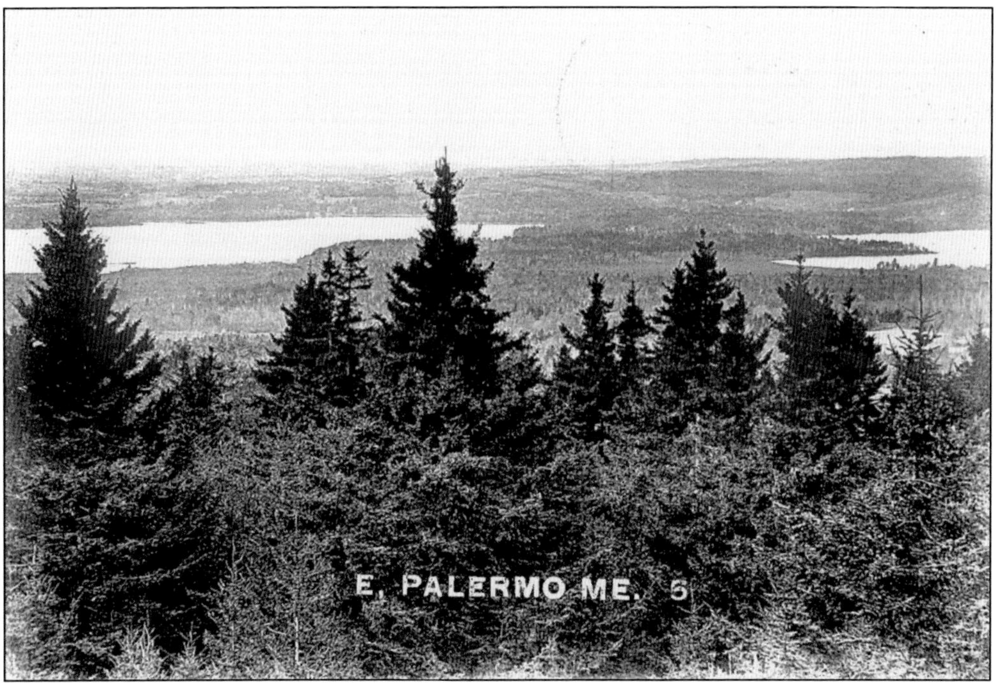

Nearly identical to the previous photograph of Sheepscot Pond, this undated image was taken just west of and slightly downhill from the earlier view. Taken during the warm weather months, this photograph also shows Deadwater Slough to the left of center on the near shore. Unseen but nearly straight ahead five miles in the distance lies Branch Mills.

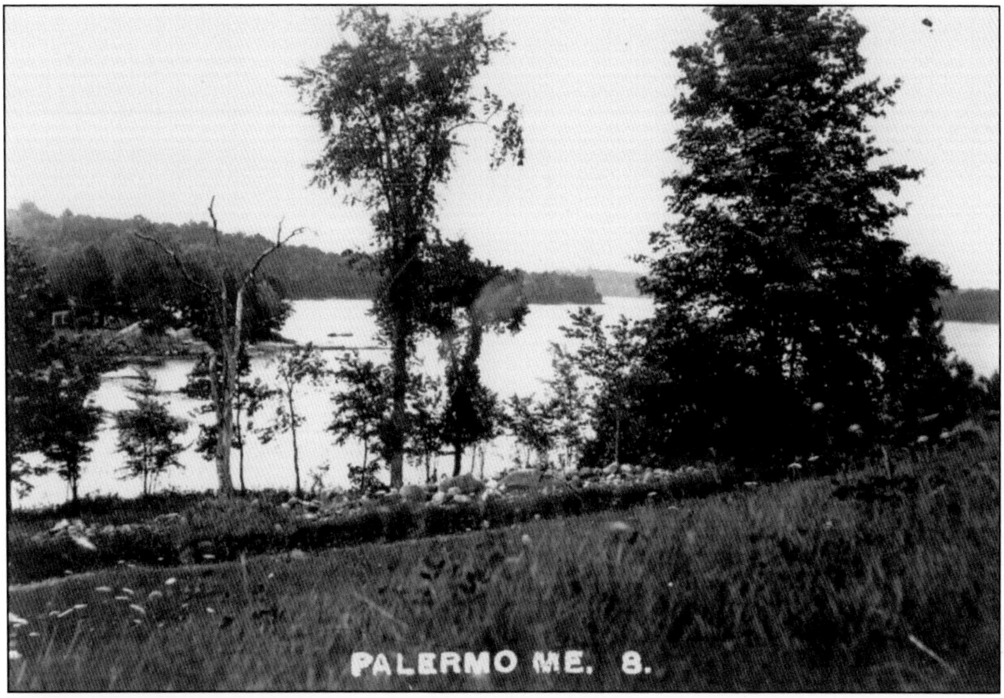

Taken alongside modern Route 3 near Greely Corner, this undated image looks south over Sheepscot Pond. The small camp seen on the peninsula in the distance no longer exists, although the view here remains very recognizable. Off to the left, out of camera view, is the location of the modern boat landing and parking area. Route 3 occupies essentially the same position today as the dirt road in the foreground of this image.

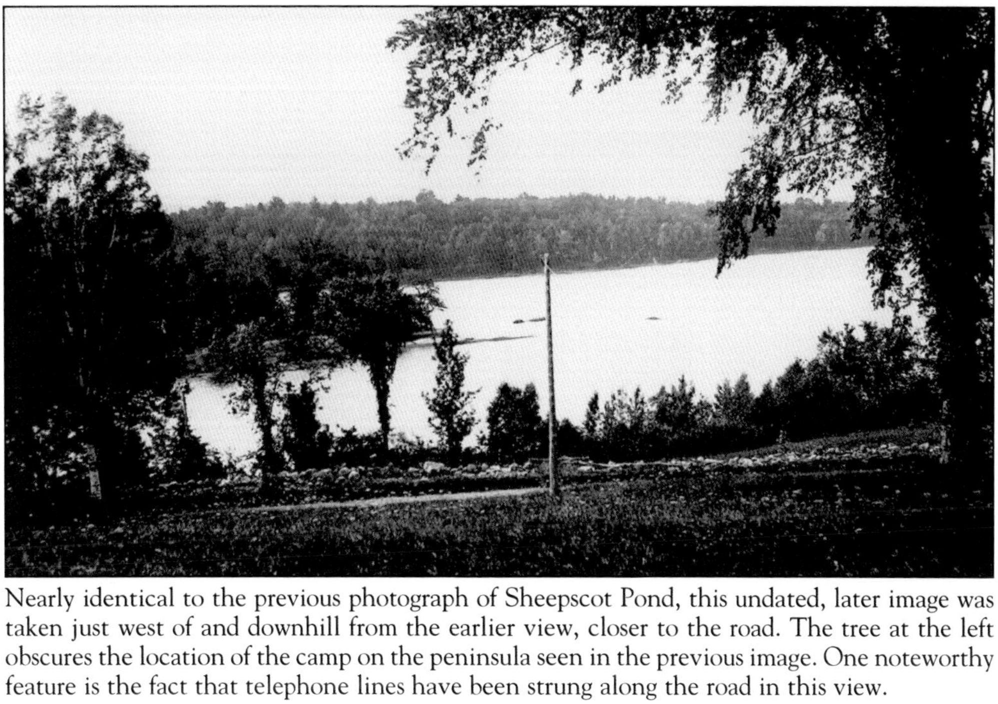

Nearly identical to the previous photograph of Sheepscot Pond, this undated, later image was taken just west of and downhill from the earlier view, closer to the road. The tree at the left obscures the location of the camp on the peninsula seen in the previous image. One noteworthy feature is the fact that telephone lines have been strung along the road in this view.

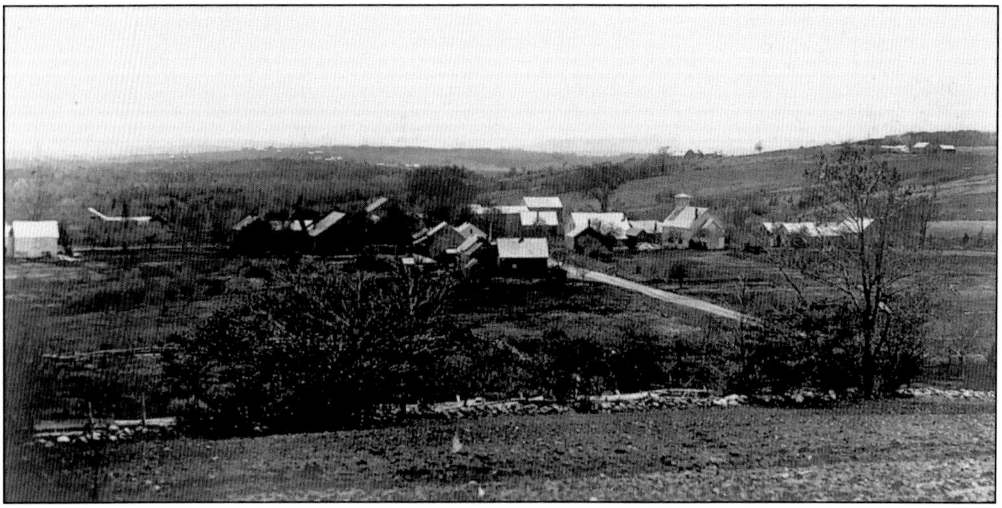

McFarlands Corner is part of the town of Montville and lies about two miles northwest of Liberty village. This undated view was taken from atop the Bolin Ridge Road, looking toward the east. Modern Route 220 crosses from left to right in the image, and the majority of the structures seen here have disappeared. The farm on the right in the far distance still stands, although the barns have disappeared.

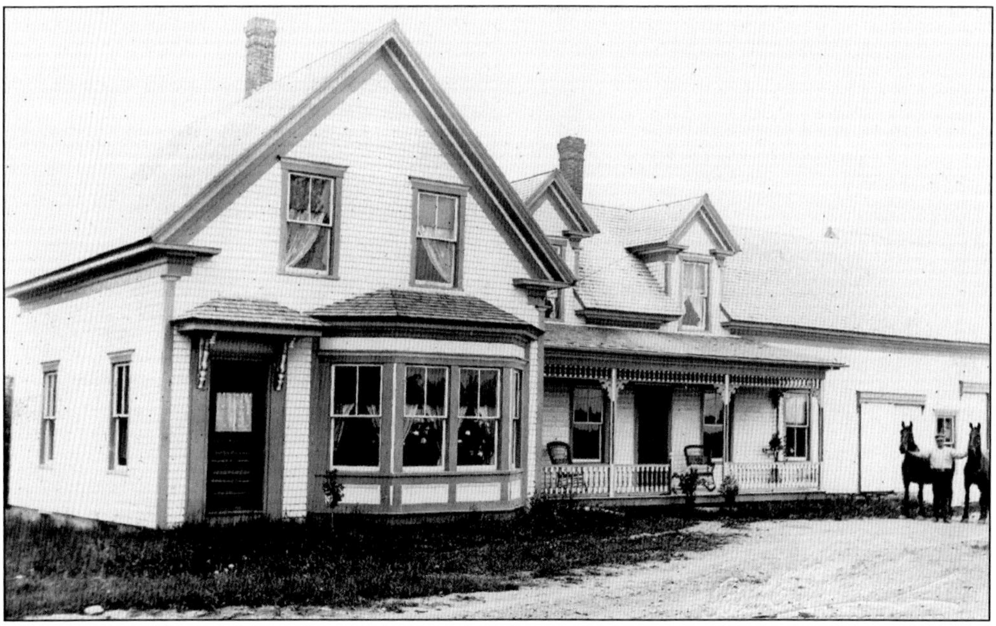

Center Montville lies five miles northwest of McFarlands Corner and was once the commercial hub of Montville. A schoolhouse, church, blacksmith shop, several homes, and more were once located along the North Searsmont Road. Today little remains, but this house is an exception. The current owner's uncle, Edgar Bean, can be seen standing in front of the barn with his two horses in this undated Bert Cunningham photograph.

Six

Individuals, Groups, and Homes

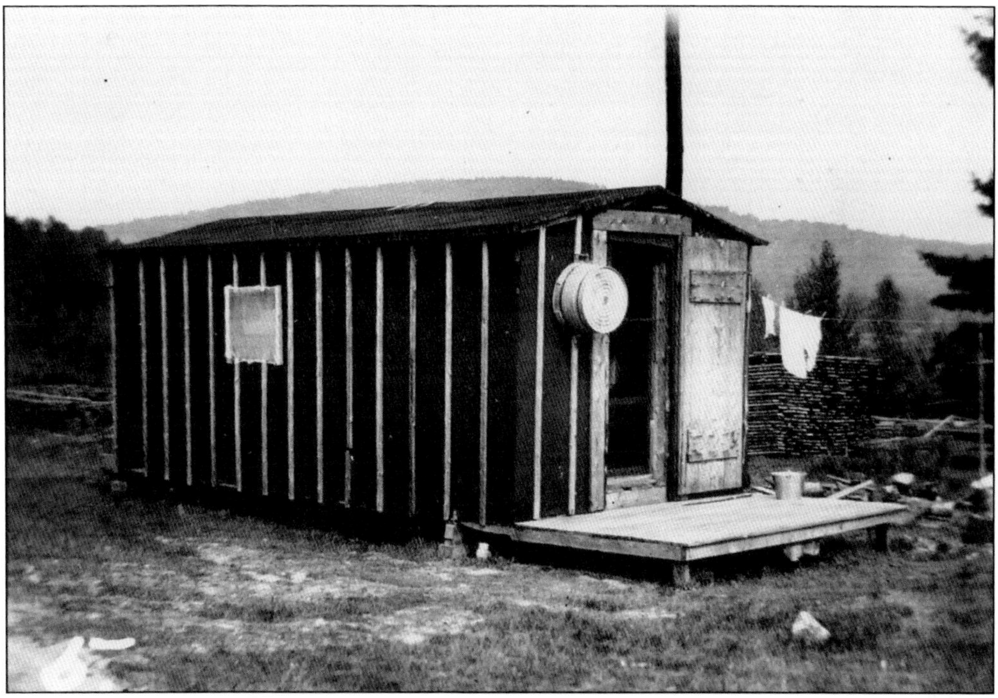

The notation on the back of this photograph reads, "This is a picture of what Nellie calls the shack." The card was addressed to Aunt Laura and Uncle Hawes from Ike and Nellie. There is no indication of the structure's purpose, location, or fate.

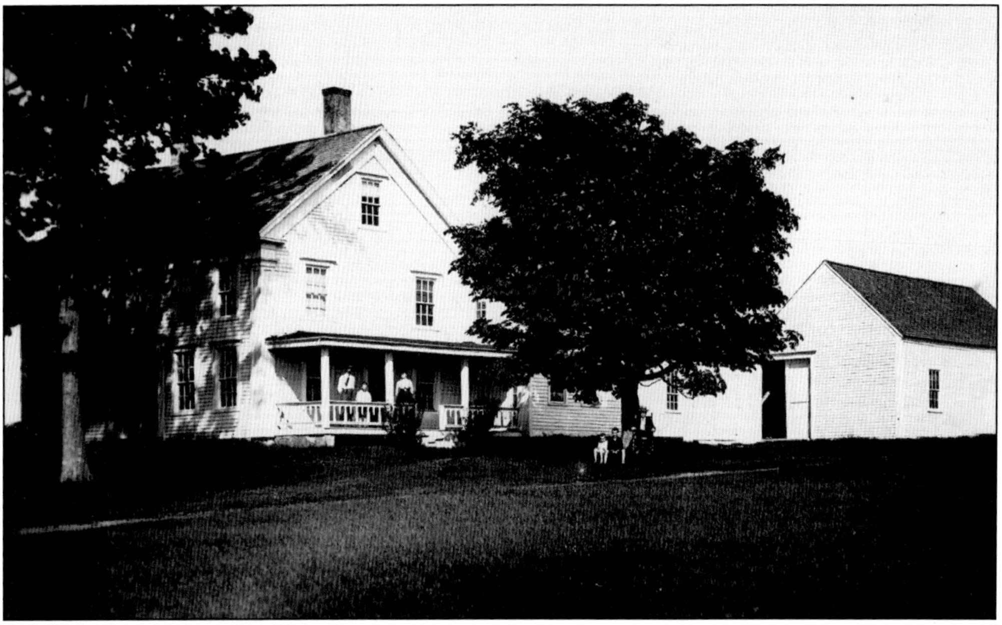

The location of this well-maintained farmhouse and whether or not it still exists is unknown, nor is there information about its occupants. Pictured are a young couple, three children, and a man who appears to be the children's grandfather, posing on the porch and lawn.

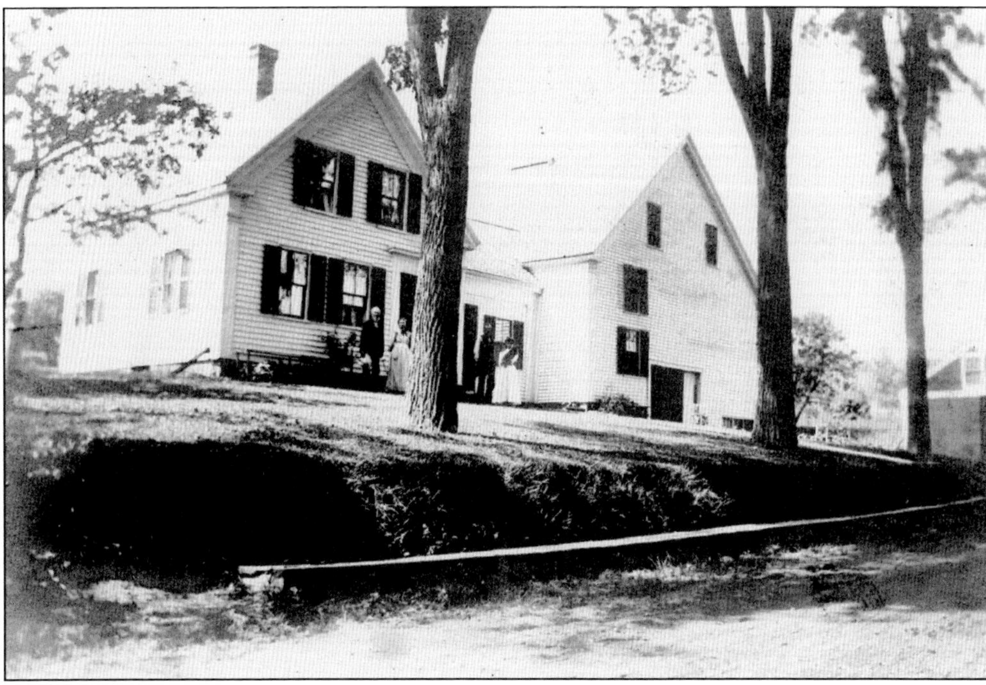

This photograph of an elegant farmhouse includes two couples posing in front of the main building. The couple on the left is definitely much older, while the younger woman on the right is holding a small dog.

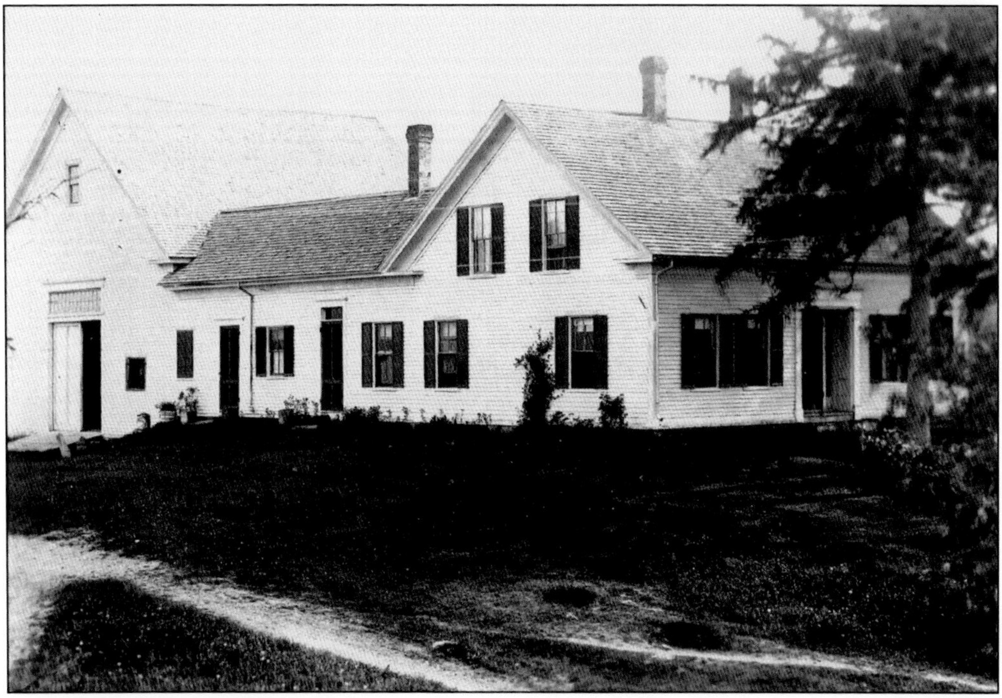

This well-kept house farmhouse has not been located, and there are no occupants visible here to provide any additional clues.

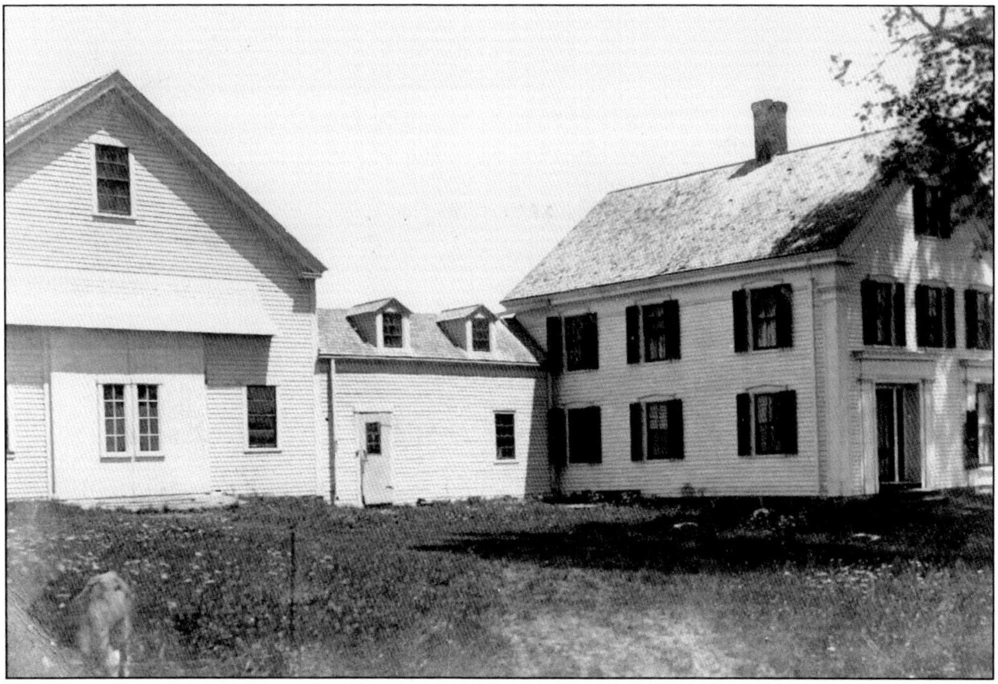

This large house and its attached barn were very well maintained, but their identity remains a mystery. As with the previous image, there are no people visible to aid in the identification, although the back is dated 1908 and has the notation "Bert's house."

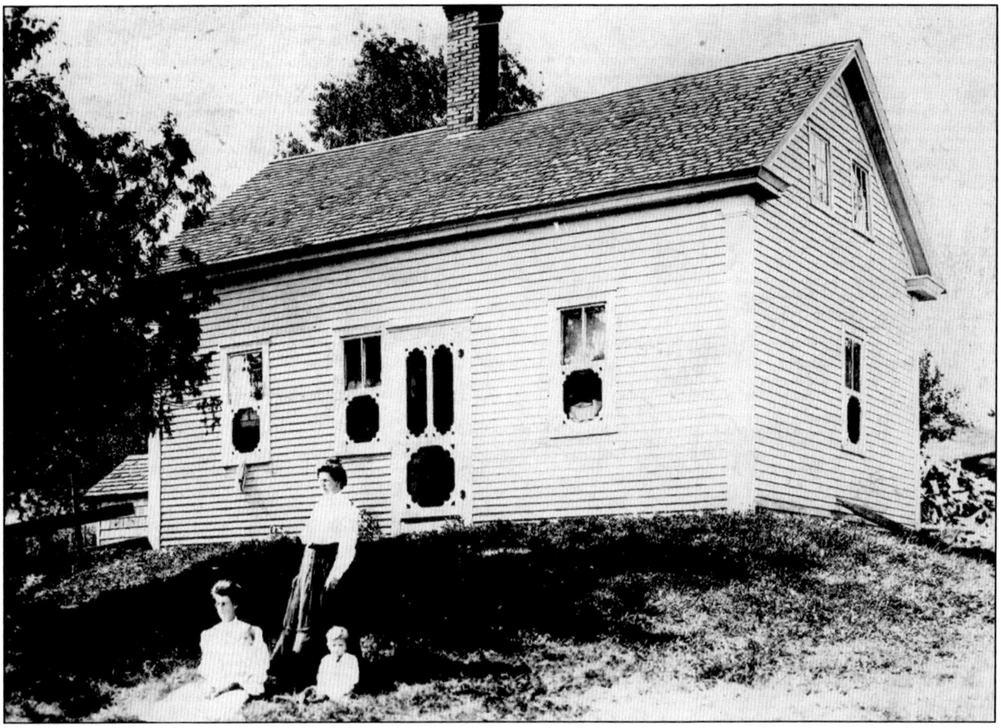

This neat little farmhouse has intriguing gingerbread trim and two young women with small children posing on the lawn but no other clues to its location or the occupants' identities.

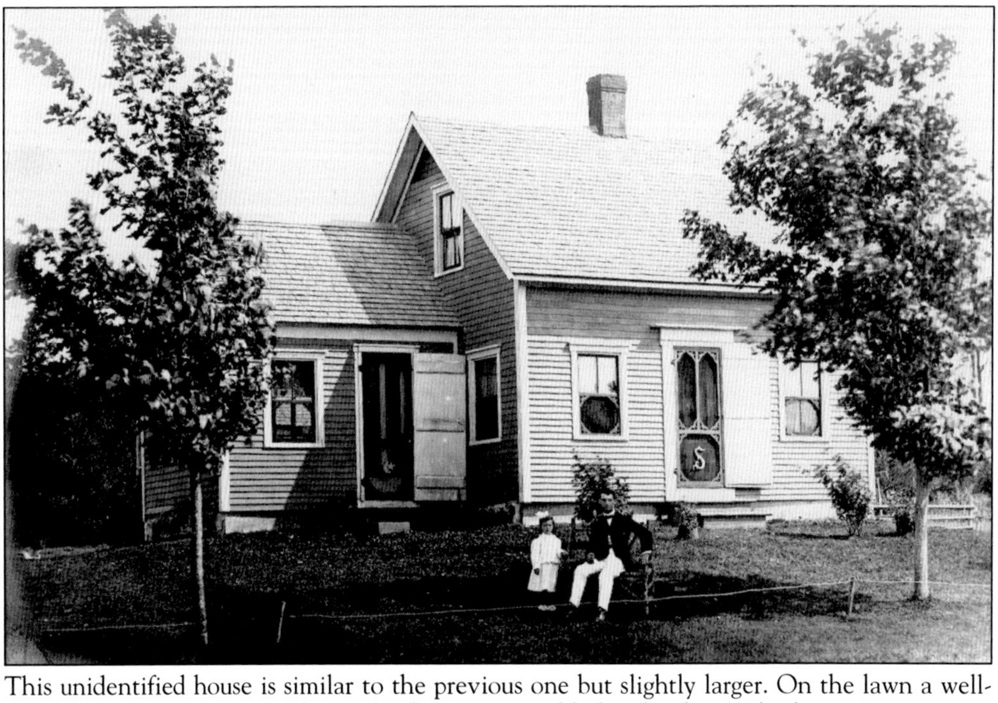

This unidentified house is similar to the previous one but slightly larger. On the lawn a well-dressed young man poses with a girl, who is presumably his daughter. The letter S appears on the screen door at the front, and the dwelling sits very close to a road in the foreground.

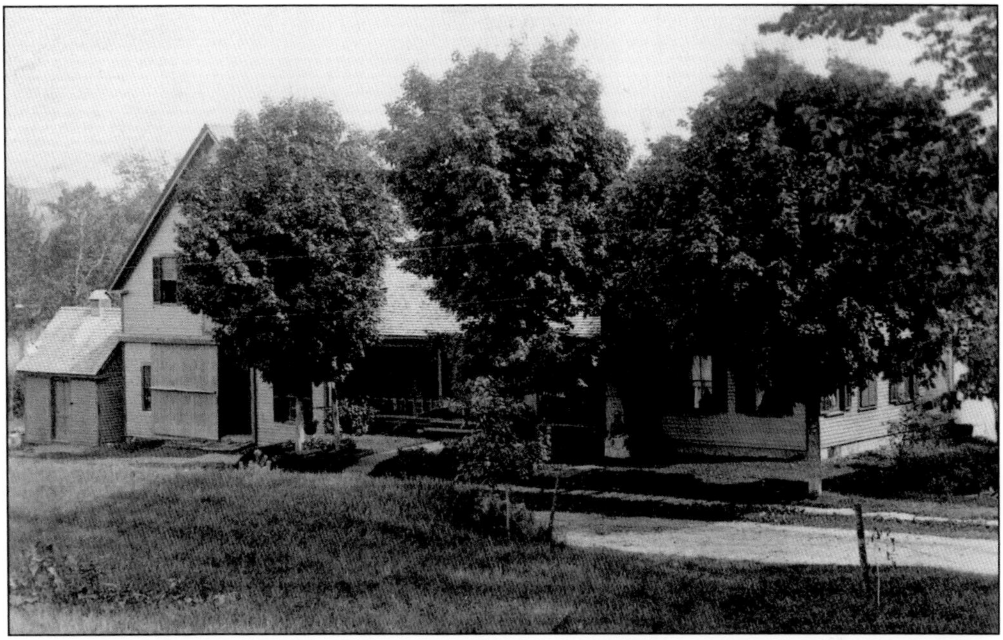

The owner of this house is identified on the back as E. Bowdin, and she lived in Washington, the presumed location of her "dear home." She mentions that her husband, father, and mother all passed away in the home. Aside from being in Washington, the location of the house is unknown, though the date on the back is 1908.

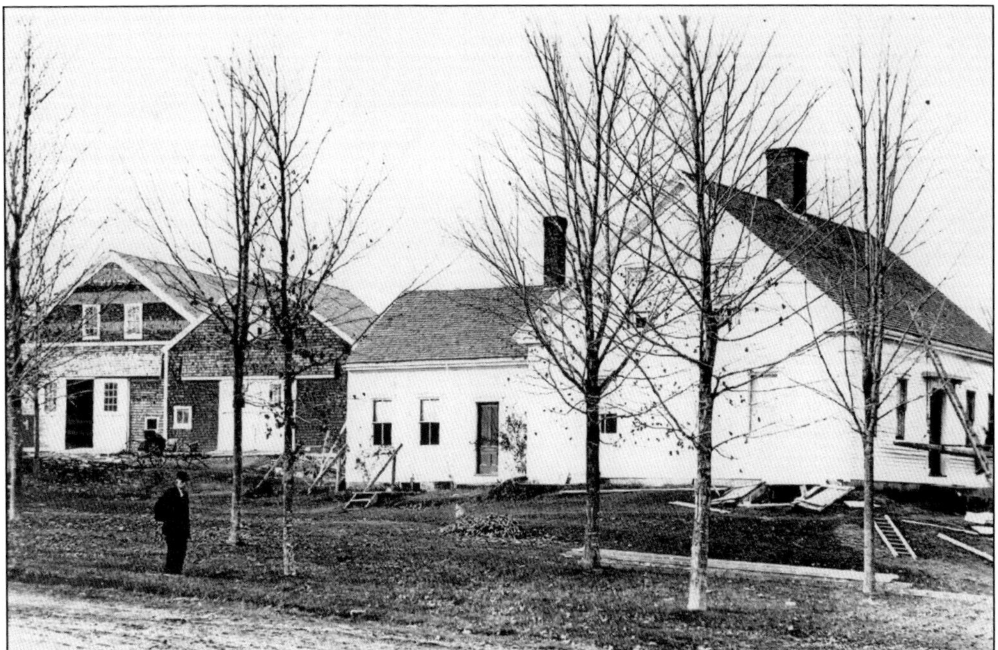

This extensive house is described as "the Postmaster's home." The postcard was mailed from North Waldoboro in 1910 by someone named Alice. In this view, the house is being repainted and there is an older gentleman on the lawn. No other clues to the location or the identity of the owner or occupants exist.

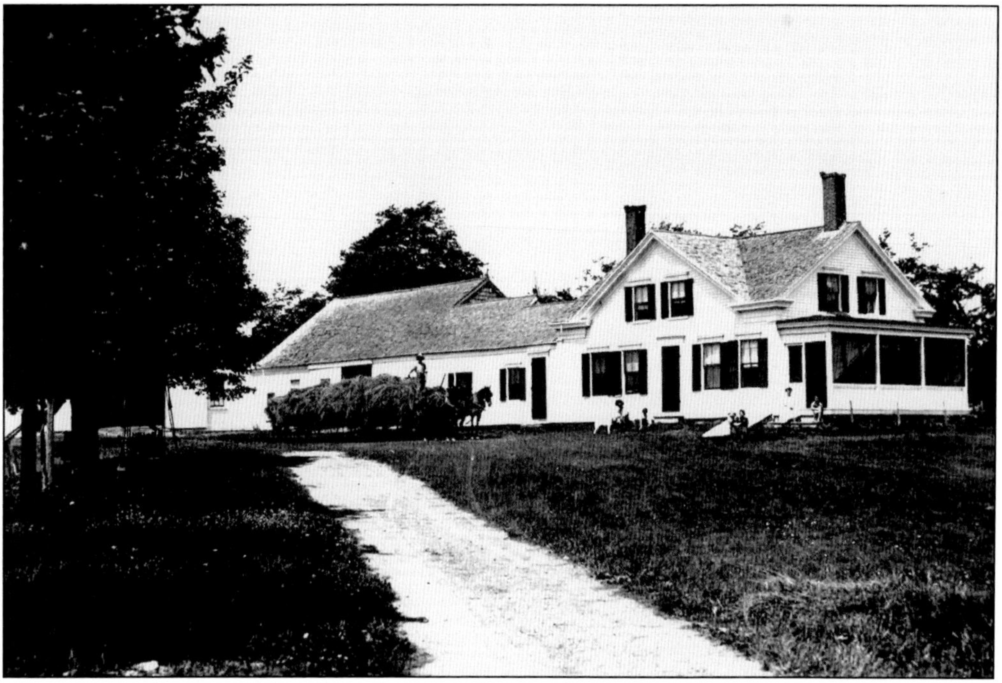

There is no indication of the whereabouts or ultimate fate of the extensive farmhouse seen here, other than the notation "Palermo" written on the back. There are six people visible in the image, including the younger man driving the large hay wagon beside the barn. In front of the house are another young man, a young woman, three children, and a dog.

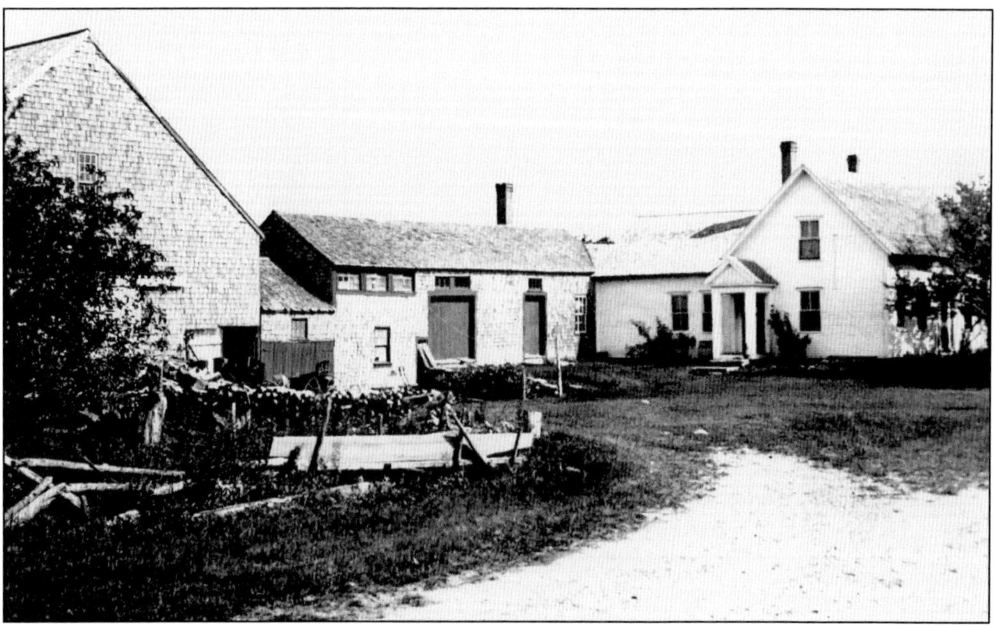

No occupants of this large and rambling farmhouse and attached barn are visible, but the property is described on the back as the "Souford Farm in North Palermo." No other clues exist as to its current existence or the original owners.

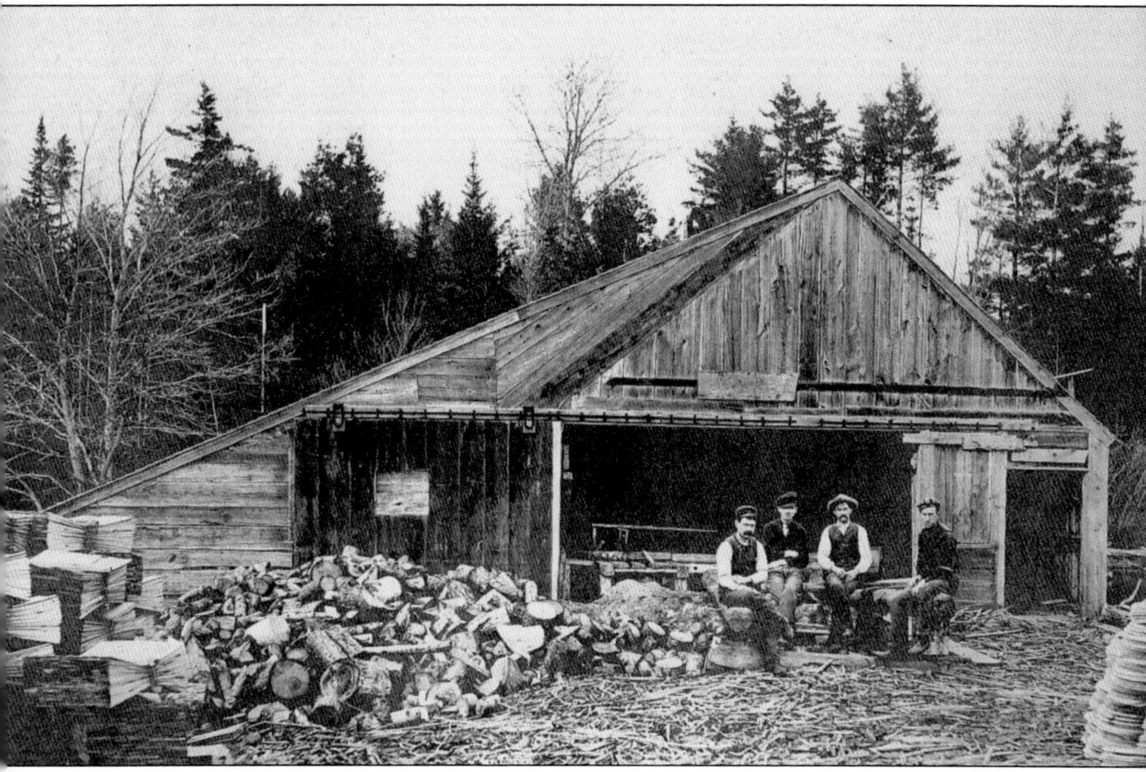

The location of this shingle mill and the identity of its four-man crew are unknown. It appears that the mill may have also made barrelheads, as evidenced by the pile to the right of the image. The original photograph is a larger cabinet photograph, rather than a smaller postcard version.

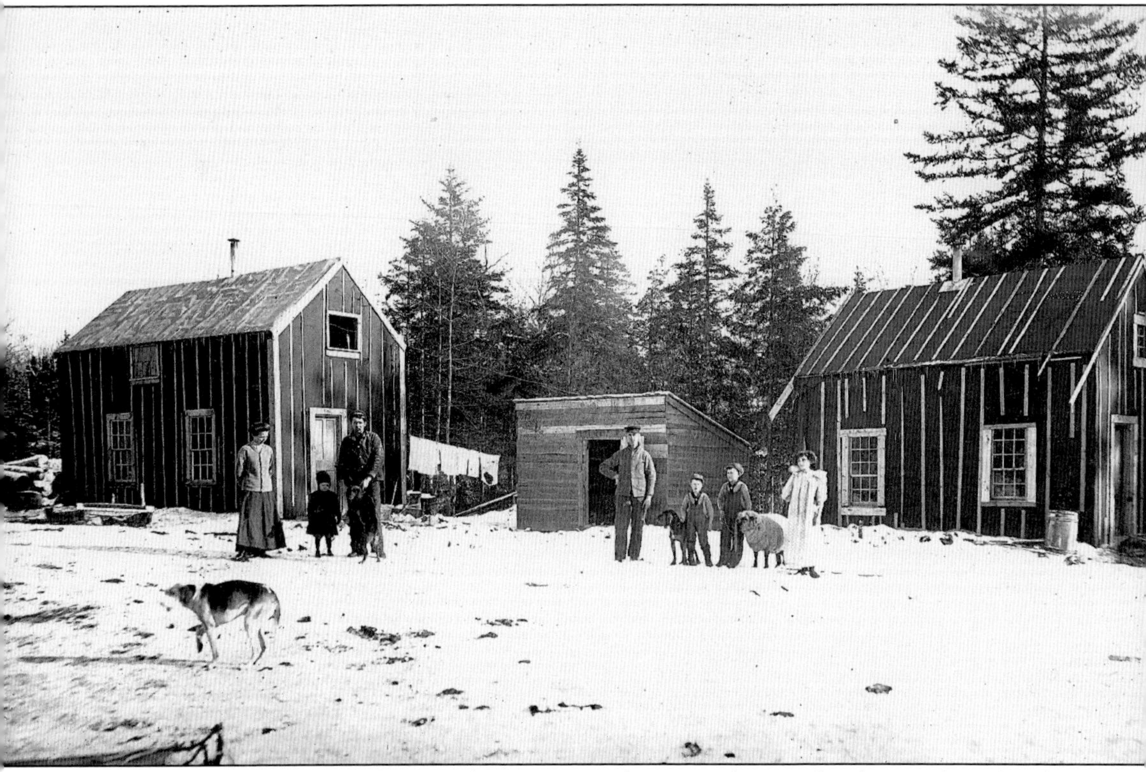

This wintertime cabinet photograph appears to show two distinct families, perhaps brothers, and their closely spaced, crude homes. On the left is a young couple with a little girl, while on the right, another young couple appears with two slightly older young sons. Both families seem to have liked dogs, and the family on the right has at least one sheep, but there is no clue as to what town this homestead was in or who the occupants were.

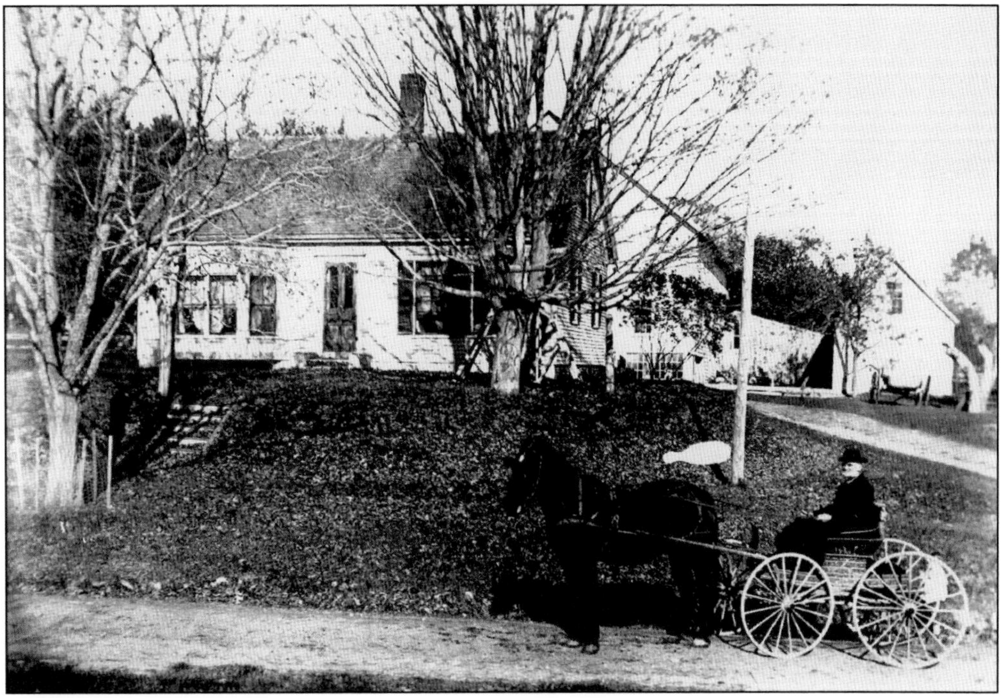

Ira Cram of Montville poses in a wagon in front of his home, a small but well-maintained house with the large barn behind it.

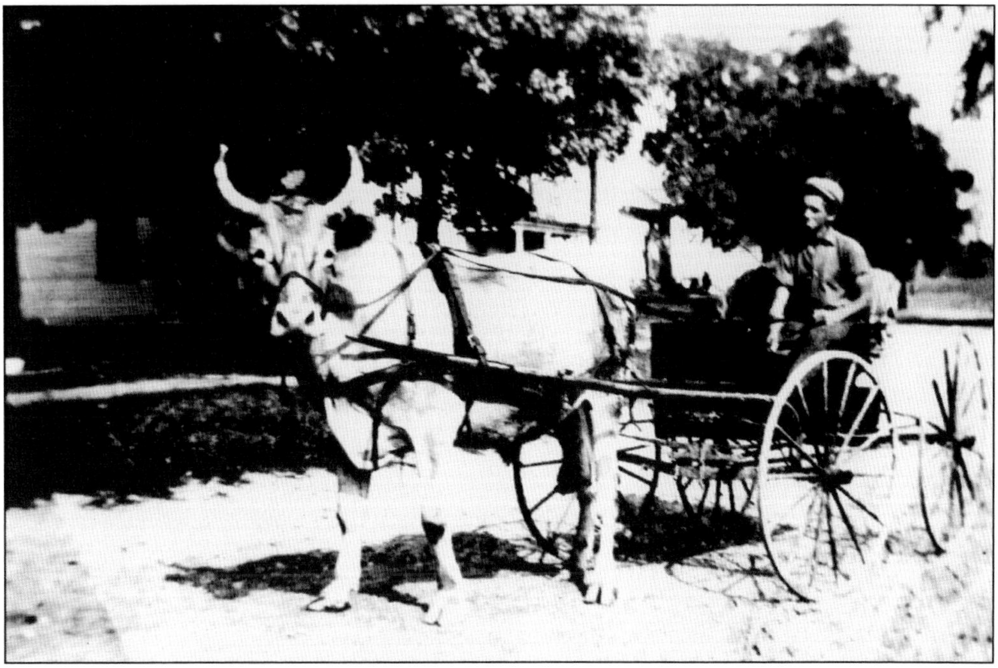

A note on the back of this picture of a middle-aged man riding in an ox-drawn buggy observes that the ox is wearing a horse's harness. There is no date or any clue as to where or when the photograph was taken.

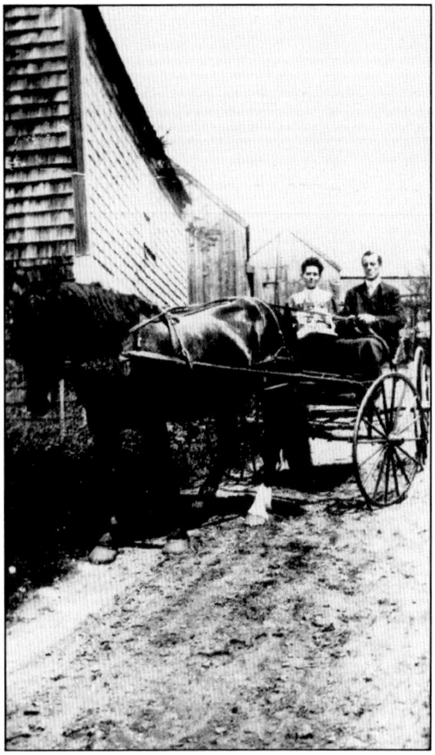

The location of this image and the identity of the middle-aged gentleman in the buggy are unknown, but writing on the back identifies the woman as Leslie Noyes.

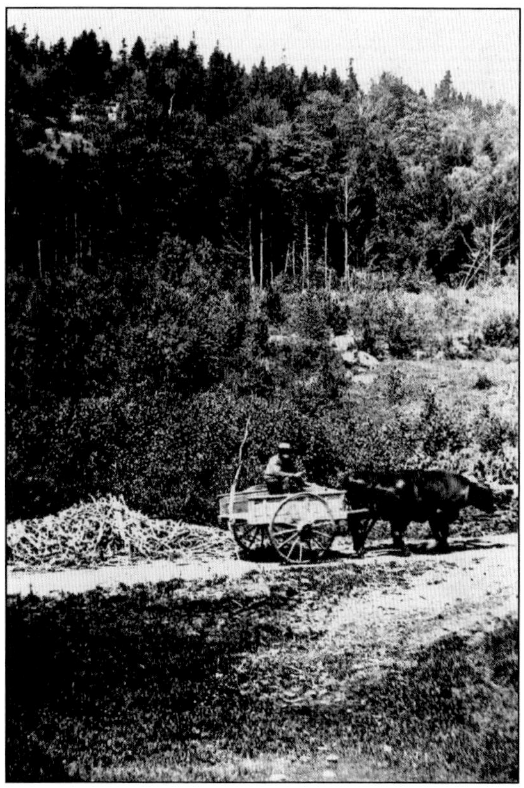

George Lenfest of Washington is shown with his double-teamed oxcart.

There is no clue whatsoever as to the identity of this well-manicured and refined young lady.

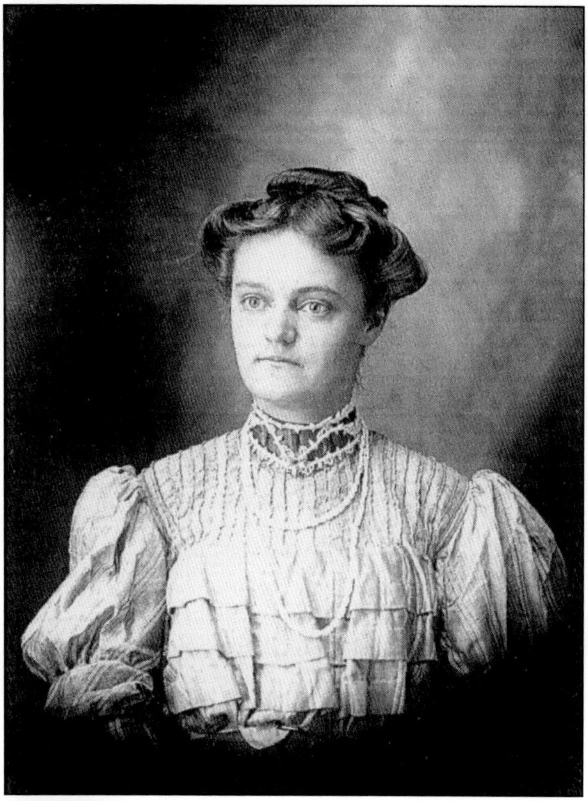

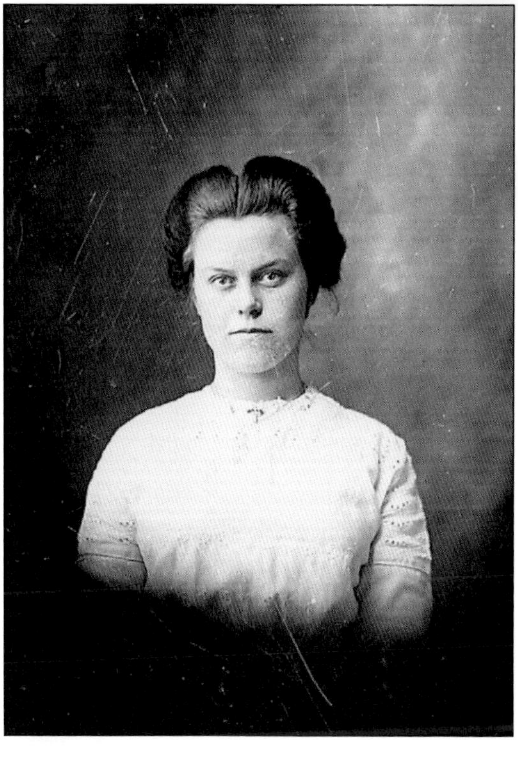

This photograph was addressed to Katherine Cunningham of Liberty by her sister Alice, but there is not indication as to whether or not the image is of either of the ladies in question. Since the card was not mailed, there is no postmark to provide the additional clue of a date.

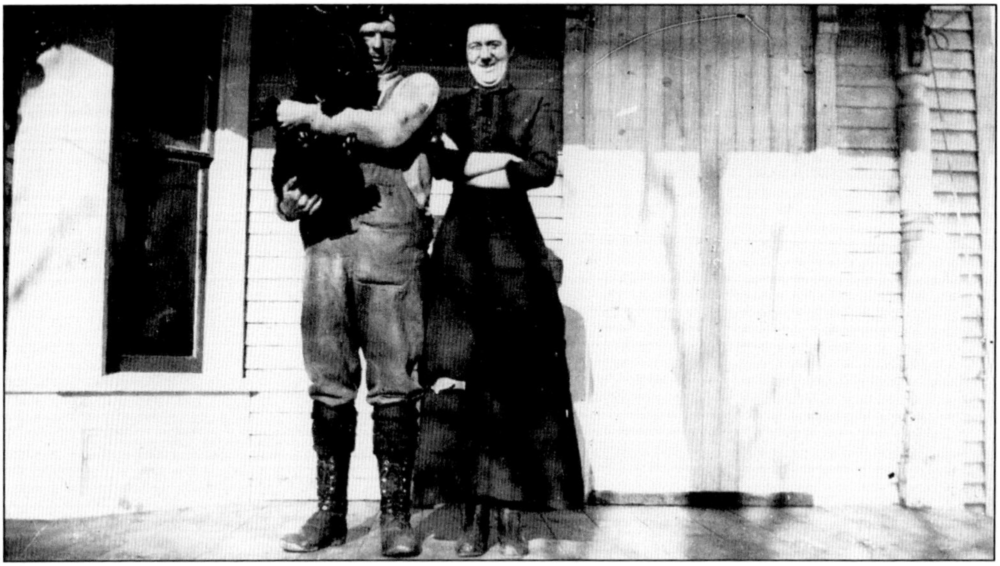

This identity of this obviously hardworking, middle-aged couple remains a mystery, as there is no indication of either their names or a date for the image. The man is holding a dog, and the couple is standing on what must be the front porch of their home.

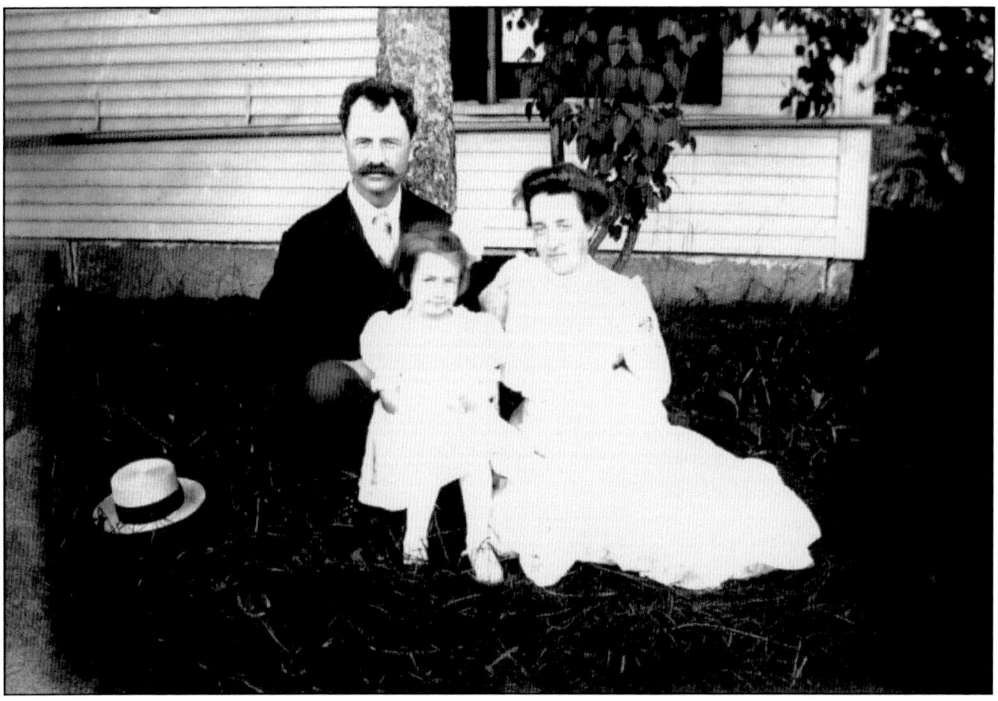

This young couple and a child, who is presumably their little girl, are unidentified, even though there is a long note written across the back of the card, which was mailed to Mrs. Bond in Jefferson in 1907. The note mentions several people who seem to have no relevance to the photograph. The names included are Fossie, Kate, R. W. Prescott, Aunt G., and C. & P. (who, according to the note, had a week-old son).

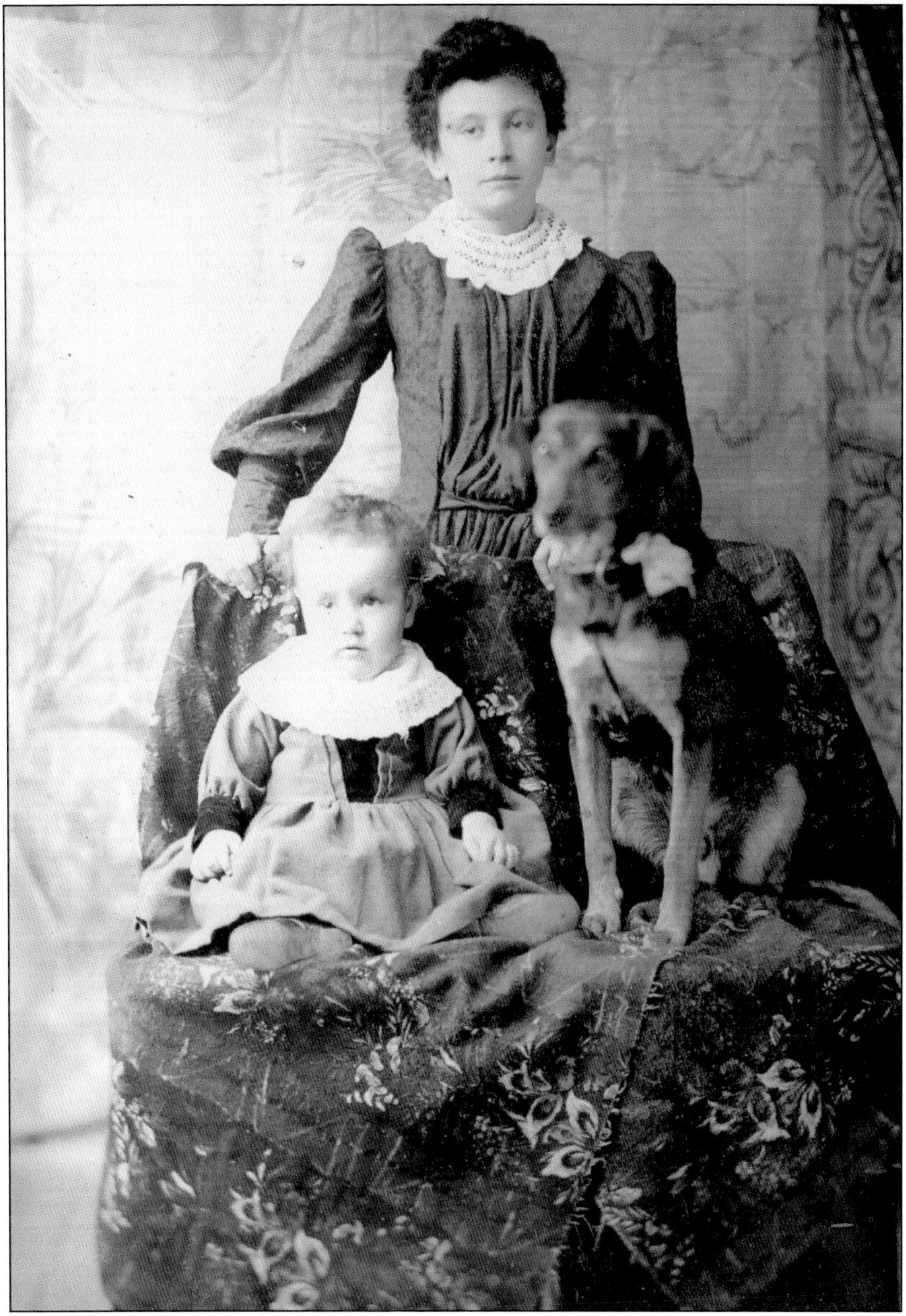

This cabinet photograph reveals no clue as to the identities of the young woman, the little girl (possibly her daughter or sister), or the dog. This undated image was taken in Frank Cunningham's Washington gallery.

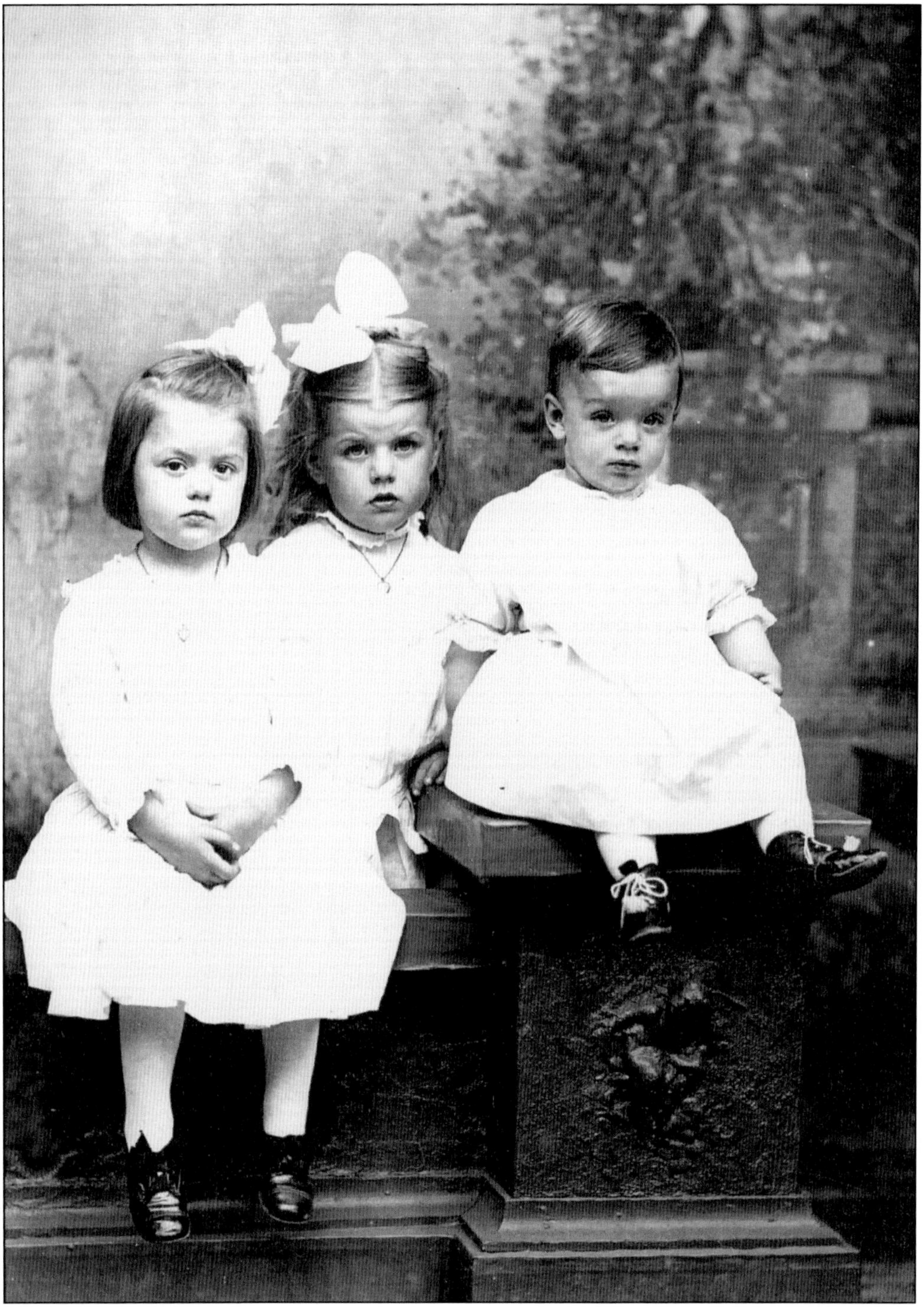

The three young children pictured in this cabinet photograph are identified on the back of the image as Claribel, Louisa, and Richardson. There is no date or last name to further identify these children or their hometown. As with the previous image, this photograph was taken in the Washington gallery of F. W. Cunningham.

These two young men are identified as Lawrence and Raymond, and the card was given to someone named Alice. No last names or dates are given to aid in identifying the children further.

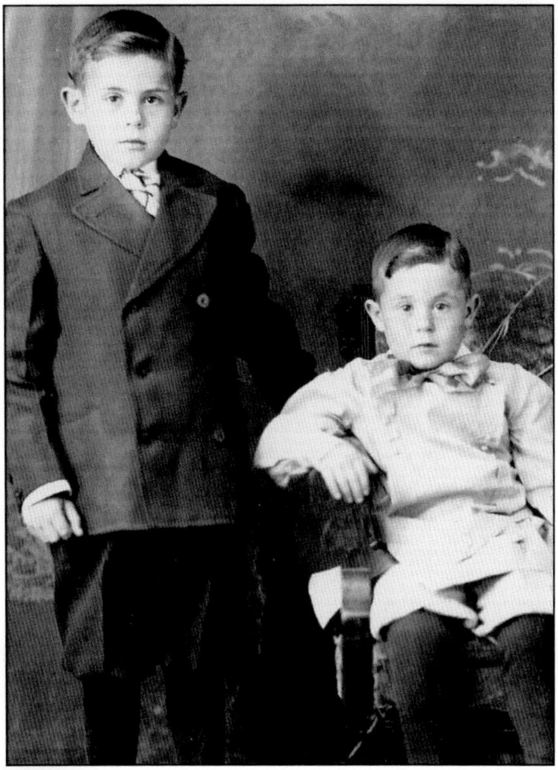

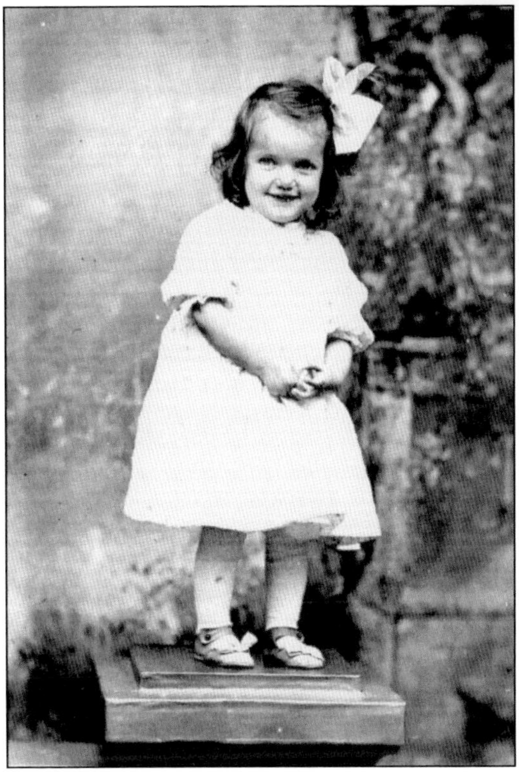

"E. M." gave this postcard, which reads, "This is pretty good after all," to Mrs. J. E. Miller. The girl was further identified as "Chloe at 22 months," by a different hand at a later time. There is no further clue as to where Chloe may have lived or what her last name may have been.

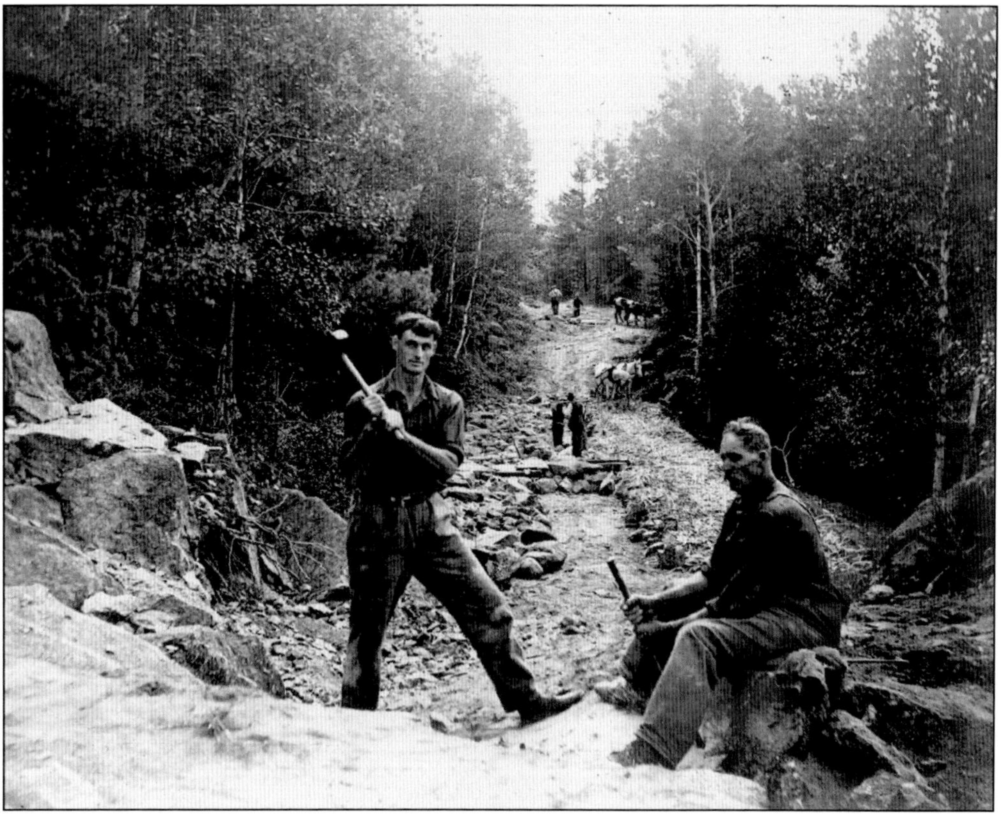

This image shows Will Prescott (left), the younger of the pair, and Edmund Prescott, both from Washington, working on a road crew in 1902. There is no indication as to whether the two men were related or not.

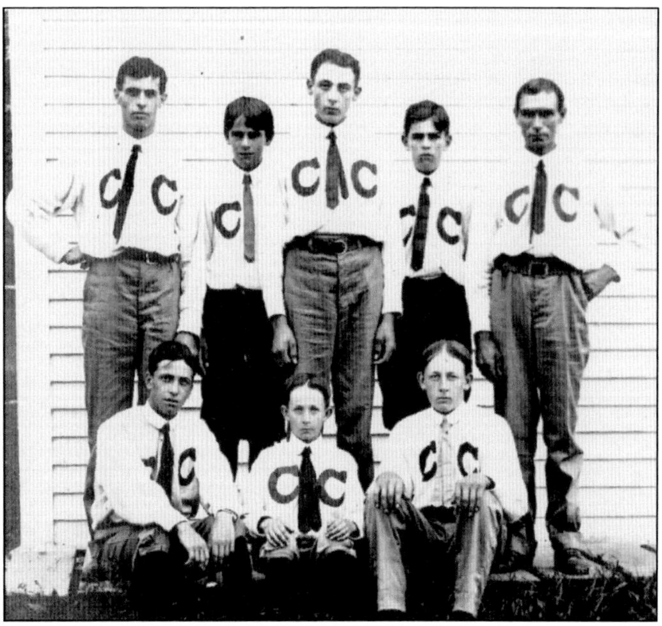

The specifics of Camp Comfort are unknown, but this is a photograph of the seven boys and one adult who attended the camp at Pemaquid Beach, in the New Harbor section of Bristol, in 1906. Pictured seated in front are, from left to right, Delo Brasier and brothers Dexter and John Brown. Standing behind are, from left to right, Frank Sukeforth, Charles Finley, Albert Brown, Charlton Finley, and Elmer Brasier, the father of Delo.

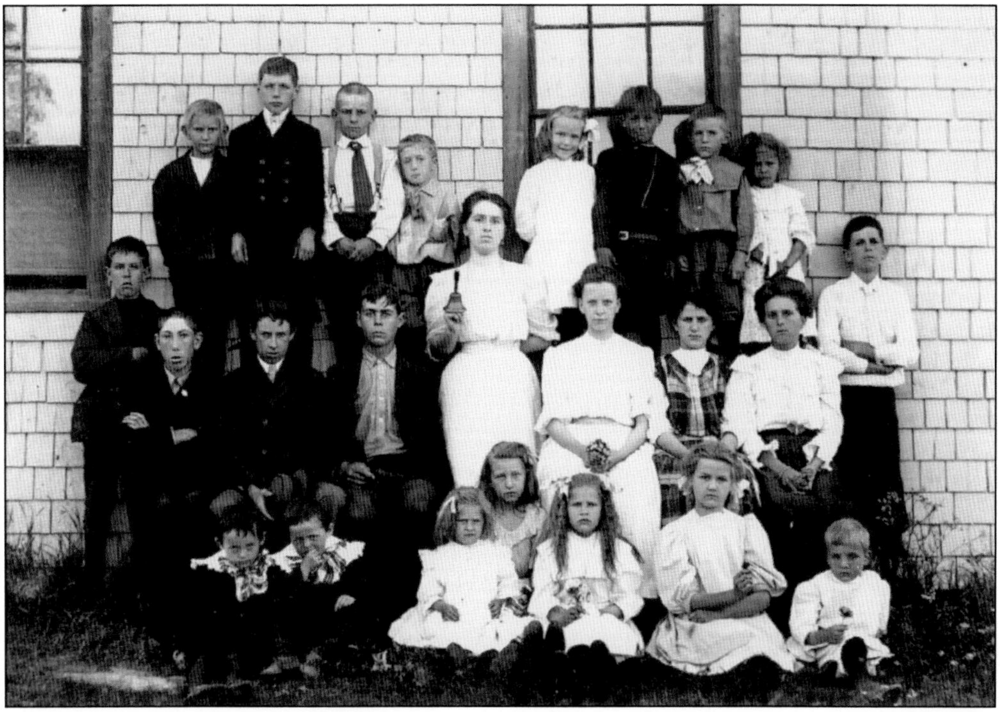

This is obviously a school group, but there is no indication as to what town, year, or school is represented. There are a total of 23 students and a female teacher in the middle, holding a bell. As with most school images from this era, a wide range of ages is represented. Of additional note are the twin boys in the front row.

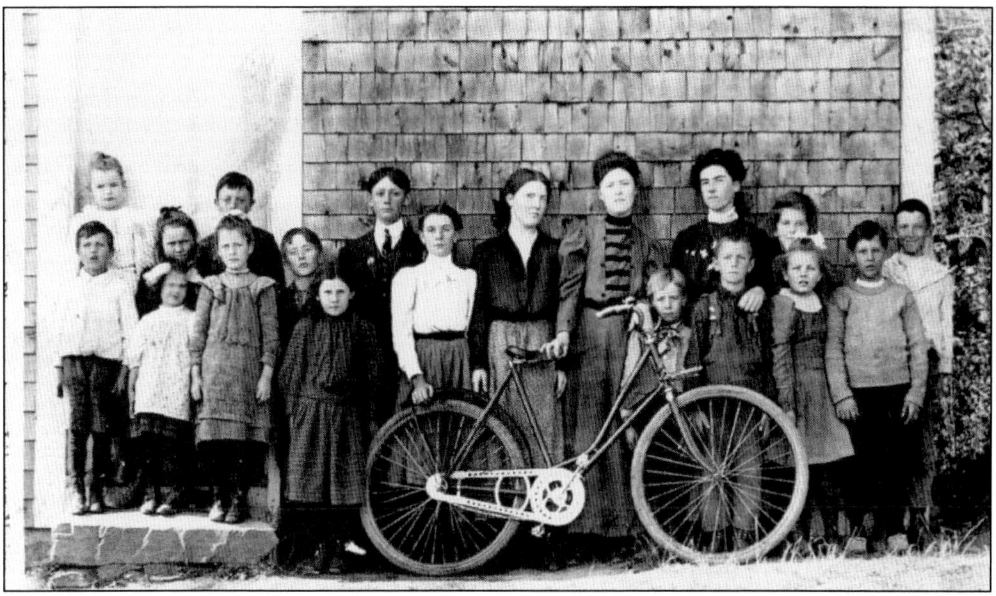

Another unidentified school group is shown here, this one with 19 people, 3 of whom could possibly be the teacher. As with the previous image, there is no date or location to provide any further clues as to the identities of the students, their school, or hometown.

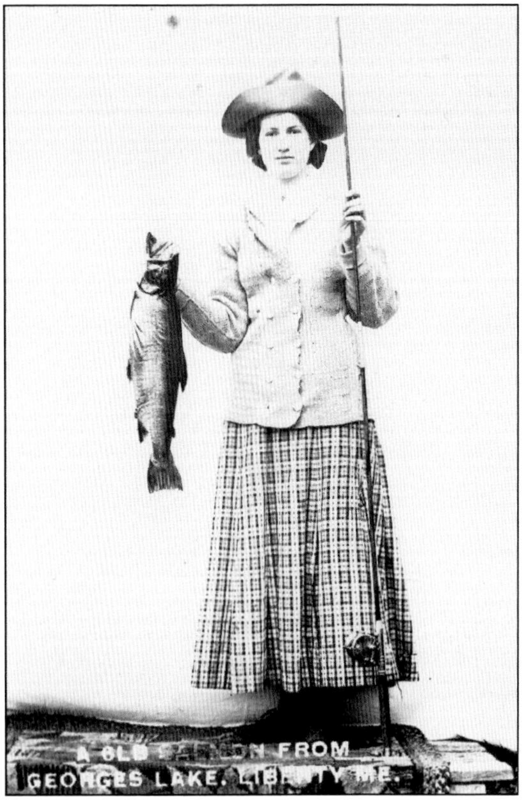

This interesting image of an obviously proud fisherwoman and her six-pound salmon was taken at Lake St. George in Liberty. The woman is standing in front of a white backdrop on a wooden step covered with a carpet. There is no date or clue as to her identity, but there is the notation "Uncle Walt" on the back of the card.

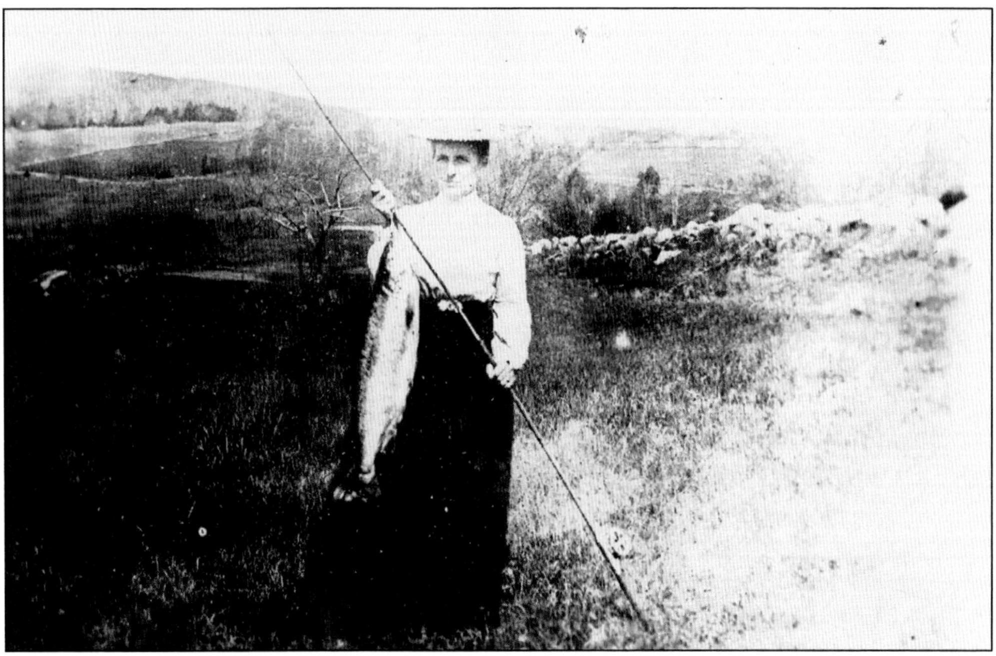

Another image of a successful fisherwoman posing with her catch, this view has no indication of location, date, or identity. The only writing on the card reads, "13 ? lbs. Salmon."

This image of a young hunter with his dog provides no clues whatsoever as to the man's identity or hometown. One interesting feature of the photograph is the fact that the man had his eyes closed at the moment the image was exposed.

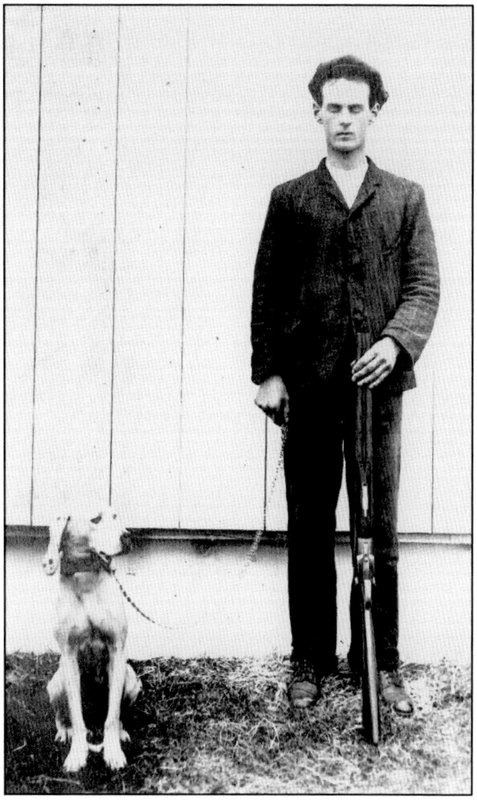

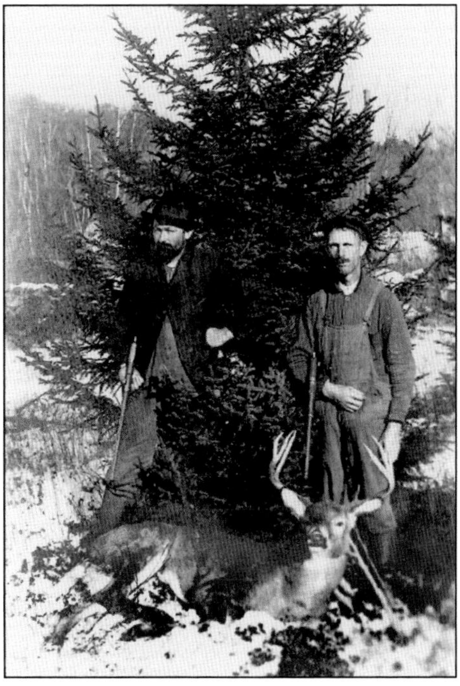

This undated view of two hunters and the five-point buck that one of them shot also reveals nothing as to the identities of the pair or where they lived.

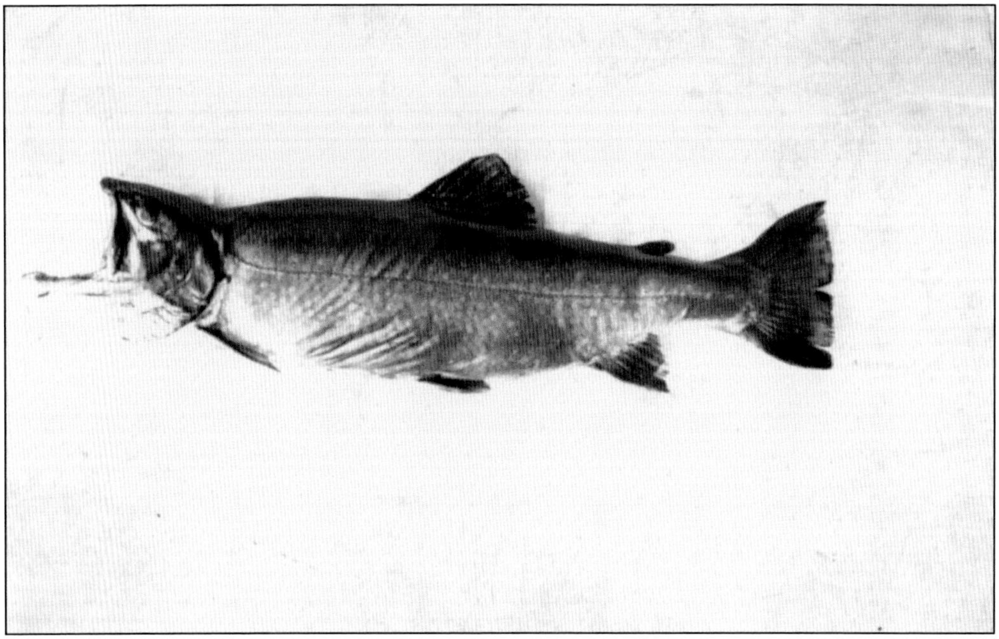

This interesting and unusual image bears the notation "6 lb. Trout," with no indication of where or when the fish was caught or by whom.

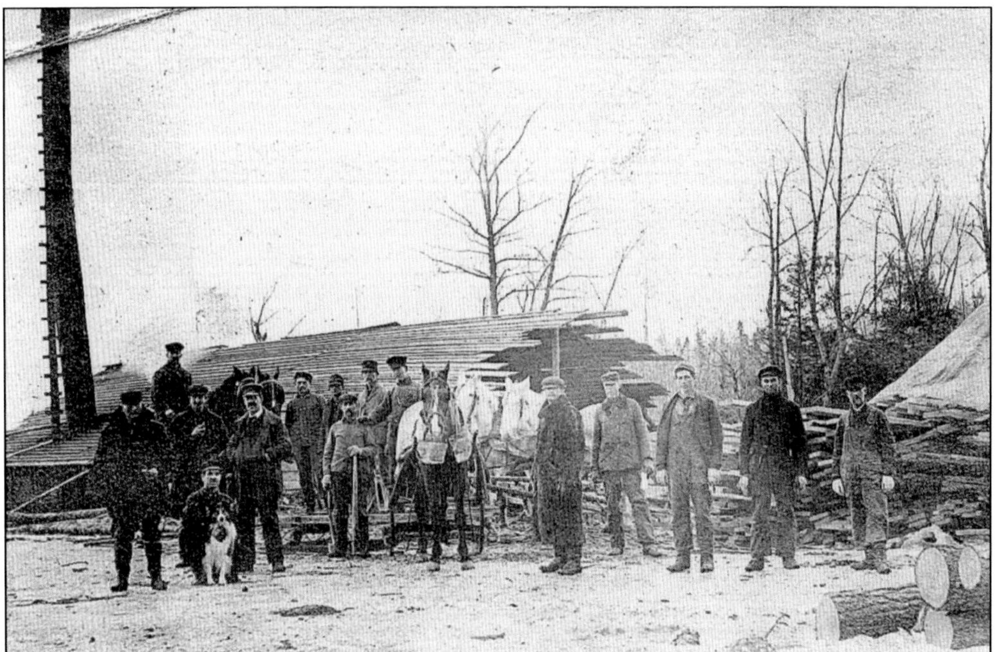

This undated image of the crew of a long-lumber mill and its 15-man crew gives no clues as to the crew's identities or to where the mill may have been. In addition to the men, there are also five horses and one dog in the photograph. Judging by the garb of the men, the view was recorded during either the fall or winter months.

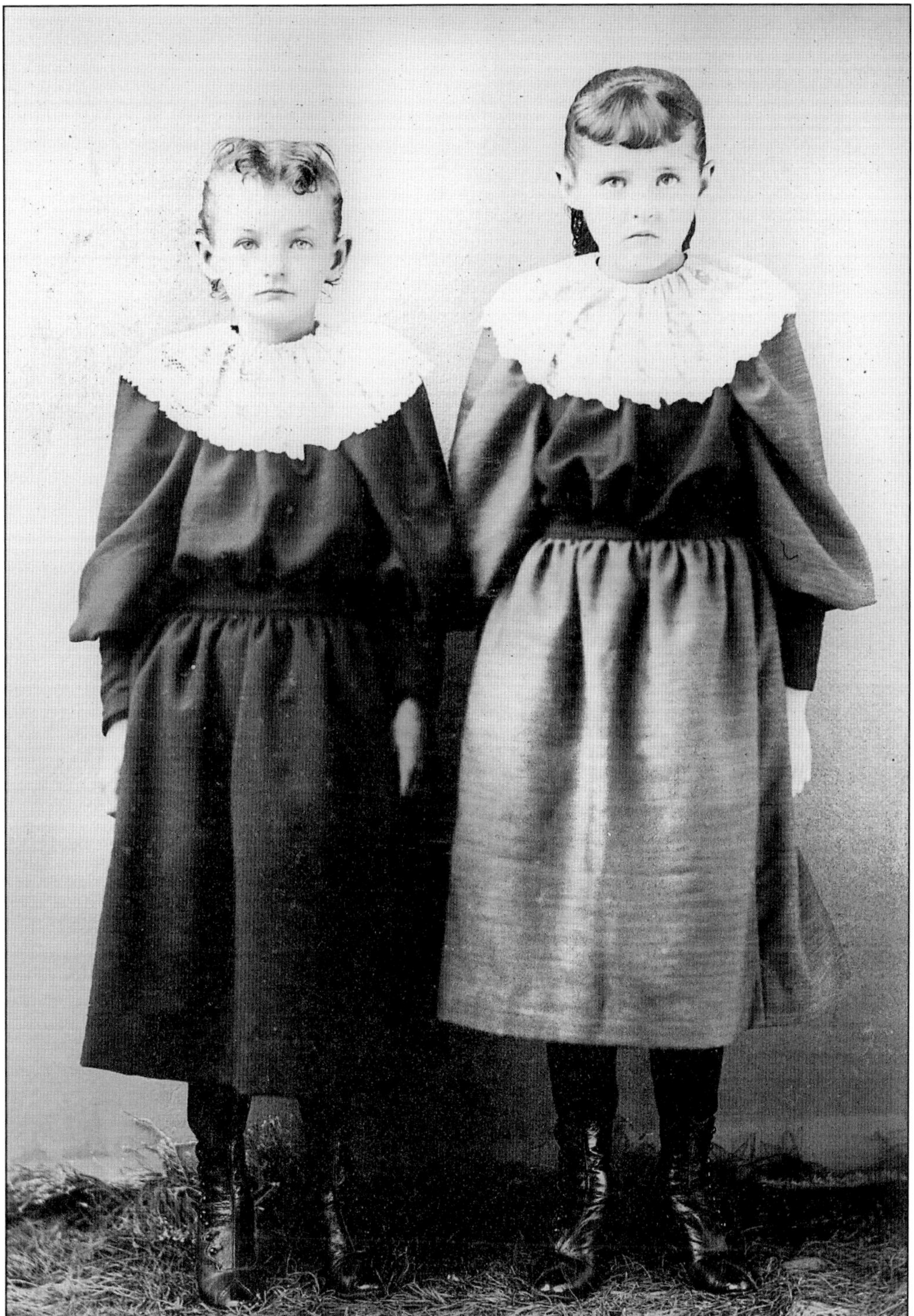

Like some of the earlier images, this cabinet photograph of two young girls was taken in the Cunningham studio in Washington but reveals nothing about the identities of the girls.

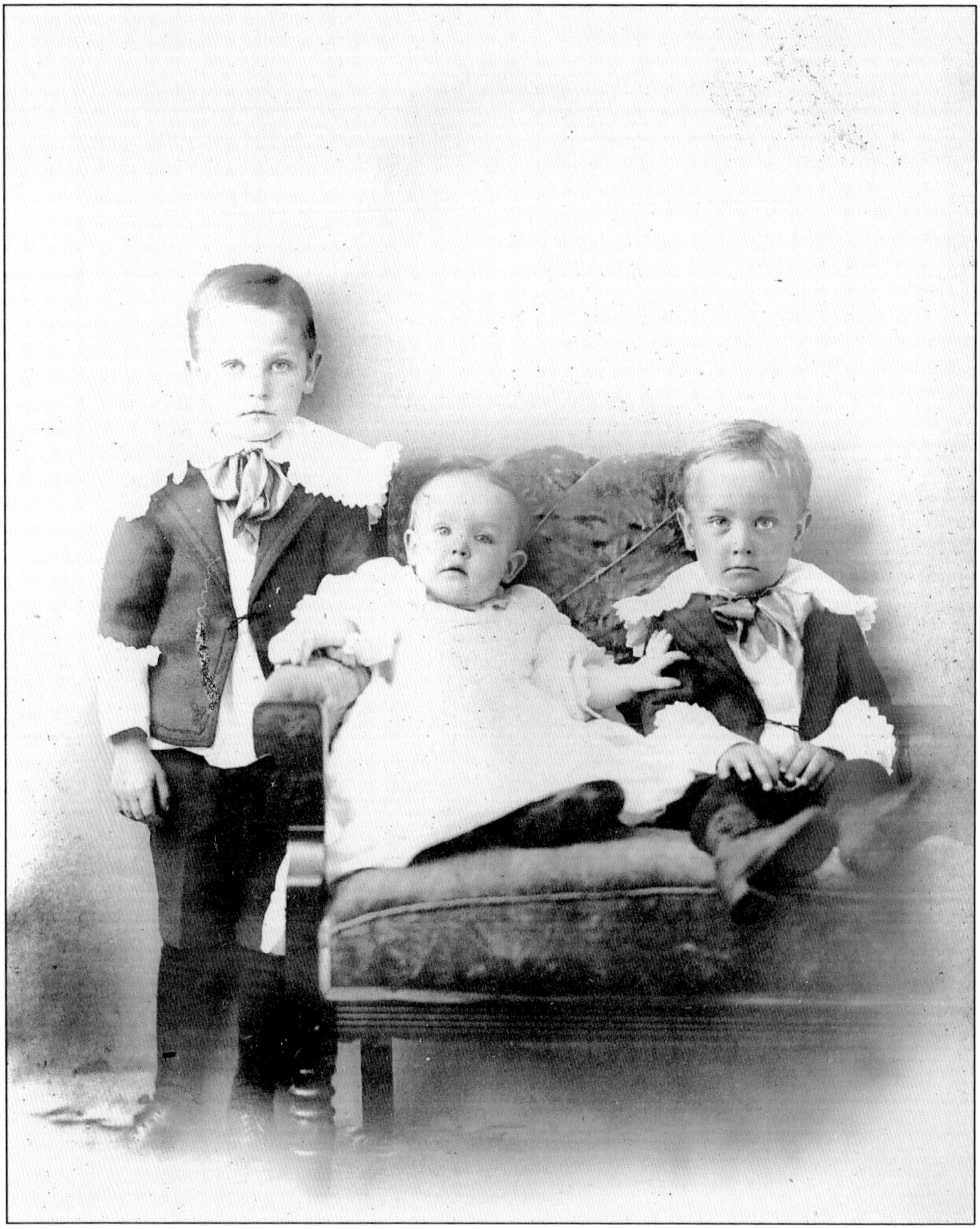

This cabinet photograph of three young children reveals nothing about any of them, other than the fact that at least two of them are definitely boys. This image was a gallery photograph as well.

Seven

Bert's Photographs

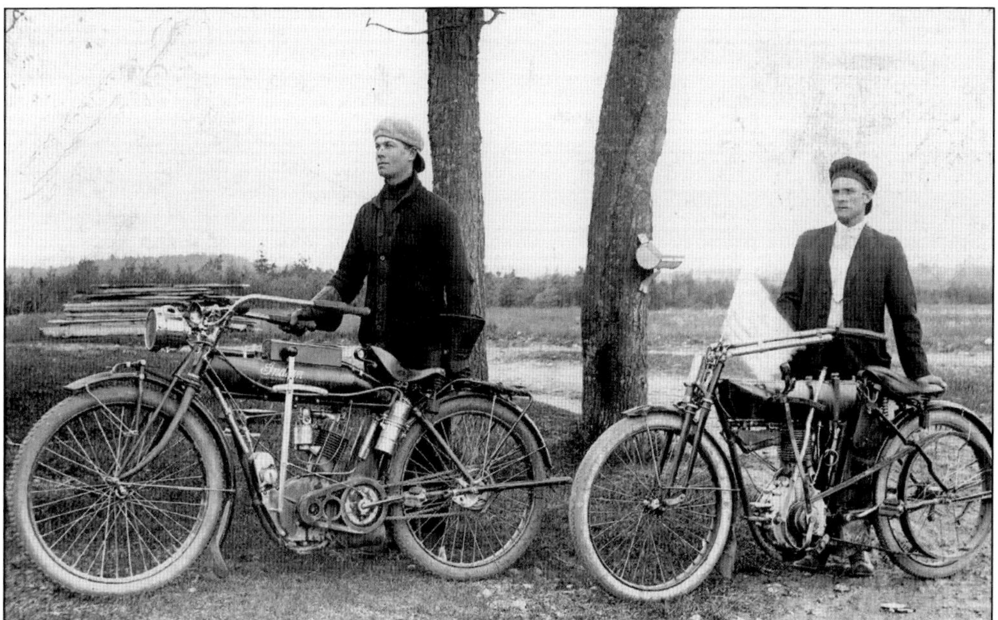

This undated Bert Cunningham photograph shows two young and obviously proud motorcycle enthusiasts and their machines, one a new chain-driven Indian. The card was addressed to Alice Fuller from Laurice Poland but has no indication as to whether or not that has any bearing on the identities of the young men pictured.

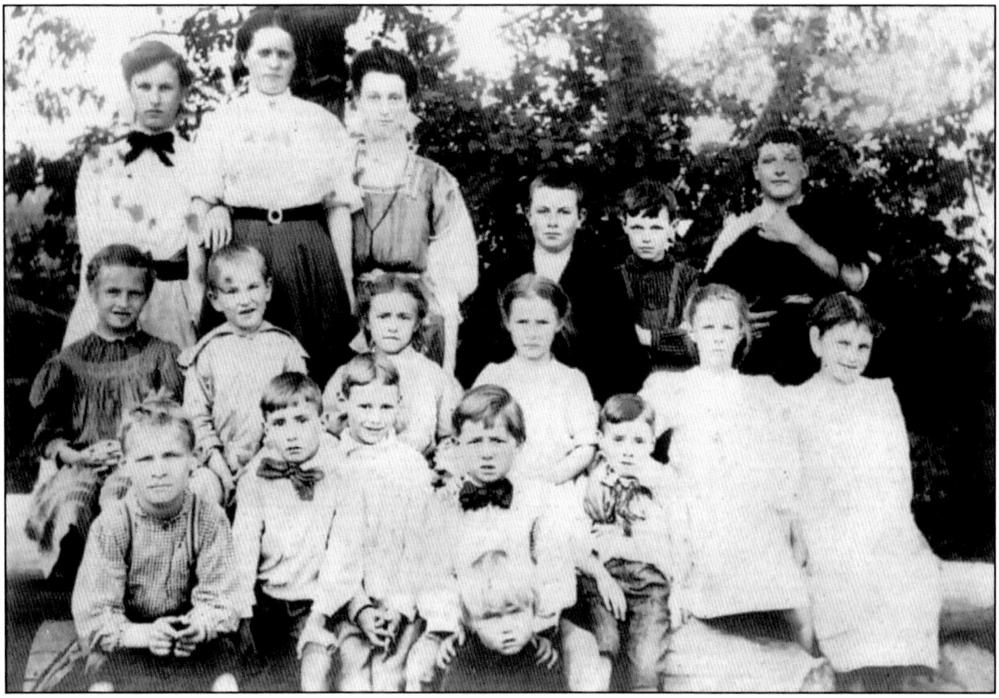

This is a school group, but there is no indication as to what town, year, or school is represented here. There are a total of 17 students and a female teacher toward the back. A wide range of ages is represented, and one of the students is holding a dog.

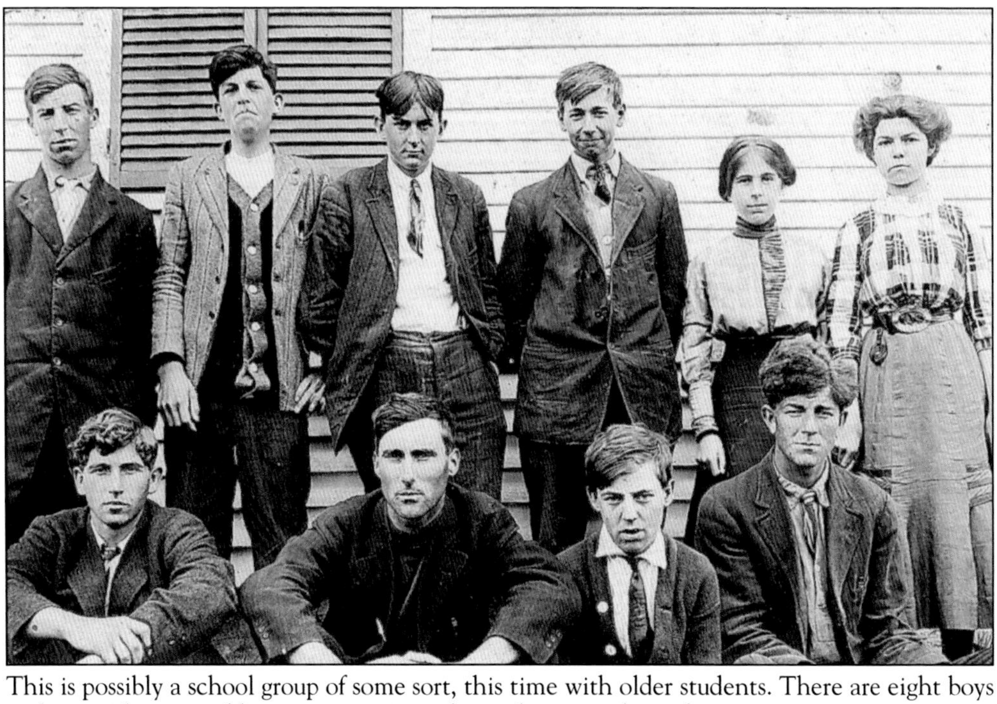

This is possibly a school group of some sort, this time with older students. There are eight boys and two girls pictured here, once again with no clue as to their identities.

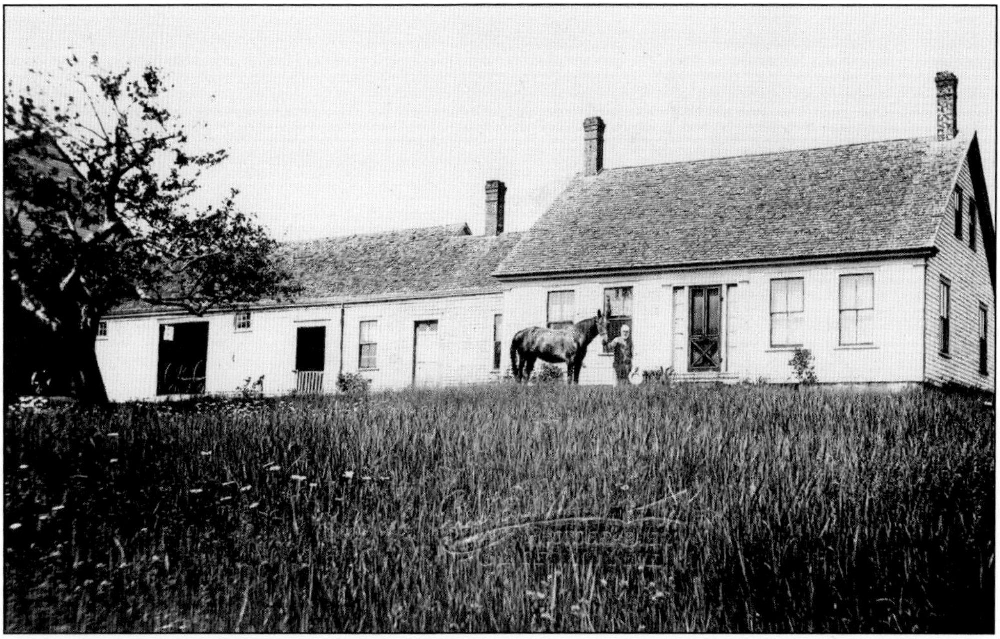

This undated image of a well-maintained house has no written indication as to where it may have been taken or who the older gentleman holding the horse may have been.

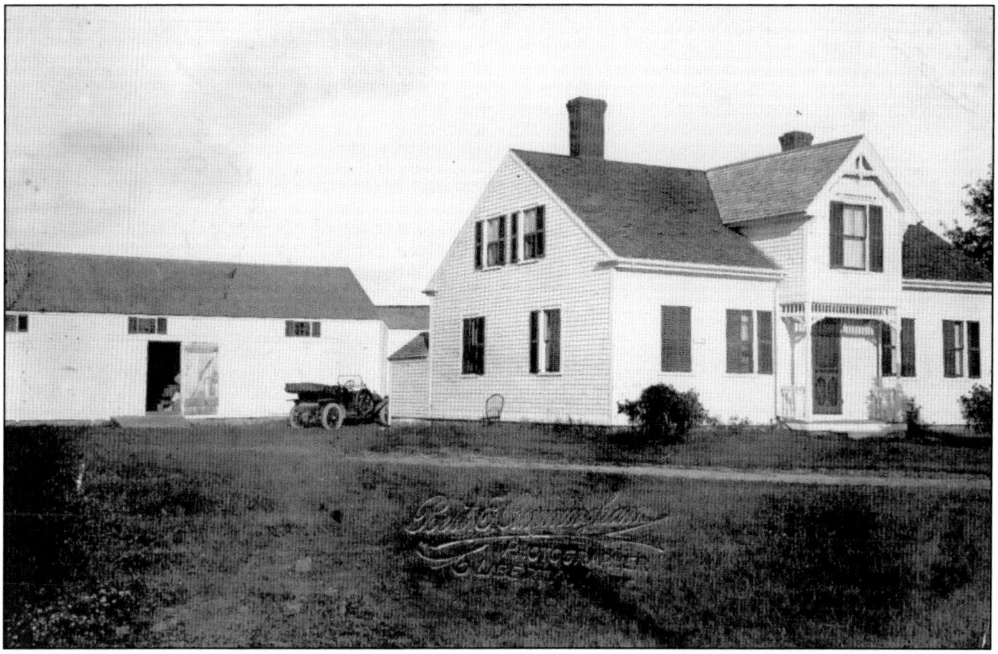

This is an obviously later photograph, as evidenced by the Model T in the yard. It bears the notation "Harrison Berry's house at Montville."

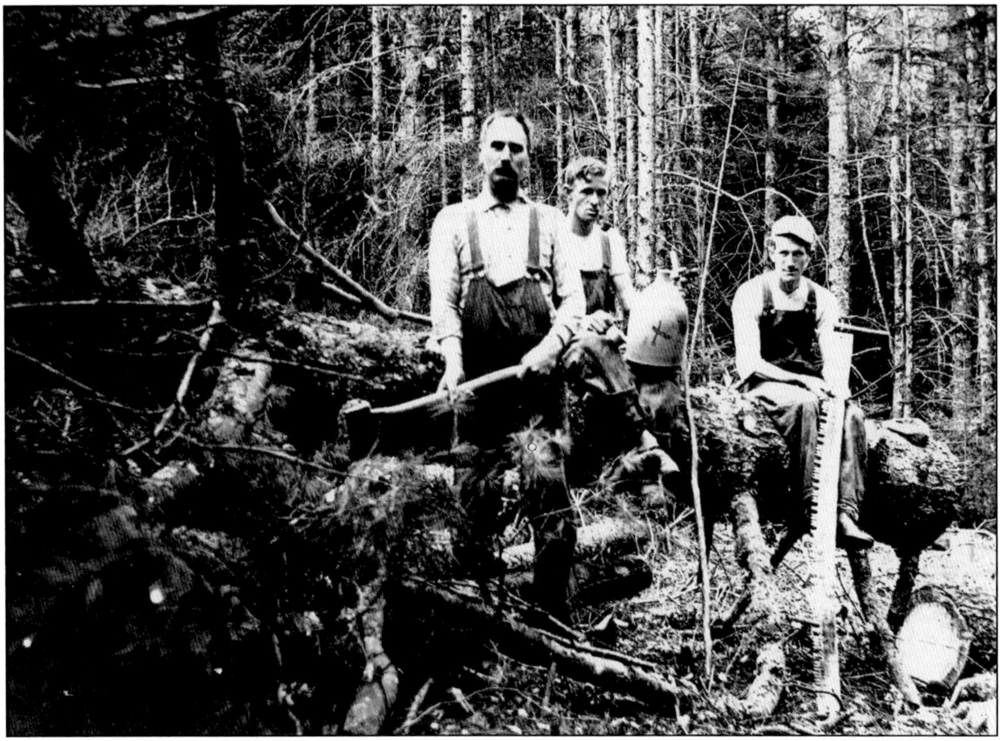

This undated image of a wood crew is addressed to "Beatrice Palmer, From Your Brother Will, When I was in the woods." Presumably Will is the one holding the jug with the X on it.

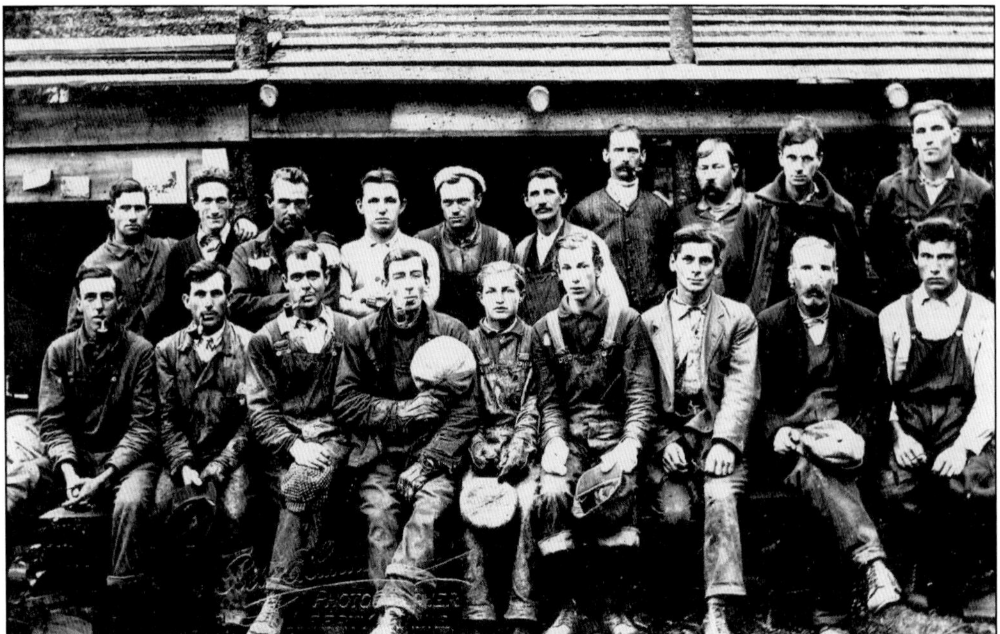

There are 19 men pictured here in front of what appears to be a sawmill. There is no indication of the identities of any of the men, when the photograph was taken, or where the mill may have been. Five of the men are smoking pipes in this image.

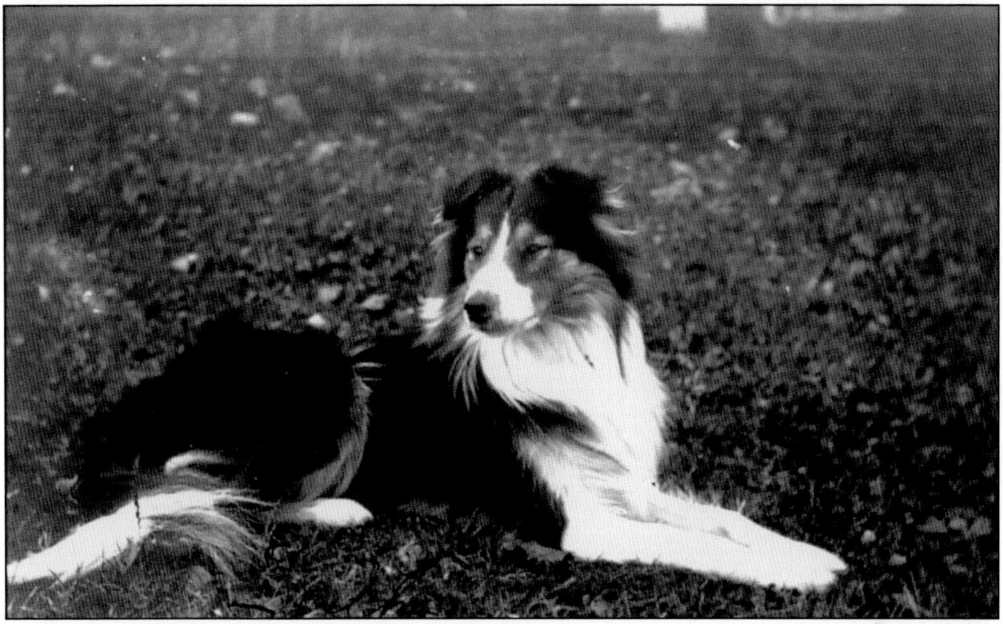

This is an interesting image of a collie, but it gives no clue as to whose dog it may have been, or when the photograph was taken. The card was addressed to "Aron McFarland in Montville" and was mailed in 1907.

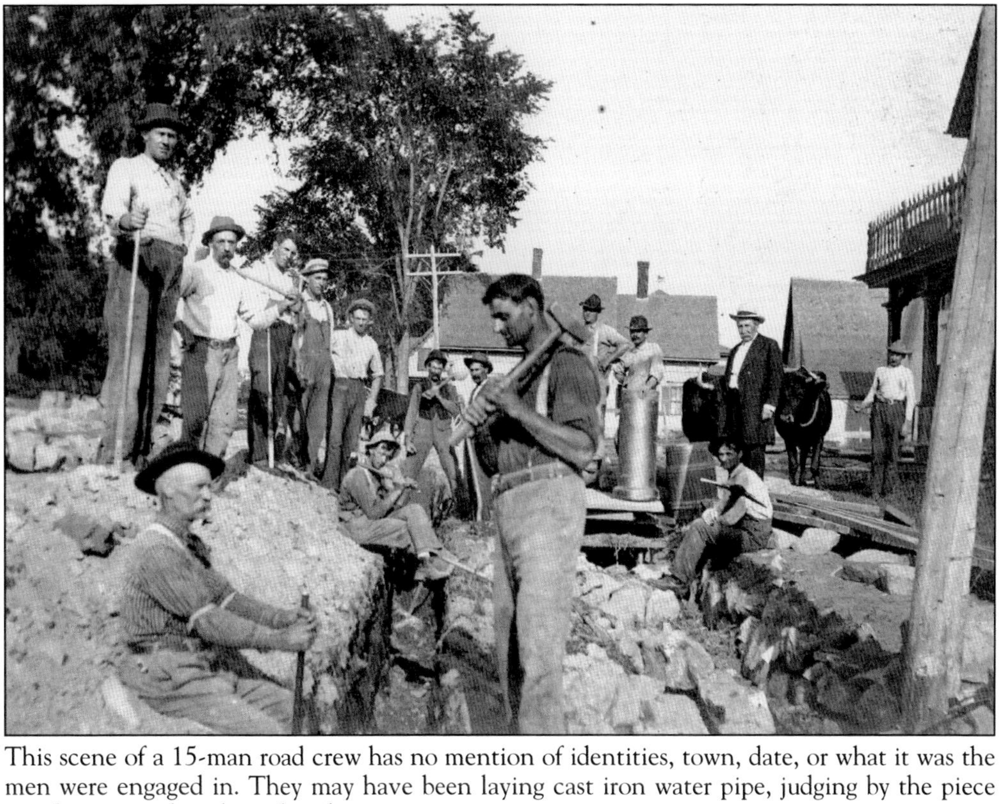

This scene of a 15-man road crew has no mention of identities, town, date, or what it was the men were engaged in. They may have been laying cast iron water pipe, judging by the piece standing on end to the right of center.

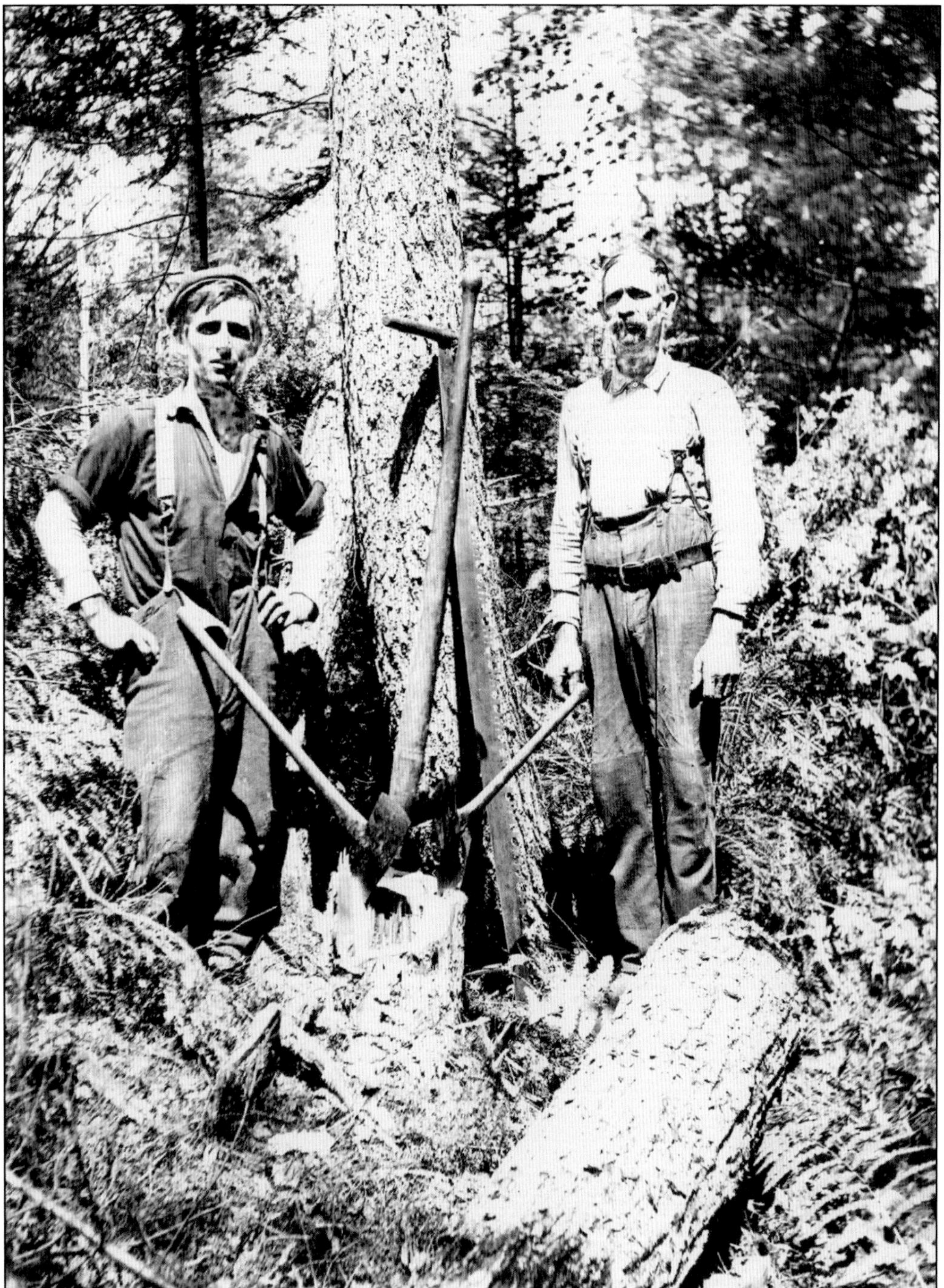

The identity of this rough-looking pair of lumberjacks remains a mystery, as there is no record of who they may have been or where they were from.